THE DARK SECRET
OF BÉALNABLÁTH

The Dark Secret of Béalnabláth
*deals essentially with particulars
of the ambush situation in
which Michael Collins lost his life.
It was written totally in 1990,
the Centenary Year of the birth of Collins,
from work in progress since 1985.*

THE DARK SECRET
OF
BÉALNABLÁTH

by

Patrick J. Twohig

TOWER BOOKS
1991

First published in 1991 by Tower Books, Ballincollig, Co. Cork

Second Edition 1991
Third Edition with Notanda 1995

ISBN 0 902568 19 1

Copyright © Patrick J. Twohig

Typeset by Tower Books, Ballincollig, Co. Cork
Printed by Shanway Press, Belfast

OTHER WORKS BY THE AUTHOR:

Filí an tSuláin: A history of Gaelic Poetry
A Folk Register: Annotated verse-history of Ireland
Of Hope and Glory: Annotated verse-history of England
Of Dinosaurs and Double Eagles: Annotated verse-history of the
     U.S.A.
Rest the Poor Bones: Commemorating the late President Erskine
     Childers
Green Tears For Hecuba: The War of Independence in Ireland
Blood on the Flag: A translation from the Irish (due for
     publication)

COVER

The front design incorporates a representation of a massive oil painting by the late Lieut. Col. George McEnery, of Tralee, symbolizing the great 'Split' of the Civil War, and the void created by the death of Michael Collins.

The back is a facsimile of R.T.E.'s aerial view of the convoy arriving in the battle area. It is from the documentary, 'The Shadow of Béalnabláth — a close approximation of 'how it must have been'.

Notanda

Dedicated to the memory
of the late Seán Daly, of
Tower Books, Cork, publisher,
historian, printer 'par
excellence', and latter-
day soldier of the
Republic

Contents

LIST OF ILLUSTRATIONS

Prologue

He did not just fight the Civil War — he invented it! His Treaty dictum — 'Freedom to fight for Freedom' — is still largely unresolved. His life was full of his times, circumstances and induced emotions, but the nature of his death is all that matters now. That in itself is more than adequate for any one man, even for Collins. Death of a hero is quite significant. In Ireland Mythology and History, alike, generate the mystique and embellish the mystery, from Cuchulainn through Brian Boru and Art McMurrough-Kavanagh to Shane O'Neill, from Owen Roe O'Neill and Wolfe Tone through Parnell and Pearse to Michael Collins. They all died strange, unnatural and even mysterious deaths, but nothing in Life became them like the leaving it.

Patrick J. Twohig,
Churchtown,
December 8, 1990.

1

The Big Fellow and the Small Fellow

Little Billy Mullins, of Tralee, walked into the Metropolitan Police Station in Brunswick Street, in the City of Dublin, and asked to see Mister Michael Collins. He thought maybe he was asking for a prisoner behind bars. It was late September, 1920, and Billy, diminutive, wiry, aquiline and somewhat pop-eyed, had been guardedly inquiring around Dublin for Collins for two whole days. Nobody seemed to know, not even old 'Ned the Boots', the Big Fellow's regular contact in the Old Clarence Hotel. Billy had been staying at the Clarence, on Wellington Quay, and intended packing his few effects, about to return home, when someone in the bar whispered — 'Try Brunswick Street Police Station!'. He did not understand and went in to tea instead. Just then another Kerryman, Tim Kennedy, of Annascaul, chief accountant of the Kerry County Council, and Intelligence Officer to Kerry Number One Brigade, strolled into the dining room. He casually mentioned that he was meeting Michael Collins at eight o'clock. Kennedy and Collins, Billy knew, were great pals. He himself had met Mick in the prison camp at Frongoch, in Wales, after the Easter Rebellion, as well as the Hales brothers, Tom and Seán, from Cork. The two Kerrymen walked along the quays together, up D'Olier Street, crossed Tara Street into Townsend Street and at the corner of

Townsend and Brunswick stood the D.M.P. Station. Billy was nervous. Kennedy had been there before. They went through a wall door into a yard and entered the first room on the right-hand side. It was not a barred cell nor a rat-infested dungeon but a spacious office with a large table and some chairs. The table was untidy, piled high with papers, documents, correspondence, whatever. If Mick Collins of the photographic memory knew the word in Irish he would probably have dismissed the lot, with a disdainful gesture and a curl of the lip, in that lovely Gaelic generic noun — 'Cáipéisí'. Billy Mullins, feeling small and bewildered, was ushered into the Presence by the strong arm of the Law. What he did not know was that Collins had been using this location for almost a year and a half, since his first meeting with detective Ned Broy of Dublin Castle, in April, 1919. Now he sat massively behind the table and looked up sharply. Beside him was a tall and slender figure standing in an attitude of waiting and listening. Collins looked at Kennedy. 'What the hell do you want now?', he said. Kennedy indicated the little fellow beside him. 'Well, what have you got for me?', said Collins brusquely. Billy walked to the table and pulling from his pocket a large bundle of banknotes and dumping it in front of the Big Fellow said: 'There's seven hundred pounds there — count it!' Billy was tough too and an old campaigner. He had been in an officers' training camp in 1915, knew Patrick Pearse personally, had tea 'and home-made confectionery' with the mother and sister in the famous house, 'The Hermitage', Rathfarnham, in 1914, long before Collins was even heard of. But the big man had his kind side for the right people. He smiled a quick one. 'All right!', he said condescendingly, but just the same he counted the money twice. Mullins issued his order for so many rifles and revolvers, so much ammunition, to be sent in regular paint containers to a certain paint merchant in Tralee, all of which Collins duly noted. Then Collins, confidential now, briefly turned and indicating the third party with a flick of his head said, 'This is . . . McNamara'. Billy did not catch the first name but already knew that Detective McNamara was one of Collins' contacts in Dublin Castle, the nerve-centre of British authority. The man smiled and said: 'You can speak freely here!'. At ninety-four (1990) Billy Mullins still cannot recall the name, but he met Captain (James) McNamara once more when, as Officer-in-Command of Tralee Military Barracks, some months into the Civil War, the captain stood at the door of Billy's little house at 55 Moyderwell, Tralee, and mutely indicating an armed escort across the way asked him in an undertone to come along as quietly as possible. Collins had been dead for quite some time and a few days later McNamara was also dead. Because of promotional jealousy and other factors he had been eliminated in a Borgia-type intrigue among high-ranking officers of the National Army in a staged military vehicle accident in Lower Abbey Street, Dublin — or so Billy Mullins told me with the conviction of knowing what he knew. 'I was a good friend of Michael Collins', he wrote in the *Kerryman* newspaper recently, 'and, as Brigade Quartermaster, I had many visits and dealings with him . . . Back in Tralee I told this merchant that he would receive supplies he had not ordered but to hold them until we collected them. That was the last time I saw Collins alive'.

Back in Brunswick Street Police Station Michael Collins concluded the interview as gruffly as he had started it. 'Good luck!', he said, and that was all. There were other brave men besides Collins. He knew that. There were other dedicated and brainy men like Billy Mullins, the little courier from Tralee in Kerry. Collins knew that too, and he died in the knowledge. He did know one thing, though — there was only one Michael Collins, there never could be or would be again. A man for his time . . .

How he met his death is still shrouded in mystery. Writer borrowed from writer as hearsay proliferated; and the arrival of the centenary of the birth of Michael Collins (16 October, 1890) bids fair to surpass all previous endeavours. Speculation has proved to be cheap as ever, surpassed only by the arbitrary fancy of the charlatan. Hard evidence is harder to come by as the years of political strictures move into the cold and unrewarding print of academic History. Two poles stand apart in a startling divergence: Billy Mullins, who spent his personal Civil War in durance vile, and Lieutenant Smith, the free-wheeling effervescent spirit, feckless and spry, who led the Commander-in-Chief down a country lane to his rendezvous with destiny. 'There was NO ambush', said Billy Mullins dogmatically — 'Nobody ever proved it! They just shot Collins themselves and drove on!'. But the lieutenant claimed, in the public press, to have witnessed a ferocious battle, of an hour's duration, in which machine-gun and rifle bullets were whirring about like Summer midges while the crash of Mills bombs punctuated the clamour amidst the cries of wounded men!

*   *   *

Opened in 1906, the Brunswick Street Metropolitan Police Station still stands and works, its magnificent cut stone façade rounding the corner in an impressive escarpment. The Michael Collins back door, on Townsend Street (to which he had a personal key, according to a Garda Sergeant historian on the spot), is sealed but intact, the little yard just as he left it except for the addition of a glass roof in the Thirties. The little room he used as an office, in the detective section at the back (while plans were being hopefully formulated for his capture, in the front offices), is now a store room, its central dividing arch sealed up, and the great oak table in the corner shows disconcertingly the multiple pen-knife cuttings of many decades past. Great Brunswick, as the street is called (in contrast to Little Brunswick, a narrow alley some distance away), is now Pearse Street in memory of the gallant Pearse brothers who were born there before the advent of the D.M.P.

2

The Dark Secret

The mystery of olden times hangs over the valleys of Ireland, over the fields, the woods, the hills, the lakes, the phosphorescent boglands. It blows in the west wind and it rolls down the mountain slopes in misty precipitation. The people of old lie buried beneath the soil. Their ghosts wander far and wide. Old paganism hangs over the trees and bushes, the fairy 'rath' and the bubbling spring-wells. But hardly ever is this old 'mystique' deliberately construed in the Twentieth Century. An exception is Béalnabláth. Its dark secret has never unfolded adequately since a low-born West Cork boy, who was to become the world-renowned General Michael Collins, a predestined whipper of the British Empire, met his death on that spot on a misty Tuesday evening, the twenty-second of August, 1922. We feel and discern, at sixty to seventy years' remove, a conspiracy of silence. That may well be. It remains to be seen. But the place itself is an enigma. An elderly man of the locality, who was twelve years old when the fatal conflict took place, denies that there is such a locality as 'Béalnabláth'. Old Tom Murray, in whose parents' house on the hill meetings were held, negotiations took place, land-mines were deposited, says that three townlands in fact meet at the historic crossroads, to wit, Pullerick (Poularick in the survey maps), Glanarouge East and

Ahalarick. Where is Béalnabláth?, he asks. What is, he inquires, this 'Mouth of the Blossoms'? Who named it?, he wonders. And he looks around as much as to say — I didn't, anyway! But still songs have been written on the theme, and a well-known poet, famous or just a poet of sorts according to the point of view, name of Paul Durcan, published a poem so-called, in recent times and in strange modern-style contra-verse, and named it 'The Mouth of the Flowers' . . .

And so he died by the River Bride. The Bride, called by anglers the South Bride (to avoid confusing it with the North Bride near Rathcormack in North-East Cork), is about sixteen miles long (according to J.C. Coleman in his *Journeys into Muskerry*) . . . 'It rises south-west of Crookstown as a tangle of townland streams and, flowing through Béalnabláth, enters a flat-floored limestone valley at Crookstown (N.B. The ambush site is in fact on the most southerly branch known locally as the 'Noneen' — the 'Daisy' — and on the survey maps as the Béalnabláth River) . . . Coming back to the now dwindling River Bride at Crookstown you see the river leaving the flat limestone valley and follow it upwards into a glen to the south-west. At Béalnabláth (the mouth of the flowers) is a tragic reminder of evil days in Ireland'. And straightway we encounter the first of the many discrepancies and amateurish in-accuracies which have bedevilled the story of the death of the man who is certain to be known to posterity as Ireland's greatest revolutionary. The mouth of the flowers, indeed! If the story were being told in the Irish language, the 'seanchaí' (traditional story-teller) would say: 'Do thit sé ag béal na blagha', and he would have said that Michael Collins had died at the mouth of the gorge. In point of fact, the Béalnabláth battlefield lies at the entrance to an enormous ravine which runs for miles.

A little research may be in order at this point. Professor P.W. Joyce, the noted historian and toponymist, gives 'béal' (in *Irish Names of Places*) as a 'mouth or entrance to a ford. Sometimes it means the opening of a glen or valley or a pass of some kind'. And so we meet about the countryside, that had a name for every field, such locations as Béal a' Mháma, Béal a' Chumair, Béal na Gága, all meaning the mouth of the ravine, depending on certain well-defined variations in the nature of the particular spot. Now 'Blagh' is a variation of 'Blogh', both Feminine Gender, both, in the most modern usage, merely feminine while, a hundred and fifty years ago, the feminine version was just an irregular variation on the masculine. All of which means that when the name 'Béalnabláth' was coined in the distant past the precise form was chosen as the most apt, the most musical (a notable feature of Irish), the one that rolled sweetest off the Celtic tongue. A wealth of manuscript material from centuries past produced a vast ambivalence in word-spelling, all too frequently just a sweeping extension of sound. So you may find such further variations as 'blaghdha', 'blaghadh', or even 'blaghadha', with suitable aspirates (i.e. the dot rather than the Roman 'h') on the current 'Gothic' script, introducing a sense of onomatopoeia. The early decades of the present century produced a literary and reasonable simplification. Misguided purists have 'sent the fool further' by introducing 'Béal na mBláth', in both English and Irish renditions, for verisimilitude. They suppose that 'bláth' being a flower in Gaelic, the Genitive Case, plural number, was the correct usage with the *B* eclipsed by *m*, giving 'Béal na mBláth', and that 'Béalnabláth' so written was a corruption. I propose to honour their zeal by continuing to use the name as indicated.

The old Cork road to Bantry, known as the 'Bantry Line', comes down the steep hill into Béalnabláth village, crosses the Noneen stream, then follows the Bride into the hills once more. Like the old Kerry road into Cork, through Ballyvourney, it keeps as far as possible to the high places and descends only when necessary to the dangerous flood regions. The name 'Béalnabláth' indicates that crossing. Three-quarters of a mile away lies the scene of the ambush, at the entrance to a valley redolent of warfare and strife long past and forgotten. Beginning at the bridge of Ahalarick (Áth an Araig, 'the ford of the conflict'), it is encompassed by the townlands of Glanarouge (Gleann na Ruaige, 'the glen of the rout') and Pullerick (Poul Araig, 'the pool of the conflict'). From there to Crookstown stretches a veritable Rift valley such as would have been of practical interest, in the brave days of yore, to noted guerrilla leaders like Fiach McHugh O'Byrne and Art McMurrough-Kavanagh, and indeed to fighters of the 'Black-and-Tans' in the not so long ago. But now the Tans were gone and the 'Enemy' was the bonny boy himself, the 'laughing boy of the Dublin women', as a foreign writer enigmatically put it, vanquisher of the old enemy, who came to die miserably, like Cuchulainn, the ancient Celtic hero, at his rock-post, 'Clochafaermore', the 'Pillar of the Big Fellow', by the entrance to the Valley of the Vanquishing. And the 'Mouth of the Flowers', in the last analysis, becomes simply the crossing of the ravine!

3

Setting the Scene

'Michael Collins was killed in an ambush in County Cork' —
thus wrote Ernie O'Malley in *The Singing Flame*. Just that. No
more. Dry, sterile, unintentionally ironic. O'Malley, the high-
ranking, much-wounded and rabid Republican, did not care
for Collins and vice versa, just like Montgomery and
Eisenhower in a later life-and-death struggle more cataclysmic
only in extent. Collins did not like De Valera; but De Valera did
not dislike anybody — he merely worried about them. And
sometimes he worried them to death. When O'Malley published his 'Black-and-Tan book' in 1936 he called it *On Another
Man's Wound*. Knowing him and knowing Collins one
wonders if, in that title, he was belatedly getting back at the Big
Fellow, like Cathal Brugha in his death rush. O'Malley was a
loner, almost a lone fighter, like Hemingway's deranged
Republican hero in *For Whom the Bell Tolls*; and O'Malley's
book could have been a partial model for the famous novel as it
was published in the U.S.A. just four years before. Hemingway,
as a young man, had taken a peculiar and disparaging interest
in I.R.A. activities (cf. *By-Line*, 1920) — and they were both
named 'Ernie'. Circumstantial? Maybe! But writers, even the
best, do borrow ideas, as indeed the 'Lives' of Collins have
shown. Likewise there are similarities of plot, incident and

circumstance, and General Michael Collins in Ireland's Civil War could conceivably have been General Francisco Franco in Spain's Civil War a decade and a half later when many Irishmen, some quite well known, fought on both sides and on the lines of the old Split. But back to the title! The sardonic old Irish proverb, 'Is furasta codhladh ar chneá duine eile', means 'It is easy to sleep on another man's wound'. Hemingway's title was also a proverb: 'Ask not for whom the bell tolls — it tolls for thee!' (Ecclesiastes). He took the republican side in Spain. O'Malley had been wounded several times, Collins never. Old republican fighter, Neilus Sheehan of Ballyvourney, still hale and hearty at ninety plus, said: 'Sure Collins was never in a major battle!' He was never in any battle, not even firing a shot in the G.P.O. in 1916. In his book, *On Another Man's Wound*, O'Malley is sarcastic about many things, the lack of toilet facilities among the Irish country people, his own people except that he was reared in a town, the excruciating 'republican itch' that afflicted so many of his fellow fighters, funny if it was not your problem. And Collins he frankly stated to be unaccountably hostile to himself, saying on one occasion — 'Earnán, one of these days I'll lose you!' (in the modern sense of 'I'll tell you to get lost!'). O'Malley and his like needed Collins, and Collins admittedly could match the British only with a profusion of diehards like O'Malley. For, as Gertrude Stein might have said but, of course, did not — Collins was Collins was Collins!

Cathal Brugha almost hated Collins, and Collins somehow feared him as a big, strong man needs to fear a small but reputedly dangerous disease, or a big, strong bishop, with all the law of Church and Spirit on his side, might take time out to fear a small but obstreperous cleric. And when Brugha rushed out into a Dublin street to die with guns blazing he saw no Free State soldiers before him but a great big shadow of a man which, at that time, loomed large over Dublin, Ireland and the world, that he so wanted to blast out of his horizon. They say Collins wept at the news. When the time was there, what could he do but the same himself! And so he did. From the moment

Cathal Brugha was killed Michael Collins had the death-wish!

*   *   *

An affable Irregular,
A heavily-built Falstaffian man,
Comes cracking jokes of Civil War
As though to die with gunshot were
The finest play under the sun.

A brown lieutenant and his men,
Half dressed in national uniform,
Stand at my door, and I complain
Of the foul weather, hail and rain,
A pear-tree broken by the storm.

*   *   *

The poet, William Butler Yeats, looked out at the passing scene on the road by his door, at Thoor Ballylee, and conjured up those lines. My father, a schoolmaster, looked out on the passing scene at Coolavokig and remembered — 'Ah, you could talk to them (i.e. the Staters) — not like the Tans!' He himself had been incarcerated by the Tans in Macroom Castle and was tried for his life but talked his way out of it. Poet and schoolmaster equally bemoaned the passing scene. They seemed to have no part in Civil War, and they would be left to suffer in futile regret when it had passed away.

Those who should know best have put it on record that Michael Collins rarely if ever carried a gun until he became Commander-in-Chief, a few short weeks before his death. Then the gun was standard equipment. The one he personally owned, during the hard times, was a little silver plated point-thirty-two revolver which he presented to Erskine Childers during the Truce and merely as a keepsake. It had the death-mark of the Hope Diamond. A replica was found in the door pocket of his motor car, just beside his seat, when he died. Still and all, Collins loomed large as a gunman in the imagination of the British. One example. Jackie McMahon had been a friend of the present writer in Maynooth College while the next war was raging. He told me that his father had been an R.I.C. constable in Clare during the 'Trouble' times. They (i.e. the police) believed that 'Mick' had a coat specially designed so that at the flick of two thumbs the flaps fell away as he reached for two concealed weapons. Perhaps it was good they thought so. They also thought the Irish were a filthy lot; at least one enormous Black-and-Tan did in that police station in County Clare. McMahon was big too, and in a notable fist fight on the day-room floor reduced the Englishman to a common denominator. Erskine carried the deadly memento while 'on the run' with the Republicans in West Cork, after the death of the Commander-in-Chief. The author of the prophetic *Riddle of the Sands*, the peripatetic printer of sedition, gave strange impressions and took strange impressions . . . Old Mrs. Lyons, of Renaniree, west of Macroom, impressed him strangely. He said: 'She is a weird, weird old woman. She is like a precious old vase one would take down from the shelf and dust, just dust!' In a sort of Anglo-Irish corruption they called him 'Shuldhurs', but not ever as a common denominator. One rough, strong country man tried to reduce him so. Fleeing across mountain regions, on the Cork-Kerry border, before the pursuing Free State soldiers, he turned back to the weary little Englishman and snarled: 'Will you come on, you little 'padhsán', or will I have to carry you!'. The little 'padhsán', who could only have guessed at the meaning, held up the headlong flight to state, with his peculiar inward sense of composure: 'My friend, when you have striven as much and suffered as much as I have done in my time, you will be a very small man — a very small man indeed!'. Erskine Childers had said many true words in his time but none truer. (If it matters, the country man's name was Danny 'Pheig' O'Leary, from Ballingeary. His brother was assistant printer to Childers in Renaniree, owned a Model-T Ford which he used for the dual purpose of conveying Fr. Burts, P.P., on occasional sick-calls and Erskine Childers on some of his 'nefarious' activities on behalf of the Republic, whom the extraordinary Irish-Englishman referred to as 'the "Feggi" man').

The little silver plated revolver eventually brought about the London-born convert-republican's death because of an hysterical Provisional Government directive on the execution of prisoners taken in possession of arms which the now dead Commander-in-Chief would never have countenanced. Michael Collins himself finally took gun in hand at Béalnabláth, fired a shot in anger, and died in the act. How it happened is our story, as well as many an ill-conceived story up till now.

*   *   *

> Odour of blood on the ancestral stair!
> And we that have shed none must gather there
> And clamour in drunken frenzy for the moon!
> (Yeats).

4

The Mike Donoghue Story

It broke in a full-page exclusive in the *Cork Examiner* on 5 November 1985. I had nursed the story at home and abroad for upwards of thirty years. Reporter Ray Ryan did it proud. Reaction was slight, recrimination 'passé'. The intention was to headline the story as 'The Dark Secret of Béalnabláth'. The newspaper thought otherwise and showed in massive type: 'THE MAN WHO STOOD NEXT TO COLLINS' KILLER'. The man was Michael O'Donoghue, of Glenflesk, Co. Kerry, Intelligence Officer to the Glenflesk (D) Company, No. 2 Battalion, East Kerry Brigade of the I.R.A. He and some others of his company had been walking home on the old Bantry road from Cork City through Béalnabláth. The trains had been running when they left home but not anymore, at least not for Republican fighters. They had fought at Cork Harbour to prevent the Free State Army from landing by sea, had failed and were now going home westwards. The battle for the harbour had at first been indifferent, then fierce, particularly in the grounds and environs of Rochestown Capuchin College. Fighting beside them had been other mountainy men from the slopes of the Derrynasagart range — the Ballyvourney men to the East, the Ballingeary men to the South, many well-known freedom fighters among them. 'Scottie' had been with the

16

Ballingeary group, but it was the Ballyvourney men who saw him fall. Jamie Moynihan, of Coolea, later County Councillor, with a son latterly in Dáil Éireann, described it to me in the long ago, how 'Scottie' had jumped up to re-attack across a roadway at Rochestown and had been hit by a stream of tracer bullets from a machine-gun. The story of 'Scottie' (Ian Graeme Baun MacKenzie-Kennedy, Scottish aristocrat and lineal descendent of Robert Bruce and possibly even Brian Boru) I have given to some little and inadequate extent in my personal 'Black-and-Tan book' which I named *Green Tears for Hecuba*, the title not proverbial but Shakespearian, with some sad classical overtones, as I saw fit. (There was a story, likely apocryphal, which said that Scottie and another republican decided to surrender, held up a white flour bag, marched across the road and were riddled in the process. The recalcitrant young Scotsman's father, a major in the British Army, was said to have offered to preside over a firing-squad at his son's execution). Poor Scottie died rather irrelevantly, far from his home territory of Lochaber, for the now fast fading ideal of an Irish Republic. He was twenty-three . . . 'Friends who heard the tracer bullets slapping into his body as it lay in a dusty by-road at Passage by the Sea have since wept for the big child innocently caught up in the ugly toils of internecine conflict that was none of his business. So he wanders onto the stage once more. For the moment we leave this blood relation of the Young Pretender tacking his sail-bike along on a south-west wind which might have carried his carefree singing back to Lochaber' (From *Green Tears*) . . . That was twelve days ago. In the meantime Cork City had fallen to Major-General Emmet Dalton who had fought so creditably with the British Army in France and elsewhere and saw some other well-known Irishmen die in those far foreign fields from Dunkirk to anywhere. Emmet Dalton had come home to fight with Michael Collins for Irish Independence. Apparently he was still doing so. This talented Dubliner had been impressed by the legitimate aims and forceful personality of Collins, like so many others, and thereafter had contributed largely to the formation and training of the new national army, which had become known as the Free State Army and whose members were to be derisively referred to, but not yet feared, as 'Staters'. They had now begun to encompass the whole of the province of Munster chiefly through sea landings from Waterford along the serrated coastline of Cork and Kerry to where the Shannon river meets the sea. Most of the big towns of Munster were being invested and taken, at least temporarily. The fields were still open country and the villages too numerous to be identified as military objectives. An exception was Ballyvourney whose village, Ballymakeera, was on the road from Macroom to Glenflesk and Killarney. Ballyvourney had been the central organization region for the First Southern Division. Liam Lynch had set up his G.H.Q. there in May, 1921, at the home of Cal McCarthy of Gortyrahilly. Just before the 'Big Round-up', fifth to ninth of June, 1921, he had gone on an inspection tour into Co. Waterford never, as it happened, to return, leaving his able adjutant, Florence O'Donoghue (author of *No Other Law* — biography of Liam Lynch), to ply a rare and busy typewriter to telling effect. Thirty thousand British troops scattered the headquarters at the beginning of June (cf. *Green Tears for Hecuba*). The next typewriter to disturb the peace of the locality would be that of Erskine Childers, and the hostile army would be an army of Irishmen with some British officers and all British equipment.

So the Kerrymen, after the battle for the harbour, and later for Cork City, had headed south and west. The terrain rose gradually, varying from five hundred to eight hundred feet. To the north of them, as they trudged along, lay the valleys of the Lee and its tributary, the Bride, carrying the two main roads to Macroom. To the south lay the watershed of the Bandon river. They travelled in late evening into early night, sleeping rough and always ready, moving in easy stages, still carrying their weapons, still free men, their main irritation (Mike remembered) being the incessant barking of dogs as they went by on the old back roads. And so they came to Béalnabláth. Still high above the village, they were greeted by the sound of gunfire along the valley southwards.

Fields in Ireland vary from one rood to forty acres but the expression, 'a few fields away', has been a constant and traditional estimate of distance in the country regions. Leaving the roads precipitately had become a constant and necessary mode of action since the advent of the Black-and-Tans. The Kerrymen left the road precipitately and dashed across the few intervening fields, heading directly towards the battle. Why? Who knows? Mike Donoghue told me they did. They were high above the valley of the 'Noneen' and the little dusty road swung around into their line of flight. In half a mile they were upon it, on a little plateau eighty feet above. Michael O'Donoghue said: 'We saw an army column stopped on the road below. Of course we threw ourselves down. The shooting was stopped now. There was a 'Whippet' armoured-car at the end of the line and there was a big man like he was standing on top of it (in silhouette?) looking around. The fellow next to me put up his gun and fired a shot and we SAW THE BIG MAN FALL. I hit down the gun like that (gesturing with his hand) and said to him — 'What did you do that for? Do you want to draw them on us!', and we skedaddled. We didn't know anything until the next day we got the *Cork Examiner* and we saw that Collins was kilt at this place, Béalnabláth!'. (In point of fact the *Cork Examiner* did not carry the story until the second next day, Thursday the twenty-fourth, but the afternoon paper, known as the *Evening Echo*, carried full cover of the sensational story on Wednesday).

*   *   *

At 7 p.m., 29 January 1990, Pádraig Greene of Ballinalee, Co. Longford, ex-national teacher, ninety years young, came on national radio and told a strange story. He had attended an Irish course at 'Coláiste na Mumhan', Ballingeary, during the month of August, 1922. Late in the evening of 22 August, he was at the 'Scoraíocht' (Irish dance) in the 'Halla'. He was leaning against the stage with Dr. Gearóid Ó Nualláin, President pro-tem of the 'Coláiste' and Irish professor at Maynooth College (uncle of 'Myles na gCopaleen') and Liam Twomey, prominent local Republican, when a number of armed men sidled into the dance hall. Liam Twomey exclaimed: 'What the hell is Mick Donoghue doing here!', and went over to speak to them. Returning a minute later he said, with tears in his eyes: 'Michael Collins was shot this evening at Béalnabláth! My mother isn't going to like this!'

*   *   *

Late on Wednesday evening, 23 August 1922, a party of six armed and weary Kerrymen arrived at Peter Sweeney's, Gortanacra, Ballyvourney. They did not give their names nor were they required to do so, but it was understood that they were from 'over the Bounds'. They had with them a motor car and were looking for petrol. A republican consignment was stashed away in a pile of mangel-wurzels (the English primly call them 'mangolds', the Irish 'mangles') at the back of the house. It may be noted that Wakefield 'Castrol' was being distributed in cans ('tins', as they were referred to) about the country, as had been the system from shortly after Lord Wakefield had re-established his failed British oil company in Belfast in 1899. These were two-gallon 'jerry-cans', painted green, with stylish brass caps somewhat like the crown on the 'King of Diamonds'. The caps invariably carried a wired lead seal. One of those empty cans is still extant at Gortanacra. It may have contained the actual fuel which indirectly engendered the death of Michael Collins. Two motor cars had been commandeered from the Muckross Estate in Killarney where at that time quite a number of 'high-class' English people were living in fine houses and on tenant farms within the vast estate. The motor cars were without petrol, so they had to be drawn to Glenflesk with horses. 'They were stashed above there in the mountain', said old Pat Riordan, pointing generally at the rugged reaches of

Fileadown and the 'Robber's Den', above the valley of the
Flesk river that the departed Black-and-Tans had known as the
'Robbers' Glen'. The Kerrymen had taken one of the cars to a
probable location in the Macroom area, and then the train to
Cork to confront Emmet Dalton in the harbour. At Gortanacra, on their return, the men were asked to stay to tea and
sat (the family remembers) in a semi-circle on the kitchen floor.
One young fellow in the group appeared strangely agitated.
From time to time he jumped up from his chair and paced the
floor in the grip of some fear or stress. Eventually the man of
the house said to him somewhat irritably — 'Is there something
wrong with you?'. The lad said — 'Yesterday we shot Michael
Collins!'. 'Well, then, if ye did', responded Peter Sweeney, 'it
was a damn bad day's work ye did!'; and the big man in charge
of the group (obviously Mike Donoghue) said to the young
fellow — 'Shut up! You're talking too much!'

'If only Tod Healy was alive, he could tell you all!', said old
Pat Riordan of Glenflesk. Of course he could, I said to myself,
and so could several others whom I could name and who were
now securely beneath the sod. 'Tod' Healy was Captain James
Healy, O/C of the Glenflesk 'D' Company, Second Battalion,
Kerry No. 2 Brigade, and Pat Riordan, born in 1904, was now
the 'last of the Mohicans', the only living member of the great
line-out of the list of fighting men from Glenflesk and surroundings which I now held in my hand and at which I vainly stared
to find a name for the man who shot Michael Collins. Why he
did it was irrelevant. Whether his name should be known,
likewise. But how he did it was important for posterity, and
would be pursued to the limit. He was, I knew, in there
somewhere. Was he battalion Vice-Commandant Jerry Kennedy of Brewesterfield House, Gortacuish? No. Jerry was not
at Béalnabláth. Thirty-odd years ago he told me himself that he
had been as far as Wexford a short time previously (where he
had 'decided' an undecided local officer with a fast draw of his
Smith and Wesson), and finally at Limerick. Nor was Tod
Healy. His wife vouched for that shortly before she died two

years ago. What about First Lieutenant Mick Murphy, or the second lieutenant with the quaintly historic name of John McGillicuddy? 'John Mac', as he was known, certainly was there. His nephew said so. He was a member of Mike Donoghue's intimate group during the Civil War. His father, Jerry, and his brother, Pat, went pro-Treaty, so he was unable to return home and lived in a dug-out at Clonkeen, eventually going to Australia and then to America, never to return. 'He was a good shot', said his nephew, John, the present incumbent at Clohane Iron Mill. Quarter-Master Michael O'Donoghue, known as 'Mick the Bridge', could have been there. So could, and probably were, section-commanders Con Quill and Mick Lynch, but probably not Adjutant Denis Hegarty because big Mike Donoghue, Intelligence Officer — an independent rank — was in charge of the group. Young Stephen McGrath might have been there. Could he drive a car? 'He could! He was good at everything!', said Pat Riordan. He was a student of some kind. His father and mother taught at Clonkeen National School, up towards the County Bounds. 'He was the only one of us', said Pat, 'who had plenty of time on his hands'. Was he, I asked myself, the excited young man who was 'talking too much' at Peter Sweeney's, Ballyvourney? And what about the two ex-soldiers, brothers Fred and Pats Healy, or any one of the forty-eight other volunteers of C and D Companies listed here who were scattered about Munster, from Kenmare to Shannon, to Kilmallock, to Passage West, fighting and dying to repel the new invaders, the Free State Army, from their home ground? Is it sufficient to know, or is it merely sad to relate, that one of those men fired the shot that killed Michael Collins? If only Tod Healy were alive!

Bernard O'Shea is ninety-four and lives on the Muskross Estate, Killarney, where he was born. In the old days he was Intelligence Officer to the Muskross Estate Company of which his brother, Tim, was captain. During the Truce he supervised the removal of the two motor cars from the estate. They were the property of two estate agents, Colonel Leahy and Major

Whelps. They were transported the back way by lovely Lake Guitane and first deposited at Hegarty's of Coosane, near the Robber's Den, Glenflesk. The engines, he remembers, had been immobilized but they were put in working order by an ex-British soldier from northern Ireland who had 'an impossible name' and was merely nicknamed 'Crowley'. Bernard's brother, Captain Tim (who later joined the Free State Army), could drive a car but was not, of course, at Béalnabláth. The driver for that occasion, he said, was another Michael O'Donoghue of Coolies, Muckross, known as Mick Dan Paddy. He was later killed off a motor cycle. Denis Hegarty, of Coosane, was — as already mentioned — adjutant to the Glenflesk Company. His younger brother, Michael, who still lives in Killarney, remembers that a fine bicycle was also taken from the Muckross Estate, the property of a Colonel Greany. It had a three-speed-gear on the handle-bar, and was his first introduction to that unique mode of transport.

*   *   *

Letter to the present writer from Mrs. Bridget M. Walker, 1211 College Avenue, Lenoir, North Carolina, 23 July 1989: 'I spent a week with them (at Ballyvourney) in 1964. We did not discuss politics, other than to say how much progress had been made since the 'Trouble Times'. It was a casual remark that he made when he said he saw the man who shot Michael Collins. He did not elaborate and I didn't ask any questions. After that it was never mentioned again'. Mrs. Walker was formerly Bridie Murphy of Barraduff, Co. Kerry, and a niece of Mike Donoghue!

5

The Jimmy Ormond Story

It begins at the end and ends at the beginning of a very strange footnote to History, which has now become the very essence of Irish History itself. It refers to the 'second wound at the hairline' which Dr. Oliver St. John Gogarty, who performed a cursory autopsy on the body of Michael Collins in Dublin, failed to mention at the time but did so many years later in America where he had gone to live. James Ormond, of Lismore, Co. Waterford, was marching at the end of an 'Indian file' of Republicans, hitherto unknown, who just happened on the ambush at Béalnabláth. For a brief moment he had Collins on his sights. All he needed in his hands was a rifle — which he had. The man directly in front of him, in the marching line, had a German Mauser automatic, a gun with which the Republicans were fairly liberally supplied — the rather notorious 'Peter the Painter', familiar enough to be referred to commonly as a 'Pether'. The ballistics of the matter will be gone into later, specifically with regard to the possibility of an invisible hairline wound on the forehead, or elsewhere on the skull, of the Commander-in-Chief. The problem is so important for posterity as to merit an exhumation of the body. It has been frequently mooted, and frequently rejected. The points have been made that it would require a legal, even a Government, order, that this would be virtually impossible to obtain, that it would take a long time to procure, that to do so otherwise would constitute a mere civil offence with a nominal fine. In this, the centenary year of the birth of Michael Collins, the matter has drifted into an ominous silence likely to remain . . .

So, was the Free State Army a 'Dublin Army', as so many men and women of the South seemed to regard it? No, indeed! No, unfortunately! Not even was it an army of 'The Pale' either in its early expansion and later constriction — that strange wall around the English in Ireland of long ago with Dublin City as its core (forerunner of the present embittered division of Ulster), the protective enbrasured parapet which has had its concomitants in the story of peoples, from the Great Wall of China through Antonine's Wall, Offa's Dyke, and many others, to the flaps of the recently demised 'Check-point Charlie' in divided Berlin. I am asked, naïvely but incisively, by a naïve but incisive mind: Were the Free State Army soldiers fighting for Ireland on England's behalf or fighting for England on Ireland's behalf? And I give the short, convenient answer: So far as the rank-and-file, and many of their officers, understood any of this, they were fighting for Collins. The regular cant of the time was: 'If it's good enough for Mick, it's good enough for me!' But Mick was told — It's not good enough for Cork! So who was Mick? From January to June of 1922 he was Chairman of the 'Provisional Government', an artificial, 'ad hoc', mono-cabinet-type Executive temporarily erected on the lines of the British Government within a Parliament-type 'Dáil Éireann' (prn. 'Dawl-Ay-Ran') which was under the presidency of Arthur Griffith since the resignation in January, 1922, of the still vacillating Eamon de Valera, and in which Michael Collins was, in fact, Minister for Finance, and in which all the confused and disturbed, but ambitious, 'Princes of Serendip' had still to catch at many fleeting notions in an effort to justify their new political existence. Politics is a city-state matter, from the classical Greek words 'polis, politiké'. Dublin was then, as always, the tail wagging the dog, and all too often the country people were merely the fleas. From July through August Mick was Commander-in-Chief of the Army which up to that stage was still being identified, by both sides in the dispute, as the Army of the Republic, its personnel still technically 'Volunteers'. And the force to reckon with was the almost inscrutable and solidly entrenched mind of General Liam Lynch, Republican Chief-of-Staff, on his incorrigible way to a personal Jerusalem and self-immolation.

The point at issue was: On the Liam Lynch, or anti-Treaty, side, were we still fighting for an Irish Republic; on the Michael Collins, or pro-Treaty, side, still fighting as-it-were for, or with-a-view-to, an Irish Republic? Words! Words! WORDS? Certainly not! A deceptive Treaty, then? Extremely doubtful, on the evidence. The British side to the argument had had their own share of blood, sweat and tears over a number of months before the signing of the document on the sixth of December, 1921. Their Prime Minister, tricky, astute, garrulous Welshman, David Lloyd George, had become somewhat hoist with his own petard, and a political career, which had rocketed in the early 'Great War' years, could have come to grief floundering in mud like the first Battle of the Somme. In June of 1921 he had laid on the 'Big Round-up' on the Derrynasagart mountain range between Cork and Kerry, to trap a reported 'shadow army' of Republicans, had found nothing and lost face considerably . . . 'More than that, it was not because there was nothing there after all, because part of a Divisional H.Q. staff, a complete "Flying Column" and many active-service men besides, that came accidentally within their sphere of influence, almost literally slipped through their fingers and got away without leaving a whiff of suspicion behind them' (From *Green Tears for Hecuba*). So, a year later the British had their troubles again over the Treaty and the implementation of it, in the Summer of 1922. And so it happened that a dour, introspective young man of few words and simple emotions, named Jimmy Ormond, from the town that gloried in the Duke of Devonshire's manorial castle, found himself in West Cork training for the future in a section of a company of a battalion of the Third Cork Brigade, under the auspices of General Tom Barry, the most famous of all guerrilla leaders of the time, first among his peers, and whose list of victorious battles read like that of Napoleon in his heyday.

The Third Cork Brigade was one of ten within the framework of the First Southern Division of the Volunteer Army which had been arranged into fourteen divisions, North and South. It was the first time in history that the whole country was an organized fighting force. The nearest equivalent was the army of Brian Boru which fought the Danes at the battle of Clontarf in 1014. The famous 'Ard-Rí' (lit. 'High-King') of Ireland, indeed, had native Irish troops ranged against him on the side of the enemy. Likewise in the Spring and Summer of 1922 the army divisions were divided in their allegiance, in a confused medley of for-and-against the Treaty, for-and-against the Provisional Government, for-and-against Dáil Éireann and, most disturbing to individual minds, for-and-against an Irish Republic. The First Southern Division was clearly anti-Treaty and comprised the counties of Cork, Waterford, Kerry and West Limerick. Its Commandant was General Liam Lynch who was also Chief-of-Staff of the I.R.A. with Headquarters first at Mallow, then at Limerick, later at Clonmel and, finally, at Fermoy before defeat and death. Transfer of allegiance was almost continuous during those vital months. Otherwise all movement was confined within single divisions depending on the whim or initiative of the Commandant. So Jimmy Ormond, with his small contingent from Lismore, found himself in West Cork training with Tom Barry ostensibly with a view to an offensive against the North of Ireland where Catholics were being slaughtered. (Jimmy Ormond's commanding officer is now an old Redemptorist priest, retired in Dublin, who confided to me that he did not particularly like young Ormond. I have often wondered why!).

*   *   *

Two Irishmen met in a 'speakeasy' in Broadway, New York City, on an Autumn evening in 1926. They were cousins but had not met each other for a considerable length of time and had no knowledge of mutual activities or whereabouts. They just happened to be working in Broadway. They also happened to be on opposite sides during the Civil War: Section Commander Edward Lane, F Company, Second Battalion, First Dublin Brigade, who was with the Free State Army in Tralee, and republican James Ormond, of Lismore. Old Ned gave me the story on tape, with a signed statement, some weeks before his death in January, 1986, at his residence in Kilcommen Avenue off the North Circular Road, Dublin. He related how Jimmy Ormond had told him that he had come on the battle of Béalnabláth from the Bandon side, had fired some shots and 'saw the big man fall'. This revelation in Broadway, in 1926, was the only one Jimmy Ormond ever made, even to his family. Conspiracy of silence had become the order of the day. Conspiracy of silence was a personal thing to young Jimmy Ormond. He was a silent man, anyway, but he did become more communicative later in life and he admitted to his wife on his deathbed, in 1978, having been at Béalnabláth on that day of days in Irish History. And he was a determined man. Some months later, as a prisoner of the Free State Army, he had escaped from Fermoy military barracks, simply by slinging some bed clothes over the barbed wire of the surrounding wall.

*   *   *

The Dublin 'Four Courts', with its six Grecian columns and single cupola, stands beside the River Liffey upstream from O'Connell's Bridge. It was completed in 1802 to a design by James Gandon. His work in Dublin had been accompanied by much controversy and even rioting. It is ironic that this magnificent edifice should have become a political foil and almost destroyed by warring Irishmen a century and two decades later. It was where the Civil War really began at the end of June, 1922. Housing the Law Courts, it had been occupied in April by an extreme group of the I.R.A. Executive under the command of General Rory O'Connor. Tom Barry had left his Third Brigade H.Q. in West Cork, where, as Director of Operations, he had established a training camp for the First Southern Division. Barry made his way to Dublin where, in an effort to join the garrison of the Four Courts, he was captured and imprisoned. The building was under shell fire for some days and the rebel officers capitulated on the last day of June. With the fall of Cork City, and the investing of the major towns by the Free State Army during the third week of August, with Barry temporarily 'hors de combat', the men from Lismore simply turned their faces to the East and began to walk in the direction of Waterford and home. They were eager for transport and were prepared to fight for it. On their way the village of Ballinascarty, birthplace of Henry Ford's father, did not have a Model-T to its name. They turned North. Meeting the Enniskeane road to Crookstown they faced North-East, coming out on the Bandon road at Bradfield's Cross. And so they came to Béalnabláth 'de shiúl na gcos' — on Shank's mare. They had given the go-by to Bandon, eight miles back, and were wondering how to give the miss to Cork City, twenty miles ahead. Distant firing was no wonder and when they heard some, in the valley beyond, they hurried to the scene in the hope of capturing some means of locomotion. They were tired, hungry and now it had begun to rain. Walking single file, and heading for higher ground, they viewed the quarry. Jimmy Ormond was last man in line. An army column was halted on the road beneath them and just as they arrived the firing ceased. From behind an armoured car, at the end of the column and nearest to them, a 'big man' appeared walking up the road in their direction. They fired some shots and Jimmy Ormond 'saw the big man fall'. Other soldiers appeared around the bend and having fired some more as a gesture the Waterford men proceeded on their way. Unknown to them, in a backyard of a farmhouse nearby, was a 'rake' of motor cars, Republican transport from as far away as Donegal and Dublin. It would have been theirs for the asking . . .

6

The Bobs Doherty Story

'I went into the army because I liked horses, and I've spent four years in and out of a stinking, noisy tank . . .' Thus spake Evelyn Waugh's Brigadier Cape in *The Sword of Honour*. The transition from cavalry to armour came gradually between the two World Wars, with a fading emphasis in the First and a firmer de-emphasis in the Second. In retrospect the disastrous charge of the Lancers up Sackville Street, Dublin, at Easter, 1916, seems almost as ludicrous as the charge of the Polish cavalry against the German Panzers in September, 1939. Chivalry to genocide was, however, an alternative gradation in the history of 'war's glorious art'. And men continue to fight and die while the world is fully aware that everybody loses in the end, occasionally cognizant of the fact that, for example, the known Commander-in-Chief lying dead on the roadside might conceivably have been the still unknown soldier who shot him from the hillside at Béalnabláth. The pawns remain perpetually interchangeable, the affiliations inexplicably complex . . .

Robert J. ('Bobs') Doherty, of Glenflesk, Co. Kerry, went to Ballincollig, near Cork City, to join the Army because he liked horses. Going to Ballincollig after the publication of the Truce Agreement (Monday, 11 July 1921) became a polarization of intent west of the Derrynasaggart mountains. Bobs

30

understood that they were forming a cavalry unit at that world-renowned ex-British Army barracks 'to attack the North'. He did not end up in a stinking, noisy tank. Fortuitously he ended up at Béalnabláth just in time to see the big man fall. Or maybe he fired the fatal shot! He has been strongly credited with the effort. In 1987, as an old man in St. Petersburg, Florida, U.S.A., deaf and almost blind, but still vigorous in voice production, he denied the questionable honour. He did, however, in a spirit of exuberance on arriving in America in 1925, claim to have done so. Undoubtedly he was there — at Béalnabláth. He revisited the place on three occasions with his Irish relatives. His two comments in recent times to his nephew, Con Doherty of Tiernaboul, Killarney, were: 'I was above the road' and 'I was covering the road'. His exact position has been identified and will be pin-pointed in time.

*   *   *

'Sagittarius' is a centaur, a classical horse-man or man-horse archer aiming to shoot a star — or is it a moon? — with his bow and arrow. Old Bobs Doherty would be confused, maybe concerned, at the analogy. Apart from the possibility of his having been a David to Collins' acknowledged Goliath, his prowess as a marksman still endures in the living memory of his locality. At Ballincollig he joined an echelon of the army still committed to fighting for the Republic, which had the mainly Protestant six northern counties of Ireland as an immediate objective. Furthermore, it was firmly believed in such circles that Michael Collins was already planning such a campaign, while border incidents and Belfast pogroms were becoming daily more frequent. Like so many others, Bobs found himself merely fighting for one army division against another . . . 'Before the middle of July (i.e. 1922) all hope of a truce in Munster was at an end and the two Irish armies were committed to war' (Macardle in *The Irish Republic*). Looking forward a little, the lovely bayside town of Kenmare, in County Kerry, fell to Free State troops on 11 August 1922. It was held precariously for a month by inadequate forces for such an important salient deep inside the Kingdom. Kerry, after a less intense preoccupation with the 'Tan War', now became seriously embroiled in the 'cogadh cois teallaigh'; the 'war beside the hearthstone', the tragic Civil War. Dublin, Cork, Waterford, Limerick — and some major towns — may have identified with the alternative 'cogadh cathardha', the inter-city or infra-city conflict as in classical times. Kenmare was held by officers of the locality, now on the side of the Provisional Government, while their companions and fellow fighters of a short while before were in the hills looking down in dismay and bitterness. Kerry was bitterest of all in the Civil War. Kerry was murderous. Kerry was tragic. Kenmare was held by officers who could live at home. Their opponents also frequently lived at home, and un-neighbourly visitations became nightly raids. Kenmare was weakly held and obviously set for a counter-attack. It happened on Saturday, 9 September 1922. It happened early in the morning and went on all day. By evening the Republicans were in and the Free Staters were out, while some of their officers were floating down Kenmare Bay to the sea in an open boat. The attack was directed by Séamus Robinson, famous Tipperary guerrilla fighter, conspicuous in his bowler hat, with local Republican commander — and later politician — Tom McEllistrim, and Brigadier John Joe Rice. Bobs Doherty led his section of a dozen men from Kilgarvan down along the Roughty Valley, renowned in song and story. A mile out of town he turned on a by-road northwards, swung west to the Union Workhouse and began his fight into town along the banks of the little Finnihy river. His advance was held up temporarily by one man, like Cuchulainn defending the Ford of Ardee. But this time Ferdia, the challenger, was victorious. A sniper, high up in the steeple of the parish church, was wreaking havoc among his men. Bobs steadied his rifle and with the sure eye of the mountainy man picked the sniper out of the eye of the parochial steeple. He thus shot his way not only into folklore but into history; for that may have been the shot which got him credited with having killed Michael Collins at Béalnabláth. Or maybe not! But he still rates one of the possibles.

*   *   *

After the fall of Cork City to Major-General Emmet Dalton the National Army did not immediately give its attention to the vast barracks at Ballincollig, five miles away. They did not have the manpower. In an urgent signal to Collins on 11 August, Dalton appealed for reinforcements. He needed some hundreds of men. 'I am at a standstill!', he mourned. Dalton's dilemma gave the Republicans time to burn down a large part of the establishment at Ballincollig. In fact quite a few of them still roamed the city streets and occupied some of the important buildings including the waiting Shanakiel Hospital. But the Army was intent on following the main body of Irregulars to Macroom and the West, leaving their lines of communication and supply rather tenuous. The British had tended to the same mistake during the previous 'Troubles'. Most of the Republicans left Ballincollig and headed West. (Liam Lynch was just then negotiating the setting up of a guerrilla base at Kilpadder in the vicinity of Mallow, and Dev was in troubled attendance). Bobs Doherty hung around Ballincollig Barracks for a while. With him was 'a clerical student from Castleisland' (in Kerry). His name the old man could not remember. After a brief but sensational episode they never met again. 'I think he went to America and disappeared', said Bobs. The student was training in munitions. Ballincollig Barracks gloried in the knowledge of having the largest powder mills anywhere, its fame beyond the confines of Empire, its ruins of exquisite stone-work, painstakingly built, now dreaming and vegetating along the banks of my own lovely Lee. College students featured in the Civil War as in the Tan War. Medical students and others, from Cork's University, were prominent in the South — Dr. Patrick O'Sullivan, of Kilnamartyra, his engineer brother Mick (author of *Where Mountainy Men Have Sown*), Dr. Frank Creedon, of Ballyvourney, Dr. Willie O'Riordan, of

Ballycotton, Dr. Eugene Callanan, of Clonakilty, to name but
a few. The clerical student was an oddity, but not misplaced in
History. Students from the great ecclesiastical seminary of
Maynooth, in County Kildare, the largest and most famous in
the world, had been hanged 'for treason' in 1798, during the
great rebellion, just three years after the foundation of the
college.

*   *   *

Bobs Doherty and his student friend eventually left Ballincollig
Barracks. They were the last to go. Inside the vast expanse of
buildings they were in comparative safety. On the outside
things were happening but military traffic was still only inter-
mittent or not at all — because of obstruction — on the road
they were to follow. Boldly leaving the main gates they moved
along the all-to-one-side main street which, at that time, was no
more than an exclamation-mark on the thoroughfare. Still
bearing their weapons they left the village behind and headed
west on the southern road to Macroom. They had a rifle apiece
and, oddly enough, a Lewis-gun slung in a wooden box between
them. They were nothing if not prepared. It was the seventeenth
of August. They had five days to go before their fateful
meeting, two or three spent in watchful meandering and resting
up as they met with and briefly touched the river of destiny, the
Bride. The first meeting was at Ovens Bridge, three miles out.
The bridge was demolished, but relief was at hand. Just beside
the bridge was the hidden entrance to the largest limestone cave
system in Munster. They had found an ideal haven for an in-
terlude. (The name 'Ovens' is a corruption of the Gaelic
'uaimheanna' meaning 'caves'). Ten years later, in 1932, an old
wooden box was discovered deep inside the caves, containing a
Lee-Enfield rifle and a Lewis light machine-gun. The Lewis-
gun was a commonplace weapon of the time, capable of being
carried by one man even with twin satchels of circular ammunition pans strapped across the shoulders. Lewis-guns were
prominent on the Republican side against the Tans at

Coolnacahera, outside of Ballyvourney, in February, 1921, in one of the most extensive and successful ambushes of the period. The Lewis-gun (like the 'Pether') became a personality weapon and it was 'a great man' who could fire one from the shoulder, just as it was 'a great man' (e.g. Dan J. Quill of Coolea) who could fire a rifle-grenade from the shoulder. The Lewis was quick and handy in an emergency, the equivalent of forty-seven (a pan full) rifles. Bobs Doherty and friend had second thoughts and decided on mobility instead, but Bobs kept his own rifle for luck. Beyond the bridge they took to the higher ground, turning left for Kilumney and leaving the Macroom road behind. The old Irish good-luck wish, 'Go n-éirí an bóthar leat!' ('May the road rise with you!'), was never before so relevant to Bobs and his nameless student companion. The road did indeed rise with them after Kilumney and they were able to view the expanding valley of the Bride and the precarious roadway possibly traversed by hostile traffic from Macroom. There was one item of great historical interest — the ruins of the fifteenth century Franciscan Friary of Kilcrea whose graveyard housed the remains of two notable resisters of hostile forces of the past: Cormac McCarthy, known as 'Láidir', the Strong, born in 1411, who captured Macroom Castle (built in the thirteenth century by the Carew family) and established it as a Celtic stronghold; and gentleman-farmer and tragic adventurer, Art O'Leary, also of Macroom.

On the sandstone ridge above the flat limestone valley Bobs and the erstwhile clerical student passed through Aherla village and shortly afterwards came upon the entrance to Annesgrove House, on the right, waiting for its hour of glory. Just there came the parting of the ways. Straight on was Crookstown and the Macroom road once more. The Bride gorge and its enveloping hills ran southwards. Far away to the west, and reading from south to north, there were four passes homewards over the Derrynasaggart mountains: Borlin, above lovely Glengarriff by the sea; Lackabawn, above St. Finbarr's Gougane Barra; Robert Gibbings' 'Top of Coom', above Coolea; and the 'County Bounds', above Ballyvourney. Still keeping to the high places they turned south, just short of Annesgrove, to the Quarry Crossroads, to Béalnabláth, and into History. Beneath them in the valley the standing-stone known as 'Clodah' (in Irish, 'Cloch Dáith' — 'David's Stone') stood inside its ring of prominence. And Goliath was over the next hill, oblivious to the impending sling-shot . . .

It was half-past seven and it had started to rain. Gun-fire was echoing along the valley. They dashed over the hill on the near (or eastern) side of the road and rather suddenly came upon the scene of battle. 'We dived for cover', said old Bobs, still remembering the feel of wet grass where they landed. 'There were some men already in position near us', he continued, 'and a little distance away. I didn't know who they were. There was an armed column below us on the road and a big man started to walk away from it. Someone near us fired just then and I saw the big man fall. I heard a man say — "I put two into him!" That's all I know!' Is that all anybody knows, or will ever know, about the death of Michael Collins? Will there always be one question to ninety-nine answers, like the camel and the name of Allah? The 'clerical student from Castleisland' was, in fact, James Sheehan of Knockatagil, Kilcummin, Killarney, born in 1901, who regarded Castleisland as his home town because he had 'huckstered' so much there as a boy on behalf of his widowed mother's little shop, during the course of the Great War. Then, in 1919, he 'went for the church' to St. Peter's College, Wexford, but left in 1921 'because of some I.R.A. trouble', his relations say. After Béalnabláth he disappeared, arrived in America, returned some years later to live a lonely bachelor existence until his death five years ago (1985), at Knockatagil, the 'Hill of the Rye' . . . Another and more famous clerical student (this time from Maynooth) was John (Jack) Stack of Ballyconry, near Listowel. His story, if investigated, could be the basis of a separate little volume. In fact he himself was to become the model for 'Michael Flynn, his second-in-command, known as Mickeen Oge Flynn', unconditional republican, celibate by inclination, half priest by training' (whose only child, Dr. Betty Stack, still lives in Ballyduff), while 'Paddy Bawn Enright, ex-prize-fighter, known as "The Quiet Man" . . .', was based (as admitted by the author himself, Maurice Walsh) on John McElligott of Listowel, and 'Castletown' (of the book rather than the John Ford film) was, of course, Castleisland, nestling comfortably in the long shadow of Stack's Mountain!

*   *   *

Bobs Doherty has now died (1989). His latest picture shows the fine old Kerry-American features still glowing with the memory of an adventurous and once deadly life-style, the rakish and buccaneer look still lighting up his face, the great hands still holding an imaginary gun to show how fields were won — and lost. Deaf and diabetic, his enormous voice bellows out the rudiments and crudiments of his long life to an indifferent tape-recorder, resounding from the Everglades of Florida to the heatherglades of Fileadown. His was not even a legitimate birth. In Glenflesk he was a 'peata fraoigh', the 'pet, or darling, of the heather' — an ungodly but lovely thought. By contrast, Michael Collins was the son of a seventy-five-year-old man and a young woman, his lawful wife — a godly but unlovely after-thought. And choir-boy Bobs was the model for the sweet singer in the classic Black-and-Tan film, *The Dawn*, which featured the *Slievenamon* itself; and Johnny McCarthy, of Glenflesk, sang, in silver Irish tenor, of 'Bold Phelim Brady, the Bard of Armagh'.

7

The Timmie Kelleher Story

Emmet Dalton said in a televised documentary in 1978: 'If you look at the map of West Cork, it sticks out a mile how you have to go!' Why, then, did it take three men to guide the Collins convoy into Carbery? First, there was the motor cycle scout, or outrider, named Smith, a lieutenant, who joked about not being a map-reader, but who rode a bone-shaking 1919 'Triumph', with rigid back springing and nerve-shattering front compression-coil suspension, all over the place in an unrecorded endurance test considering the condition of the roads of that era, when all roads were dirt roads and pot-holes were filled with piles of hand-broken stones, and the dust in dry weather formed treacherous ridges and in the rain was furrowed mud. Then there was the Mallow man, John O'Connell, who left home to guide them into West Cork and did not know the way but joined the Army in the process, fought at Béalnabláth and afterwards talked about it as if he were Field Marshal Foch discussing the Battle of the Marne. And, finally, there was the taxi-driver, the type who knows the roads so well that he gets as near as possible to how the crow flies, regardless of merit, and who led Michael Collins and his band to Bandon through an intricate system of by-roads that almost baffles description. He was Timmie Kelleher of Macroom. This is his (somewhat extended) story . . .

Mr. Timothy Kelleher, at the time of his death, was a prosperous garage owner in the town of Macroom. He began his career as a driver, being employed by Mr. R.C. Williams, the Protestant (with the incongruous initials) and popular proprietor of Williams' Hotel (now the Castle Hotel), Main Street, but familiarly known to one and all as 'Dickie'. In this hotel began the Truce incident which was to become a 'cause célèbre' in the House of Commons, in London. The Republican forces were in occupation in Macroom Castle. Their police were about the town. One of them noticed a car without a licence plate parked in front of Williams' Hotel. The driver, sitting at the wheel, had an English accent. Adjutant Charlie Browne (author of *The Story of the Seventh*) was in charge at the Castle in the absence of Commandant Dan Corkery who was attending Dáil Éireann in Dublin. Charlie marched out and found three strangers, who had previously been drinking at the bar of the hotel, now moving about the town. One of them he recognized as a 'tough egg' from his prison days in Cork. He took all four to the Castle for interrogation. They were on a fishing trip, they said. No fishing gear. Civilian clothes. Concealed weapons. Brigade Headquarters, in Cork City, in response to a telephoned inquiry, sent a firing squad . . . An angry young colonel, the youngest in the British Army, brought his troops out in force from Victoria (now Collins) Barracks in Cork, where they were still in residence despite the general withdrawal since the signing of the Treaty in the previous December. His name — Montgomery! He was looking for his men whose fate was still not known despite assiduous inquiries. He surrounded the Castle. Members of the Sixth, Seventh and Eighth Battalions surrounded the British. Monty advanced to the gates of the Castle. Niall O'Leary, an effervescent young returned-American, pushed his rifle through a window in a turret above the gates, where he was on sentry duty, and told the future Field Marshal to 'put your bloody hands up'. After an unsatisfactory parley the British retired. Monty tells it in his memoirs. In London Mr. Austen Chamberlain, as Lord Privy

Seal and Leader of the House, asked an angry House of Commons to 'remember the difficulties under which the Provisional Government is labouring'. After the Civil War the bodies of the executed men were exhumed and sent back to England. The *Cork Examiner* expatiated on the touching scene of a feeble old man, who had travelled from England with great difficulty, standing alone and wordless while his son's body was being removed from a bog in Clondrohid. C'est la guerre, or something . . . 'Macready believed that the Republican garrison of Macroom could have been more helpful . . . Mr. F.J.R. Hendy, father of one of the British officers kidnapped and murdered at Macroom, wrote to *The Times* blaming the British Government . . .' (Calton Younger in *Ireland's Civil War*).

About Macroom Castle: The actual owner was Lady Ardilaun (the Hon. Olivia Charlotte White, widow of the first Baron Ardilaun — Mr. Arthur Guinness), a highly respected lady of charity and culture, living in Dublin since her husband's death in 1915. Her father, she proudly told the Town Park Committee of Macroom, was a direct descendent of Cormac McCarthy 'Láidir', and the Castle always remained in possession of families allied by blood, except for brief exchanges of hand. Unfortunately (because it was one of the most magnificent structures of domestic architecture in the British Isles, and one of the oldest inhabited) the hand-changing always involved burning. Previous to the McCarthys were the O'Flynns (after whom Mid-Cork was known as 'Múscraí Uí Fhloinn' or 'Muskerry-Flynn') and apparently before that were the Norman Carews who were said to have built the Castle, or its prototype, in the thirteenth century. When the Free State Army arrived, after the fall of Cork City to Emmet Dalton, it was once again a smouldering shell. That was how Michael Collins found it on the evening of 21 August 1922, when he made the first of two inspections in the town. Perhaps his remarks on seeing it have survived in some junior officer's notebook, yet to be discovered. It is unlikely that he observed a dignified silence. Preoccupied with related matters, particularly the billeting of his troops within and around the fire-blackened walls (some were placed in the Victoria Hotel across the Square — one private put on record that he had never been in a hotel in his life before — while the Commandant's H.Q. was in the historic Market House), he paid but a brief visit to the old workhouse, the 'Union' at the top of Pound Lane (cf. Chapter Sixteen — 'The Tom Daly Story') and returned to Cork . . .

Timmie Kelleher, taxi-driver, seems to have been functioning in a world of his own regardless of circumstances. His first driving licence was issued by the 'Office of District Inspector, R.I. Constabulary, Macroom, 22.2.20' and 'Renewed, 18th. March, 1921, T. Dolan, 1 Di.' (i.e. before and after the Coolnacahera ambush), which authorized him to 'drive a Motor car, P.I.63 and W.I.77' for 'Owner R.C. Williams, J.P.'. His next licence was issued '24th. October, 1922' and signed 'J.E. Dalton, Major-General Officer, Competent Military Authority' (Dalton's initialled signature comes as a surprise!) for a 'Ford Touring, Regd. No. IF 219'. (Cf. Chapter Eleven, 'The Itinerary', for continuity) . . .

On the morning of 22 August 1922, Timmie Kelleher was awakened at 5.15 a.m., and asked to accompany Michael Collins as a guide. (James Cooney, *Macroom: People and Places*). The time is the man's own word. It is disputed but probably erroneously. For such a stirring occasion the rude and early awakening is understandable. Collins could not have arrived from Cork at that time, and he certainly did not leave the town before 8.30 a.m. Was Macroom on 'Old Time'? Was Collins on 'New Time'? The convoy, according to Kelleher, consisted of a motor cycle scout, two Crossley tenders with eight men in each, Collins' motor car and an armoured car. The convoy proceeded to Béalnabláth 'via Doonisky and Kilmurry'. Doonisky, on the main road to Cork, has to be incorrect in the light of further evidence. At Béalnabláth, Kelleher continued, Collins and a section of the convoy lost sight of the scout and the first (and second?) lorry. This also has to be a loose statement. Lieutenant Smith, on his motor bike, arrived at Béalnabláth with the Commander-in-Chief's touring car (or alternatively waited for it there). It was obviously in full view when the scout made his inquiries in the middle of the crossroads (cf. Chapter Nineteen: 'Five Local People'). Mossgrove Cross had to be the parting of the ways, while the intervening rising ground may have created further problems for the unfortunate Leyland Eight.

Contrary to some published accounts, Major-General Emmet Dalton did not leave Macroom in style seated beside his Commanding Officer. He travelled in the (first?) lorry just behind the motor cycle scout. Timmie Kelleher sat between him and the driver, Captain Conroy . . . 'When the scout and the first (and second?) lorry reached Mossgrove crossroads Kelleher signalled the scout to keep left for Bandon. When Collins and the rest of the convoy came to the Cross they turned right for Newcestown. Kelleher and Dalton soon realized they had lost the rest of the convoy. They turned around and went to Newcestown where Collins was waiting for them in the churchyard. Then they all continued directly to Bandon from there. At Bandon the motor cycle scout said he "could navigate the return journey" (N.B. "return"). Collins kindly secured a taxi to get Kelleher back to Macroom. Returning to Béalnabláth "about midday", Kelleher says there was "an awful lot of Republicans around" '. (From *Macroom: People and Places*. Timmie has left two other published accounts of his experience, to Meda Ryan — *The Day Michael Collins was Shot* — and to the *Sunday Independent*, 5 July 1970) . . .

The probability of 'an awful lot of Republicans around' did not seem to bother General Michael Collins as he returned to his native countryside, that fine morning in August, 1922, as he possibly prayed in the parish church of Newcestown village, as he tossed a handful of coins (local tradition) in the air and gleefully watched a small group of school children scramble for them in hectic confusion, as he stood in a country churchyard in County Cork thinking about Life and Death:

> The boast of heraldry, the pomp of power,
> And all that beauty, all that wealth e'er gave,
> Awaits alike th'inevitable hour:
> The paths of glory lead but to the grave.

8

'I Could a Tale Unfold'

Like the ghost of Hamlet's father, the man of slight build, courteous manner and watchful eye, who sat in a corner of the 'snug' in the Victoria Hotel, situated in an alcove of the Square, a stone's throw from Macroom Castle gates, might have added, 'But that I am forbid to tell the secrets of my prison-house!' It was the morning of that fateful day, 22 August 1922, and Florence O'Donoghue, until recently, but now resigned, Adjutant-General of the Irish Republican Army (author of *No Other Law*, and whose further memoirs and sundry papers are under legal lock and key until this, 1990, the centenary year of the birth of Michael Collins), was unarmed, neutral and alone. The Victoria Hotel! Why did that British queen, he mused, who ruled the greatest empire the world had known, and which was now apparently giving at the seams, have to be so avidly remembered in this island of restless rebellion and tentative republicanism. That name 'at which the world grew pale' did not point any moral, he thought, but adorned many a military barracks from Cork to the Matto Grosso. It was true, he granted, that Irish soldiers now trundled their weapons of war into and out of those formidable gates across the Square. He hoped they were there for a good purpose. He doubted it. William Penn had been raised, possibly even born some said, in that castle and had retained a regard, if not for its symbolism, at least for its 'local habitation'. He had left it only to go up to Oxford in 1660. Ten years later he again visited Macroom when, according to his *Irish Journal*, he 'stayed that night (18 April 1670), lay at Chris Gould's . . . stayed there that day (19 April) by reason of the rain. Saw the Castle and gardens. At the Widow Gould's bespoke seven and three-quarter gallons ''uisce beatha'' (whiskey).'

For just about a hundred years previously the inn (now the Victoria Hotel) had been known as 'The Widow Gould's' (the Gould family is still in the vicinity), a recognized stop for coaches, as well as being a favourite haunt of rebel rapparees and recalcitrant highwaymen where they rendezvoused, conferred and planned. Florrie liked the dusty, ectoplasmic atmosphere of olden times. He wondered, as he waited, how the interview he was about to partake in would rate with those desperate fellows of long ago who also had lived by the sword and frequently perished by the sword. Already his expected guests were on their way from Williams' Hotel in the main street, two figures in army uniform walking rapidly, rounding the corner at Harry Murphy's chemist shop, one a big man, burly and bustling, talking intensely, the other slim, of medium height, and silent, listening, intensely watchful, the 'famous bodyguard' of Treaty days in London, gun-flap unbuttoned, hand resting lightly on holster. Florence O'Donoghue stood up as the door was flung open . . .

'Florrie!'

'Good morning, Mick!'

'How are you?'

'Oh, I'm fine! Well, fair enough, you know!'

'This is Emmet Dalton!'

'Good morning, Sir! I've heard a lot about you!'

'Cut the politeness, Florrie! There'll be another day for that and we have a tough job before us!'

'Just as you say, Mick!'

'Not that we can't handle it, mind! But we could do with a

helping hand. To save more trouble, you understand. There's enough dead, dammit! That's why I asked you, yesterday evening in Cork, to come on out here.'

'What can I do?'

'You're well in with them. I tried Seán Hegarty, in Cork, as you know, but he wouldn't budge. You know how Seán is. Anyway, P.S., his brother, is with us. You're not against us, are you?'

'I'm against nobody, Mick!'

'Godammit, neither am I! But the thing somehow got out of hand.'

'Isn't it going right for you, now — you in charge and all that. Cork is gone, Limerick, Waterford, Carrick-on-Suir, Clonmel, Fermoy . . .'

'For God's sake don't say "Gone!", Florrie! Where are they gone to, I ask you?'

'Sorry, Mick — my mistake!'

'But I can tell you they're getting impatient in Dublin, threatening murder, in fact. Arthur's gentility died with him the other day. Emmet here is sound. While he's around there'll be control. No reprisals. Just a good, clean job. But I'm worried about the fellows down here. If I could only get through to them!'

'I'll do my best!'

'Good man — do that! Talk to Charlie Browne and some others. 'Colder', I mean Dan Corkery, could be difficult. You heard his crack in the Dáil, about upstarts who never fired a shot. I met a local bunch down below there, last night. I forget their names, but they're in favour. Outside the crowd went wild. But this town is split, isn't it?'

'About fifty-fifty.'

'Damn! As bad as that? However, I'll be back here in the evening. Is that all right, Emmet?'

'Whatever you say, General! Just one thing . . .'

'What's that?'

'We've only got a small escort. Couldn't he come back to

Cork, if we went straight on after we're through? Innishannon Bridge, I hear, is patched up. And that little place, near Crossbarry, on the road to Bandon — what d'ye call it? Kill-something. Oh, yes! Killeady. That's clear! It would be best that way. I could give him a pass'.

'No - No! I must have an answer — I couldn't sleep the night!'

'May I say something?'

'Yes, Florrie! What is it?'

'What will Winston say if you start negotiating privately?'

'Winston can go and . . . . himself, at this stage, as far as I'm concerned! There's too much trouble brewing on the Border. Fitzpatrick being shot was a serious business. Only thing, he took four of the "Specials" with him. Up there is where I'd like to be at this moment. But I can't leave these fellows down here. I know them. They're too dangerous. Try to put them off, will you, Florrie? I'll agree to anything — anything in reason! Otherwise I'll have to kill them. Bloody Sunday!'

*   *   *

He watched the two soldiers walk away around Harry Murphy's corner, without a glance towards the Castle gates — one talking, the other listening. He got on his bicycle and started to ride away to anywhere, carrying a dead weight of responsibility . . . 'I only remember one slight incident, of very little importance, which was spoken of when we were very young children. I believe that Michael Collins did give my mother a present of a Kerry-Blue dog when he visited them (Dad and Mother) the day before he died'. (Letter from Rome, 28/1/90, from Mrs. Breda O'Donoghue Lucci, sculptress daughter of Florrie O'Donoghue). And thereby hangs a tale!

9

The Emmet Dalton Story

This above all: to thine own self be true,
And it must follow, as the night the day,
Thou canst not then be false to any man.
(Polonius).

Emmet Dalton was a soldier. What is a soldier? you ask. Definition follows. Mine! Yours! Lloyd George's! Anybody's! Yes,
but (you say) Dalton resigned from soldiering at what is known
as the peak of his career. Can one resign from soldiering? On
the definition, or otherwise? Yes? How, then, did he do what he
had to do as a soldier just the length of one document away
from 'civvy street', or the thickness of a piece of 'bumf'? Is
there a question of morality in soldiering? He who takes the
sword shall perish by the sword, Scripture says. Or HAMLET
once again — 'that the Everlasting had not fix'd His canon
'gainst self-slaughter', nor, indeed, against hetero-slaughter.
Or is there now an absolute principle for the gun-in-hand just
because Stone-Age people found a need to protect themselves,
and their new-found property, from others of their kind? Or
was there an earlier emotion created when Neanderthal Man
found himself just too soon for civilization, with Cro-Magnon
Man (and Woman) already about to take possession of a few
points of the Law?

Literary giants of the twentieth century have found it convenient (in the classical sense of 'conveniens') to refer to an apparent early change of styles in life and human behaviour as 'pre-1914' or 'pure 1914', while we who had not had the experience were noting, with the single-mindedness of youth, the scarred faces, the shell-shocked nerves, the strange pallor of ex-soldier postmen and road workers, the sad one-leggedness of sideline entertainers and, contrarily, the tall, swinging gait of the Driscolls, O'Briens and Sheridans, the straight-backed tinkers of the Munster Fusiliers. We were still to learn that the tarnished images of the Rupert Brookes had even pre-dated the upheaval known as 'The Great War', despite the general adulation accorded to them. Anyway, a slightly built, average-sized young Dublin man, named Emmet Dalton, went to war and by the circuitous and tediously muddy route of the trenches of Picardy and Flanders worked his way into Irish History. Was he a great man? 'I don't know', said daughter Nuala — 'I only knew him as "Daddy"!'. What did others know him as? The daring would-be rescuer of Seán McKeon? Frank Pakenham's 'famous bodyguard' of the Treaty Debates in London? The quiet, unobtrusive conqueror of Cork City — the Napoleon of Patrick's Hill? Or . . . the unbelievable 'mole' of John Feehan — the paid and vengeful slayer of Michael Collins, the avenger of 'Bloody Sunday'? With a hundred or so private opportunities, did he have to wait and calculate for a chance ambush and public exposure, leaving Winston Churchill to explain to the world? Perhaps he shot Tom Kettle at Givenchy (on the pretext that he was a too idealistic Irish intellectual in a world of war), and buried his body in the seething chalk! Preposterous, you say? What is the essential nature of being preposterous? And what does Emmet Dalton mean to a somewhat newer generation? The bearer of a famous name who, unaccountably, became a film maker? — who, in the process, displayed the flair as well as the intense eye and sideways-leaning head of a John Ford, with an almost film star daughter named Audrey? Questions! Questions! Questions! What does he say of himself? . . .

In the Summer of 1921 Emmet Dalton had been appointed Assistant Director of Training to the reformed Irish Republican Army, and now, in the Summer of 1922, he was Director of Training to the disjoint Free State Army; and the British major had become the Irish major-general. In 1978, two years before his death, he contributed to a documentary film on his life and times, made by Cathal O'Shannon for Irish Television. (I am indebted to R.T.E. for accommodating me with regard to this later portion of the documentary) . . .

Cathal O'Shannon: The anti-Treaty side were now gathered in counties Cork and Kerry, and to this theatre of war were dispatched Tom Ennis and Emmet Dalton . . .

Emmet Dalton: Between the hopping and the trotting, anyhow, it was decided that we should do something about it (Cork), and Collins suggested to me that . . . or rather asked me what I thought would be the best way of approaching, and I said, well, I know the River Lee and I said I've been to Cork, and I believe that if we went down there quietly, with a landing force, that we could get up the River Lee and capture Cork while they were asleep.

Cathal: To go down by sea?

Emmet: To go down by sea . . . because we couldn't go (by rail) since the Mallow viaduct was up. The whole place had been cut off. And, accordingly, we took over a couple of B & I boats and I marched my troops aboard. I had some of the Second Battalion of the Dublin Brigade and I had a hundred and fifty men of the new army which had been fitted out with uniforms and rifles only a matter of a week beforehand — not experienced troops! My total complement was four hundred and fifty. I had an armoured eighteen-pounder gun and an armoured car aboard.

Cathal: So you sailed to Cork?

Emmet: So we sailed duly for Cork, and it was a non-eventful trip until we got outside the Queenstown Harbour, as it (Cobh, prn. 'Cove') was known at the time. When we were challenged it was nightfall. We were challenged and there were searchlights thrown on us. The captain of the ship that I was on was a bit nonplussed by this and he said — What are we going to do now? So I said — You just tell them who we are and what my intention is!

Cathal: The challenge was coming from where?

Emmet: From the British Navy — it was a British naval vessel outside. They were still using the port, and as a result of this conversation, anyhow, they said - Well, good luck, and they kept out of range. So we moved on in and then decided we'd have to get the deep-sea pilot. We knew this and we called in (by wireless? megaphone?) for one, and the deep-sea pilot came to us. He came aboard and when he came on the bridge and saw me in the uniform — the others were hidden down below decks — he said: What IS this? So the captain said - We (the crew?) are only just driving [sic!] the ship. Now I told this man — You've got to drive this thing and bring us up the River Lee! He said - I can't DO that! He said - I'm a deep-sea pilot. You'll have to get a river pilot to take you up! I said - No, I'm sorry, I can't wait for that! He said - I don't know the river! He said - I can't take you up! And this is the only time (Dalton continued) I think I've had to do this: I took out my revolver, pointed it at him and I said — If you don't take us up we're all in trouble! I said - If you take us up there is a chance of avoiding trouble. (Calton Younger: 'Dalton came to the conclusion that the pilot was involved with the Republicans . . . If he refused he would be shot, Dalton told him'). I said - You can't have been twenty odd years (he doesn't say how he knew) down here and not know the river. (Calton Younger: 'If I make a mistake it's your fault', said the pilot after a pause. 'So be it!', snapped Dalton). Well, luck was in our way. He conveyed us up the river, anyhow, to a place called Passage West and, as it turned out subsequently, that was the only place we could have landed. It wasn't mined. And it was right opposite Rochestown. (Garrulous old Charlie Nash, presently curator of the Cobh Maritime Museum, was even then one of the pilots. He is still an expert on Morse Code, both telegraph and flag, as well as the international flag system for shipping. The Capital-S flag, he says, with blue centre and white border, means 'I require a pilot'. Dalton, however, says that it was already nightfall, and so a flag would be practically invisible. There were eight pilots in all who lived at the boat harbour in the famous 'Holy Ground' and worked to a rota. They were more correctly known as 'Harbour and Coastal Pilots', the harbour pilots being normally permitted to proceed as far as Passage West. Billy Higgins was a coastal pilot. It was he who had the historic altercation with the Major-General who, in the final analysis, proved more lucky than clever. From 'Arrivals' at Queenstown, for 8 August 1922, it appears that the S.S. *Porlock Head* and the S.S. *Finola* could not proceed to Cork because of two block-ships at Blackrock Bend, and that the S.S. *Lady Wicklow*, of the City of Dublin Steam-Packet Co., was able to proceed, with the aid of a pilot, only as far as Passage West where she landed some troops. It is also stated that on 9 August the Fishguard-Cork passenger vessel, the *Classic*, which eventually transported Collins' body to Dublin, was compelled to load passengers and mail at Cobh deepwater quay. The block-ship, S.S. *Gorilla*, was eventually towed away from the same deepwater quay on 15 September). However (Dalton continued), we got out. There was actually a guard of the opposition, of the Irregulars, in the building right beside where we landed. And we landed our troops, and one of my officers went in and we captured the enemy, and while he (i.e. the officer) was there the telephone rang, and he answered the telephone and it was from Union Hall Barracks ('Union Quay' is correct) which was then the Cork City Headquarters (of the I.R.A.). They wanted to know what the shooting was about because they heard our fellows shooting in the initial capture.

Cathal: This was the Irregulars ringing?

Emmet: The Irregulars, yes. They called themselves otherwise but . . . One of my officers, Liam Tobin it was, who originated in Cork, and he answered the telephone, and he said, 'Ah, there's nothing — just an incident on the river'. He had a lovely Cork accent. And that was that. (Mrs. Lankford pays a glowing tribute to Liam Tobin as an intelligence officer in the happier early days, including a curious cameo on the diocesan priest, Fr. Tom Roche, professor at St. Colman's College, Fermoy, who applied for a commission in the I.R.A.). I had already arranged how to advance on the city of Cork, in waves and with continuity, connections, armoured car; and they set off under the control of General Tom Ennis. And, well, the rest is . . .

Cathal: History?

Emmet: The rest is history! We were not really seriously opposed. We were opposed at Rochestown where there's a monastery of sorts — some kind — I don't . . . but we had some casualties there, and they had some casualties. There was one particular one outstanding. There was a young man . . . funny enough he wasn't Irish. He was a Scotsman — but he stood to die. He said nothing would . . . he wouldn't give in — wouldn't surrender. So he died. His name was MacKenzie-Kennedy. I salute bravery wherever I see it.

Cathal: The campaign in Cork, and around Cork in the county, was going on, of course, and, although you didn't know it, Griffith was dying in Dublin.

Emmet: Well, we were occupying . . . you see . . . we had landed in Cork on the night you speak of and within four days — within three days — we had occupied every town in Cork. It was quite an achievement. We had spread out. There was a nucleus of Volunteers here and there — Seán Hales had a big brigade of Volunteers — who were true to us, and there were others, some in the city of Cork, some in different parts of West Cork. And they amalgamated with ours, and we took over the various towns, and we were in charge.

Cathal: The news of Griffith's death came to you then. What were your feelings when you heard that Griffith had died?

Emmet: Well, one was very shocked at Griffith's death because Griffith was to everybody . . . he was the pioneer of 'Sinn Féin'. The very term 'Sinn Féin' was Griffith's. He was a man who died of a broken heart, I would think. His problems weighed heavy on him and he had worked hard. He was obsessed with his love of country, and he was a man whom I knew fairly well from my visits to London. I got closer to him then because we were in the same place. And he was a very likeable person. I was very, very, very grieved at his death.

Cathal: Within ten days of Griffith's death, of course, Collins was on his way to Cork.

Emmet: Yes!

Cathal: The twentieth of August, I think, he arrived.

Emmet: He arrived in Cork the twentieth of August.

Cathal: Were you expecting him? I was going to ask you that — you weren't aware that he was . . .

Emmet: I wasn't expecting him at that stage. You know, I . . . he sent me any advice.

Cathal: Did you think it was wise of him to come to Cork at that particular time?'

Emmet: You never think in terms of what was wise and not wise when you are talking about Michael Collins. He was a law unto himself. He was very considerate with everybody else, but he made terrific demands on himself.

Cathal: Were you alarmed to see him there?

Emmet: I was concerned to see him there because I knew how . . . how boyish he was. I mean, I knew the warmth and extent of his heart; and he had so many connections and associations with Cork, and West Cork particularly. He had a devout love for his people. They didn't understand that at all! And he felt that . . . I told him that he was taking an unnecessary risk in this journey; and he said — 'Surely they won't shoot me in my own county!'

Cathal: Did you oppose him in it?

Emmet: No! . . . No, it's no secret!

Cathal: What was his mood at the time?

Emmet: Worried! Depressed! He was depressed that so many of his good friends were on the 'wrong' side. He was depressed because Griffith had died, and he was very fond of Griffith; and he was depressed because he didn't like to see the Volunteer

Force disorganized as it was; and I think that if there was a weakness in Collins it would be that he would make a compromise to try and save — or create — a unity. It has been said since that he had this in mind but he didn't discuss it with me. (Note: it is feasible to think that Dalton knew Collins was to meet Florrie O'Donoghue in Macroom, but kept his own counsel to the grave. Florrie's family knew, and Dalton had the closeness and single-mindedness of the born soldier).

Cathal: His plan was to go the next day, the twenty-first, and tour the area?

Emmet: Yes . . . which we did, and we went as far as Macroom. He spent so long in Macroom that it was nightfall, maybe, and we had to go back.

Cathal: Back you came into Cork?

Emmet: Into Cork City, yes. He had things to do there later on.

Cathal: Your headquarters was at the Imperial?

Emmet: Yes, the Imperial Hotel.

Cathal: And with you he stayed at the Imperial?

Emmet: He stayed at the Imperial Hotel.

Cathal: And you made plans to . . .

Emmet: We made plans to tour the area the following morning. You see, he wanted to do too much in too little time. The roads had been harassed. I mean, they had trees cut across roads, ditches dug across roads, to make transport more difficult. There were quite a number of people who were opposed to us, you know, and they used every means in their power to make life difficult. (The possibility of a counter-philosophy seems to have totally eluded Dalton as it did General Seán McKeon, in the Civil War. When he killed, McKeon said — 'We have had our graves — now they can have theirs!'). However, we started out the following morning and we went to Macroom again, and we went from Macroom to Bandon, from Bandon to . . . I forget the list of the tour. Went to Skibbereen . . .

Cathal: Did he choose the route himself? Did he say - 'I want to . . .'

Emmet: No! There were people he wanted to meet in different places; and the route was . . . sticks out a mile when you're looking at West Cork. You see how you've got to go. The question was — we had to take alternative types of roads because of the obstructions.

Cathal: The escort was — ah — adequate, I suppose?

Emmet: Not at all! Totally inadequate! I would never have permitted it for one second if I'd been in Dublin.

Cathal: Why did you permit it there (i.e. in Cork).

Emmet: I didn't permit it there! I couldn't change it. His escort came from Dublin. It may have appeared adequate. To me it wasn't. (N.B. If there were any question of Dalton's disloyalty I believe it would have shown here).

Cathal: And did you let Collins know that?

Emmet: Oh, yes! I did!

Cathal: It was no good, I suppose, to try to discourage him from making this tour at all?

Emmet: No! None whatever! None! NO! NO! NO! He was determined to make this tour, and I think he was rightly determined. I mean, after all, he did meet his fate . . . It was a fluke — you know what I mean. It was a . . . Well, it should never have happened!

*   *   *

Sometime after the above interview Major-General Emmet Dalton stood on the site of the Béalnabláth ambush with his interviewer. Cathal O'Shannon begins as follows:

On August the twenty-second (1922), at seven-thirty in the evening, the convoy, consisting of a motor cycle outrider, two cars (one, in fact), a Crossley tender and an armoured car, was halted by a barricade on this road. The place — a well chosen ambush site. (N.B. The error of the 'chosen site' still runs through every publication. It is the fallacy of the apparent). Its name — Béalnabláth — the 'mouth of the flowers'. (But cf. Chapter Two). It is on the road between Macroom and Bandon . . .

Cathal: So your vehicles would have stopped, General, on the far side of the road, but in roughly this position? (They were standing in the new parking lot by the stream, and the 'far side of the road' (i.e. from the monument) was where the original road swung in a wide arc. The placing of the monument on the opposite side was a matter of convenience. Collins died about forty yards upwards of it towards Bandon. See pictures from *Pathé Gazette*).

Emmet: Roughly this position (i.e. about thirty yards downwards).

Cathal: Yes . . . So yourself and Collins got out of your own car and took shelter on this side of the road.

Emmet: Well, he and I got out and some people got off the Crossley tender (Notice how he mentions only one), and we lined up on that ditch which is not here any longer because they've changed this place. It was a small ditch — maybe it just passed along here (pointing with his walking-stick to the centre of the present roadway. It was changed in the early Fifties when the public showed a renewed interest which had lapsed for many years).

Cathal: And it gave you a certain amount of shelter from the right . . .

Emmet: Yes! It gave you (i.e. us) cover from the angle from which the firing was coming, which was up there (pointing with his stick at the parallel by-road across the stream).

Cathal: Which is what — a hundred — two hundred — less than two hundred . . .?

Emmet: Around two hundred yards, I guess.

Cathal: Would you have any idea how many men were firing on you at this stage?

Emmet: Well, to assess the firing from the volume that there was, there were only about half-a-dozen at the most.

Cathal: Hm!

Emmet: Firing rifles. (In his statement in 1923, Dalton mentioned 'a sudden and heavy fusillade of machine-gun and rifle fire').

Cathal: Did you feel, at the beginning of the action, that you were in a perilous situation?

Emmet: Oh, yes! (Laughing). A chosen ambush is always perilous; and this was obviously a very bad (military) position. There was no area for retreat. The one thing we could have done was drive on. Which I said to the Commander-in-Chief: 'Drive like hell!' But he (Collins) elected to stop here and fight them, you see. So we did.

Cathal: The first part of the convoy had gone around the bend there?

Emmet: Well, there was a motor-cyclist who had gone on in advance . . . scout. He was followed by the Crossley tender. Then we came in our touring car, and behind us came the Rolls-Royce (armoured) car.

Cathal: Right! So that there would have been men virtually all along this bank?

Emmet: We were stretched out, you know. We weren't quite on top of one another. (The bank was then a continuous curve of about 250 yards).

Cathal: Some of you would have been down there, and you and Collins . . .

Emmet: Yes! You see, there was this continuous bend . . . the spot where we were was this continuous bend of bank, and there were various other members taking shelter down there, and they were completely across it.

Cathal: So as well as a certain amount of fire coming on them (who were down there), there was fire coming down on your little party (it included two drivers) here too; and you could see the men occasionally behind those . . . . (Early photographs show much less scrub than at present.)

Emmet: Well, we saw action, and saw indications of where the fire was coming from. (An interesting feature is Dalton's quaint use of words and phrases even to the extent of referring to men and soldiers as 'people' and 'members').

Cathal: How long did it go on altogether, the action . . .?

Emmet: Not very long. I would say fifteen or twenty minutes maximum. (He seemed to have lost all conception of time. It was exactly forty minutes from first shot to last. cf. Chapter Twenty: 'The Tom Foley Story'). There was a certain amount of movement with my people down here because the motor cyclist came back and said that the obstruction had been cleared so that it was then possible for us to be gettin' on. At the time I felt that there was a little fire coming from up there (Dalton swung round and pointed his stick in the exact direction where Mike Donoghue's group had lain), from that hill up there.

Cathal: Yes . . . which would have made things very . . .

Emmet: Nobody seemed to have agreed with me (actually Lieutenant Smith, the motor cycle scout, did, but in an exaggerated manner, in a newspaper interview two days later), but I felt at the time that there was!

Cathal: So that you were getting fire from . . . the main fire, and possibly from that little place on the hill.

Emmet: Well, very little from there, but certainly . . . definitely some! (This categorical declaration on the Kerrymen's position is vital to the issue.)

Cathal: So Collins got up at some stage and walked along the . . .

Emmet: Yes. After about ten minutes of our engagement here he got up and saw movement. He moved to the back of the armoured car. He used it as protection to have a better sight of what was happening on the hill above. AND THEN HE MOVED FROM THERE UP AROUND THE BEND OUT OF MY VISION. But he was firing from up there and I was firing from here.

Cathal: Was there any conversation going on between all of you who were here?

Emmet: No-No! No! (On Scotsman John McPeak's evidence, someone, possibly Commandant Seán O'Connell or Captain Joe Dolan, kept shouting at him to 'keep that gun going', meaning the Vickers machine-gun in the armoured car, while guide John O'Connell had much to say on the matter later).

Cathal: Were you shouting things like — There they are! and things like that?

Emmet: No-No! There was nothing of that description whatever, except to get on with what we could and shoot. (It is possible he did not hear above the din.)

Cathal: So Collins was out of your sight, slightly round the bend?

Emmet: Yes!

Cathal: Under cover?

Emmet: Well, he was under the same cover as I was, under the bank, such as it was. (This is a reasonable surmise from Dalton. However, it has transpired that Collins was standing on the roadway, on the far side from the bank, rifle in hand, about twenty-five yards on the Bandon side of the armoured car, when he was hit).

Cathal: At what stage, then, did you learn that he'd been killed?

Emmet: Well, I heard — I thought I heard — the voice calling me, and I jumped up, and at that stage O'Connell (i.e. the Commandant) had come up the road to me. He said - 'Where is the Big Fellow?' So I said - 'He's round the corner, round the bend', and we both went up there and he had been shot. He was lying there with this very gaping wound in the back of his head. So I called the armoured car back (i.e. to reverse), and we lifted him and took him onto the side of the armoured car (He probably means the back. Despite being a Rolls-Royce creation, the 'Whippet' carried a crude wooden back-section much like an old-fashioned donkey cart with rails. Captain Joe Dolan held this unenviable position up to the time of the first shot); and moved behind the armoured car — with the armoured car between us and their firing position — got him to the (safer?) position on the side of the road and, under the protection of the armoured car, we bandaged the wound — I bandaged the wound and O'Connell said an 'Act of Contrition' to him. We knew — I knew — he was dying if not already dead. We did the best we could to cover it up; and all action at this stage had stopped because the firing had departed practically, except that, while we were lifting the body onto the armoured car to move it, the motor cycle scout, Lieutenant Smith, had come forward to give us a help (Smith later said that Dalton called him for the purpose) and in doing so there was an odd shot (others say a renewed burst of firing) and he was shot through the neck (This had to be the Jimmy Ormond group heading home to Lismore. They would have been a hundred yards or so distant from Collins, and at his back to the left, when he fell). It was a clean wound and he carried on helping us.

Cathal: What about Collins' wound? There has been some dispute, possibly, about this from time to time. You say it was a big wound, a bad . . .

Emmet: It was a very large wound, an open wound in the back of the head — just there, and it was difficult for me to get a 'First-Field-Aid' bandage to cover it, you know, when I was binding it up. It was quite obviously to me, with the experience I had of a ricochet bullet, it could only have been a ricochet or a 'dum-dum'. (The original 'dum-dums', made for the British Army in a town in India of that name at the end of the last century and later outlawed by international law, could not have been present at Béalnabláth, unless captured from the British themselves. In the I.R.A. context, the term referred to the supposed notching of bullet points for the sake of more damage, but considering the wild inaccuracy that would ensue the term was merely pejorative and propagandist with frequent references in the Black-and-Tan times. The bullet that ricocheted — if that is so — had to be a large, soft, round-nosed bullet from a German Mauser .317 rifle, such as were being used by the I.R.A. at the time, with a strong possibility of a Martini-Henry .450, as will be seen later. John Feehan, in *The Shooting of Michael Collins,* persistently spells the term 'dumb-dumb', a common misconception).

Cathal: There was no exit wound?

Emmet: No exit wound . . . well there was this wound . . . there was no entrance wound (either) other than this (injury).

(The question of an entrance and exit wound in the skull of

Michael Collins is still, and likely to remain, a crucial point in Irish History, until his body is taken up for examination).

Cathal: Just a great gaping hole?
Emmet: A gaping hole, yes.
Cathal: Did he talk to you at any time?
Emmet: No-No! I felt that he was dying or dead at the time I reached him.
Cathal: And you got him over to the far side of the road?
Emmet: We got him to the far (i.e. western) side of the road, and I dressed the wound, just as I have said (i.e. after moving the body on the armoured car to where the Leyland Eight touring car still stood. The black 'X' shown in the photographs taken on the following day, as indicating where Collins fell, is in error. It is where he lay after being dragged across the road. The drag marks in the mud are clearly visible). O'Connell said an 'Act of Contrition' for him. We were both very upset, as you can well understand, emotionally, and the word had gone round to the rest of our column. We got them together and moved quietly down the road. And we moved Collins' body from the armoured car situation onto the touring car back (seat), and I sat in and carried his weight on my shoulder in the car, and we drove off back towards our home base in Cork. It was a troublesome journey and we encountered a lot of trouble and bother on the way because roads were blocked, and we had, at one stage, to go through a farmyard and come out on the other side. (cf. Chapter Thirteen: 'The Aftermath'). It took us quite a long time because we didn't reach Cork City until twelve o'clock, midnight. (The time reports vary considerably).
Cathal: And the action had stopped here . . .
Emmet: Had stopped here between seven and eight — I don't know. Round about eight o'clock. Personally I was holding the body of the Commander-in-Chief in my arms, and the rest of the cortège was moving ahead as best they could; and it was a sad, sad journey. When we arrived in the city of Cork there was consternation at my Headquarters. We had my doctor,

attached to my division, and he took charge of the body and brought it to the hospital. I thought it was to the — I'm not quite sure which hospital it was — I think it was the Mercy Hospital that he was taken to and nuns there took care of him . . . . [Dalton's original hospital error seems to have stuck in his mind. He must certainly have heard of Shanakiel private (military) hospital in the meantime. He had probably intended sending the body to the Mercy Hospital. Shanakiel is much further away, and in a more difficult position on the high ground across the River Lee, though it would be more accessible if, as a good authority has claimed (cf. Cormac Mac Carthaigh's critique of *The Day Michael Collins was Shot*), they had deposited the body on the Crossley tender in the Western Road. Otherwise nobody seems to know why they went to Shanakiel. There were, of course, some British military personnel still in administration in the new army, which might explain it. There were also some Republicans still in occupation of Shanakiel, still carrying their side arms. In an altercation with the bearers of the body, they said - 'Go down to the flat of the city; there are plenty of fellows still there who will give you a fight if you want it!'. This from old Jim Phelan, a retired bone-setter from Cork City, who now lives in Limerick, and was on the spot at Shanakiel. Old Jim, bright and testy, with a brilliant family, saw the wound in Michael Collins' head and vouched for the fact that there was only one and that a very large one, behind the right ear, which the linen towel from Cloughduv failed to cover. It is reasonable to think that he should know, being a bone-setter and all. His constant response to any other suggestion, as indeed to most other matters, is simply - 'All lies! All lies'. But to get back to Emmet Dalton's account . . .]. I had to keep on running my outfit. I had to get in touch with Headquarters in Dublin, and this took a roundabout route because I had to send . . . we were working on a shortwave radio which was contrived for us by young Dowling whose father was Edward Dowling of the Royal College of Science Lab. (Built in 1904, it is now the College of Engineering, Merrion Place). And he was very competent, and we had these shortwave radios all the way. I had to get in touch with Waterville (elsewhere he said Valentia), and the message went from Waterville by cable to New York, and back from New York to London, and from London to Dublin.

Cathal: And that's how they learned in Dublin that the Commander-in-Chief was dead . . . Your own officers in Cork City must have been appalled at the whole situation. What was their mood?

Emmet: Their mood was very difficult for me to define because my own mood was . . . very upset. I was not in a fit position to judge other people really. I was completely grieved. However, I got an emergency call from the female prison (near Shanakiel, it was being used temporarily for Republican prisoners, and was later to house Irish Radio's first transmitting station in Cork), that some of my officers were up there trying to force an entrance.

Cathal: And get at the Irregular prisoners?

Emmet: I think so! They were looking for some form of reprisal, I should think. So I went up there and after arguing at gun-point with some of my friends, I argued them into reason and they dispersed and went back to their units, and the crisis was avoided.

Cathal: The following day was Wednesday, the twenty-third of August, and it was decided to take the body back to Dublin by . . .

Emmet: We were ordered to take the body back by boat which was the method of transport anyhow at that time, and in the afternoon, the evening, we proceeded down to the quays. The remains were taken on board and landed on the afterdeck, I think, and at eventime — it was dark and all — a sorrowful journey down the river. There were tears all over the place; I mean, everybody was grief-stricken, including even the members of the crew and the members of the guard that were on (duty) doing honour to the 'Chieftain'. The boat proceeded very slowly down the River Lee, and when we were coming out into the harbour I was surprised to notice that the British destroyer fleet was in line astern and dressed, the sailors dressed alongship, and we were greeted with a salute of trumpets, the 'General Salute', and this was fantastic over the waves, unbelievable. At any time music is resounding over a big water space, and as we quietly went further out they saluted and then they sounded the 'Last Post', and I have that memory with me still, and it always will be. It is something that is hard to describe. I was moved, and looking around the harbour, Queenstown Harbour, I noticed that all windows all around had lights in them, candles or lights of some description, as a sort of a farewell tribute. It was a very emotional time. (British warships, British sailors, British military music — and Irish window lights! 'If you have tears . . .') . . .

Emmet: My love of Collins — I use no other word — hasn't altered one iota with the passage of time. He was a man whom I didn't know all that long, but whom I knew terribly well in a very short time. And, whereas I don't think he showed me any of his special favours, he was always very kind to me and very understanding, and he placed, or seemed to place, a lot of trust in me and in my judgement. And this is a most rewarding feeling coming from one whom you admired so much.

Cathal: A man of ability?

Emmet: A man of immense ability, untiring energy, and thoughtfulness for others. At the end of the day, when most people would look for a rest, I have known him to go round looking for relatives of people who had suffered a loss, to try and give them some comfort. And this was from a man who never had a free moment to himself. He was a patriot, a most courageous man, and a great, great gentleman.

*   *   *

Cathal O'Shannon continues: After the funeral, the Civil War continued sporadically, if viciously. Dalton returned to his command in Cork. It was at his Headquarters here, in the Imperial Hotel, that he married his childhood sweetheart

(Church weddings were not necessarily the rule for Catholics in those days — the present writer's parents were married in a country farmhouse kitchen); and learned also that a new Act (of Parliament) had been passed enabling commanders in the field to hold courts-martial and imprison or execute captive Republicans. He was not happy . . .

Emmet: I communicated with my Chief-of-Staff (Richard Mulcahy), and he granted me an interview at which I explained to him that I didn't see eye to eye with this sort of thing, that I had a prison in Cork with eighteen hundred prisoners in it, all caught in possession of arms and so forth. Was I expected to court-martial these people and have them executed, or what? Words to that effect — and that was only part of it. He said, No, that was not expected of me, but the situation had reached the stage where the Government had decided to take strong action. They had already taken some strong action (he was likely referring to the attack on the Four Courts in Dublin, on 28 June, an operation of which Dalton was in charge). And I said -'Well, how do I get out of this?' I said - 'The only honourable course for me to take is to resign!'.

Cathal: The war was still on?

Emmet: Oh, yes! The war was still on — but it was in safe keeping. My resignation was accepted. Mulcahy said that . . . he was understanding, he was friendly (he was, in fact, Commander-in-Chief in succession to Collins) . . . he said that if I had occupied positions of importance like his, or similar situations, that I might not be so broadminded (Collins' resentful understudy, Dick Mulcahy, with whom there had always been a strained relationship, tended to excuse rather than reason). However, he said - 'There is still work for you to do. I'm going to send you over to Mr. Cosgrave (William T. Cosgrave became Acting Chairman of the Provisional Government on the death of Arthur Griffith) in Government Buildings. He is reforming the upper house of the Parliament, the Senate, and I think that maybe Mr. Cosgrave would suggest to you to become Clerk of the Senate'.

Cathal: But here you were, a young man with a new bride, your future surely as a soldier assured, high rank, and really you had known very little but soldiering for most of your adult life, first of all in France, the Middle East, and then in Ireland.

Emmet: Yes!

Cathal: And you were giving up an awful lot, on a matter of principle!

Emmet: Well, I have made many decisions during my lifetime that have not benefitted me, but I have been running along what I consider to be my principles. There are certain principles I will not violate, and this was one of them. I had no alternative!

10

The De Valera Story

My time in Washington, D.C., was the Kennedy Era. It was also the era of that outstanding television newscast, the 'Huntley-Brinkley Report', with a seated Chet Huntley, in New York, being responded to by a standing David Brinkley, in D.C. 'This way of an evening', as they say in Ballyvourney, David and Chet had taken, as an extra current affairs feature, the changing diplomatic scene in the Capital, specifically the comings and goings of world figures, the welcomes, the farewells, the protocol, the White House lawn photographs, and especially the quick change as people of note followed one another unknowingly and in rapid succession; the whole (their own word!) razzamatazz. I remember it was David, standing awkwardly and shy but bitterly incisive as always, who said: 'And now, just as you-know-whose cavalcade moves slowly down Penn Avenue out of sight, on its way to Andrews Airport and the great world beyond, up goes the first of the new banners with - WELCOME TO THE PRESIDENT OF IRELAND!'
'Good-night, David!'
'Good-night, Chet!'

* * *

On that occasion, Eamon de Valera — none other — was accorded the signal honour of addressing the combined houses of

Congress, a latter-day 'Great Compromise', as it were. His voice was poor, his projection weak, his material average, but he received a long, standing ovation through which he maintained his accustomed statuesque 'sang-froid'. He was eighty-one, spoke off-the-cuff for half an hour, and even though John F. Kennedy was dead (this was the Spring of 1964), it was still 'Irish Time' in Washington. If sarcasm were allowed in whatever afterlife Michael Collins reposed he would have remarked wryly - 'Live, Horse, and you'll get grass!' If obscenity were permissible, which is doubtful, it would have been: 'So the Long Huar (his phrase!) finally made it!' But President de Valera remembered times, perhaps even on that historic day on Capitol Hill, when it looked like that he would not make it. One such was 22 August 1922, the day Michael Collins lost his life at Béalnabláth. Dev's Diary supplies certain items of itinerary. There are some omissions and some shadings, but the long day's journey into night is clear nevertheless.

*   *   *

As General Emmet Dalton was fighting his way into Cork City, on August the Tenth, Eamon de Valera was having tea with Liam Lynch, Chief-of-Staff of the I.R.A., in the canteen of the Military Barracks in Fermoy. The barracks was being prepared for burning. It was the last Republican stronghold. Lynch had decided on a renewal of the old guerrilla warfare. Established Republican Army posts were no more. On the eleventh (before or after the burning is not said) both men moved on to Mallow, which was still in Republican hands. That night de Valera stayed in the home of an un-named 'Assistant County Surveyor' (From the Irish of Thomas P. O'Neill's extended version of Lord Longford's definitive biography of Eamon de Valera. Cf. Chapter Eleven: 'The Michael Collins Story: The Itinerary' for details of the visit). On the twelfth Dev paid an historic call on the seventy-year-old and now retired nationalist politician, William O'Brien, a native of the town — students of History will readily recognize references to the 'All for Ireland League', and the slogan, 'Conference, Conciliation and Consent' — who had spent his political life working for the ideal of an united Ireland. Surprisingly the older man counselled an even more energetic denunciation of the Treaty, but De Valera was having second thoughts, especially with regard to the viability of physical force. They moved on. Bringing the motor car with them they arrived at Kilpadder, near Dromahane, three miles south of Mallow. The Chief-of-Staff had an idea of setting up a guerrilla base for the continuation of the struggle; but this was also where ex-President de Valera changed his mind about the war and where General Liam Lynch changed his mind about Eamon de Valera. And here an extraordinary discrepancy appears in Dev's Diary (quoted by Lord Longford for the first time), which writers have followed ever since. The house was Pat O'Connell's. Like the O'Sullivans of Gurranereagh, near Béalnabláth, the family were now pro-Treaty but the two great men were somehow unaware of this. Dev had been there before. The family wrote (to the present writer): 'Eamon de Valera stayed for the most part of a week in the old house at Kilpadder, Mallow, during the Black-and-Tan period of Irish History. He was 'on the run' at the time. He slept in what we called the 'Upper Room' which was kept for visitors. My grandmother told us as children that he came down early each morning to the kitchen to help her light the fire. A 'sop' (a bundle of dry straw) which was brought in the night before was used to kindle the fire in those days. De Valera said he was used to doing this with his grandmother in Bruree. One thing that we remember is our grandmother's shock at the fact that he did not go to Mass on the Sunday — of course he was probably afraid of being caught. To her it was a terrible thing and I feel she never forgot it. One important thing — she always said he was quiet, unassuming and very easily pleased. He really should be as he was virtually at her mercy, but she never felt that. Kilpadder was a relatively isolated place in those days. Eventually he escaped through the back window of the Upper Room as there must have been a tip-off that the Tans were on his trail. He took

the Mass Path to Kilcolman and went across the fields to
Casey's Bridge. He is supposed to have stolen — or taken — a
shirt off a clothes line 'en route' to replace the one which he tore
getting out of the window in haste. While he was in Kilpadder
(i.e. on the present Civil War occasion) our father borrowed
two horses from Newmans (i.e. the big house where Nazareth
Home is now) and went riding with De Valera who was a good
horseman. Evidently he thoroughly enjoyed his stay at Kilpadder and was forever grateful to our grandmother. Cathleen
clearly remembers grandmother getting a card with a £5 note
from him one Christmas. Five pounds was a lot of money at
that time.'

The discrepancy in the Diary, or perhaps I should say the slip
in the great mind, must have been due to the horses — a cavalier
association of ideas. Dev wrote: 'Kilpedar near Ballincollig'.
Lord Longford quoted this and Professor T.P. O'Neill (who
had originally collaborated with him) adapted it in the Gaelic
version (and others followed) to the interesting known fact that
Seán Hyde had established a cavalry unit near Ballincollig
(close to Cork City. cf. Chapter Six: 'The Bobs Doherty
Story'). The Hydes of Toureen, between Ballincollig and Innishannon, were horsey people 'par excellence'. Siobhán
Lankford writes: 'After Adare the Republican Army withdrew
to Mallow . . . At their head rode Seán Hyde, gay and
debonair. Dressed in civilian clothes, he wore a slouched green
hat. Around its crown flowed a beautiful purple ostrich
feather. His mount was a spirited hunter. He looked an officer
to lead an army'. Seán Hyde was more than a great horseman;
he was also a hurling star in his day. Starting with the U.C.C.
'Collegians' in 1915, he then played for Cork County, as right-
half back, in the same year. His team was beaten by Laois (Leix)
in the All-Ireland Senior Hurling final. Then he moved to
Dublin to become a veterinary surgeon, and in 1917 won an All-
Ireland Senior Hurling medal with Dublin (on the Collegians
Selection) as full-back against Tipperary. In the same position
with his adoptive team he lost to Cork in 1919, and Seán

returned to his native county to take a more serious part in national affairs, eventually becoming Divisional Intelligence Officer, and finally O/C Western Command, during the Civil War. Dev's slip is obvious and rather disastrous in that T.P. O'Neill extended the Ballincollig theme and also that Kilpadder is vital to the issue because it was there the fugitive leader did some serious thinking and inserted in his Diary the now famous meditation or soliloquy: 'Any chance of winning? If there was any chance, duty to hold on to secure it. If none, duty to try to get the men to quit — for the present. The people must be won to the cause before any successful fighting can be done. The men dead and gloomy — just holding on. How long will it last?' (Also quoted by secretary Kathleen O'Connell). It was at Kilpadder that he heard of the death of Arthur Griffith and thought ruefully of the tragic condition of affairs which was quickly turning the old-style struggle into a new-style disaster. Dev did not like Liam Lynch's idea of a camp at Kilpadder for the purpose of a continuation of guerrilla warfare. He wanted one last token stand at Ballyvourney, and finish. Michael Collins, he believed, was about to establish some kind of military dictatorship in cahoots with Britain. After three days he moved on to Gougane Barra, not, strange to say, because Dalton was in Cork but because Collins was on his way there. But the lovely Gougane, the rocky enclave of St. Finbarr, in 'Sweet Valley Desmond' where, according to J.J. Callanan,

> A thousand wild fountains
> Rush down to that lake
> From their home in the mountains,

held no solace for the tormented intellectual. News came to him there that John Devoy, Judge Daniel F. Cohalan and their 'Friends of Irish Freedom' in America had rejected him as the Republican leader of the future. It was Tuesday, 15 August 1922, just one week to destiny with the two protagonists circling towards each other as if manipulated by some external power. Ballyvourney was just over the hill from Gougane Barra, but Dev moved elsewhere. He had heard of a Republican conference to the south-east!

*   *   *

Gortafludig, the 'field of the mud puddle', is as remote as one would ever wish to be. It lies three miles upwards from Gougane along a tricky by-road off the by-road, just one of 'all the little winding roads among the hills' that so intrigued H.V. Morton, a decade later, while *In Search of Ireland*. This was where Eamon de Valera, 'the once and future' President ('Rex Quondam Rexque Futurus', from the tomb of King Arthur, seems apposite), took refuge while on the run. The Gaelic phrase, ' ar a choimeád', means 'on his keeping'. In this instance his keeping was in the trusted hands of the O'Leary family of Gortafludig. Madge, one of the girls, was a particular friend. Before her death in 1988 she put on record some of her fast-fading and fascinating memories. Dev loved frogs, to the extent that she thought 'he had never seen any before'. There was a colony down by the lake side where he sat for hours watching their antics, gleaning a solace from the vital things of nature. Many years later, when she was a settled hotel keeper in the faraway seaside town of Youghal and he was the highly regarded elder statesman of Europe, they met once more, and Dev said, 'Tell me, Madge, are the frogs still down there by the lake shore at Gougane?' Other important visitors also frequented Gortafludig in those historic times — Erskine Childers, for one, whose son would be a future president. Childers arrived from Ballyvourney one day on his white horse, bringing with him his 'two typewriters' and stayed on as 'Dev's secretary' in a room reserved for them both. He had bought the horse in Ballyvourney. He had been a British cavalryman in the Boer War and a naval officer in the Great War. His typewriter and tiny printing press were constant companions as well as the fatal little handgun, a present from Michael Collins. Previously a constant visitor had been Daniel Corkery, the great littérateur and artist, teacher and future professor. The lamed genius carried a torch for Madge, but in vain. She was twenty while he was forty-two. But he enshrined the precious hour in one of his stories in *The Stormy Hills*, where the ageing and home-returned dandy tries for the affections of the pretty 'colleen' already bethrothed to the local commander of the volunteer freedom fighters . . .

There were two escape routes from Gortafludig, one up and one down. Dev used both from time to time. Dan Thady O'Leary, Madge's brother, and Jimmy O'Leary of Gougane (whose father, Batty Kitt, this writer's paternal granduncle, was immortalized by Robert Gibbings in *Lovely is the Lee*), were the two 'look-out' men. On Sunday evening, 20 August 1922, Dan Thady had his turn on the lookout rock at Gort-napéiste beside the River Lee. A messenger from the East arrived with an urgent communication. He took it to the house and presented it to the Republican leader. Dev 'read it quickly and left immediately without explanation'. Madge said he 'took the road upwards' which is more than likely as the Gougane way would have exposed him to two miles of open road cycling to Inchanossig bridge, though it would have its compensations for a romantic as he apparently was — the Gort-napéiste Rock, for example. He had his own rock look-out to the west of O'Leary's house, where he sat endlessly thinking and watching for signals from Gougane. It is still known as 'Dev's Rock' with some distance away the flat, bullet-pocked side of another rock showing the result of his target practice. Coasting down the hill to the junction of the Ballingeary-Bantry road, he would have thought of the noted Gaelic poetess, Máire Bhuí Ní Laoire (Yellow Mary O'Leary), who had lived just there and had recorded, in beautiful verse and melody, the running battle through that frightening glen of Keimaneigh in 1822, a century ago exactly, which she had witnessed between some local 'Whiteboys' on the one hand, and landlords Hedges and White and their entourage from Bantry House on their way to Macroom Castle, on the other. He would have known about the imperturbable 'Scottie' who had died at Rochestown near Cork Harbour, a few days before, and his cave hide-out at the back of Twomeys, Tooreen Duv; even how Scottie had blurted out in a rare burst of exasperation, when his flagstone door had proved intractable - 'Oh, damn you, John Bull!' A man of rare obscenity himself, Dev might have said to his immortal soul as he rode by - 'Oh, damn you, Michael Collins!' But he took the other way, passing the house where the last eviction in Ireland had failed in 1906, then out onto Inchanossig Bridge and the southern shores of that lovely, unspoiled Lake District, to Bohane's Cross, south of Inchigeela, and then Kilmichael, scene of Tom Barry's famous victory over the 'Auxies' from Macroom Castle, a few short miles away. But now the Free State Army was in Macroom and tomorrow Michael Collins would be inspecting at the Castle. And so to bed!

Bed? That is the question! In later years Dev's De Gaullish appearance and attitude frequently created a sense of fun, lending material to many cartoonists in comic publications, not least Ireland's own *Dublin Opinion*. I like to think of the 'Long Fellow', despite his many troubles, stretching his weary length in a hayloft near Kilmichael, or even the pub at Cooldorrihy Cross, a little short of the famous ambush site; but he cycled on and late evening found him approaching Terelton village where he was met by Commandant Paddy O'Sullivan who was to conduct him to Richard Woods' of Moneygave. Thirty-six hours later, on a parallel road three miles away, Michael Collins, unknown and unknowing, would be moving to his doom . . . And now the Moneygave (prn. 'Moneygaff') problem as encountered in Meda Ryan's *The Day Michael Collins was Shot* (1989)! The particular region was strictly Republican and anti-Treaty. Three houses contained the Staff of the First Southern Division — Richard Woods' of Moneygave (then known as 'Ellenville'), Walsh's farmhouse close beside it (which also housed the historic pony-trap, the property of Father Treacy, P.P., Crookstown), and O'Sullivan's of Gurranereagh, two miles away, which was now technically pro-Treaty and which the author makes an effort to 'exonerate', as it were. On the one hand she affirms that there were present at 'Ellenville', at the one time, Eamon de Valera, Liam Deasy, Erskine Childers and Riobárd Lankford [sic!]. On the other hand all of those men, except Riobárd L. (his name will be discussed later), were elsewhere at the particular time, which was the day before Béalnabláth. Moreover they are stated, all of them and together, to have proceeded directly to Béalnabláth, on the 'Bantry Line', on the morning of the ambush. One needs to assert that this is an important issue as the activities of those men, and the implications of same, are vital to Irish History. In his 'improvised diary' (the Earl of Longford's phrase) Dev recorded a preferential set of his movements and some of his troubled thoughts. In conjunction with this he informed his biographers that he arrived at Joseph O'Sullivan's of Gurranereagh (three and a half miles from Béalnabláth), an old rebel stronghold, on the afternoon of Monday, the twenty-first of August. Liam Deasy tells of receiving him there (in *Brother Against Brother*, written between his interview with Meda Ryan in 1973 and his death in 1974), 'towards evening', having himself come from his home at Ballymacsimon Quay (near Bandon) to O'Sullivan's early that morning. Erskine Childers was in Gougane Barra, at O'Leary's of Gortafludig. Dev and he had shared a room there for the previous few days. Mrs. Madge Goggin of Youghal (née Madge O'Leary of Gortafludig) put this item on tape shortly before her death in 1988. Also from Dorothy Macardle (in *The Irish Republic*) who had been one of Dev's itinerant secretaries: 'He (Childers) was attached as Staff Captain to the Republican Army in Munster. After they had evacuated Fermoy (11 August) and Cork (12 August) he set up his printing press in a deserted barracks at Ballymakeera, near Macroom; forced from that position (a company of the Free State Army from Macroom, under the command of Captain Dan Dineen of Peake, near Coachford — a cousin of the present writer — had captured the village), he moved to a vacant two-roomed cottage near Ballyvourney (actually the home of Maurice Healy of

Renaniree, on the way to Ballingeary — its photograph appears in George Morrison's illustrated history of the Civil War), and after that westward towards Kealkil (near Bantry, but by way of O'Leary's of Gortafludig and, when the chase became too hot, west again over Borlin mountain where he gave his famous answer to the running countryman who referred to him as a "little padhsán"). In October he was sent for (by De Valera) to come to Dublin to act as Secretary to the (tentatively) reconstituted Republican Government . . .' Childers was in Moneygave in the latter half of October and left for Dublin — and death by execution — at the beginning of November. Helping him in his printing operation in the West had been Seán Ó Faoláin, Frank O'Connor and Seán Hendrick (well known literary characters). Macardle: 'An untiring campaign . . . was waged by Erskine Childers . . . in the South . . . When moving about with the Columns he carried with him a little printing press on which the *Republican War News* was printed' (Ref. *Irish Press,* Christmas No., 1932). Meda Ryan: (Notes pp. 186, 188): 'Riobárd Lankford . . . formulated the press, operated the machinery, and had the paper organized weeks before Childers arrived in West Cork. His brother Joe Lankford also helped with the printing press . . . After the Civil War Siobhán Creedon married Riobárd Lankford . . .'. Sadly, no! Riobárd Langford (note spelling!) was from Cork City. In 1932 (cf. last chapter of *The Hope and the Sadness*) Siobhán Creedon of Clogheen, Mallow, married Séamus Lankford who had worked — like Collins — for the British Civil Service, returned home during the 'Troubles' and did trojan work for the destitute and demoralized in Cork, as a member of the Board of Guardians and as Commissioner of the Union (i.e. the workhouse).

And here is where the plot thickens. Riobárd Langford did not have a 'brother Joe', but he was helped (he later founded the 'Lee Printing Works' in Cork) with his operation in Moneygave by Dick Langford, a noted Republican from Callinafercy, Milltown, Co. Kerry, who, as a Staff Officer of the First Southern Division, represented the Kerry Brigades and eventually became Liam Lynch's personal information officer, being with him to the end. In other words, the Moneygave printing operation was before the fall of Cork City and long before Béalnabláth. Protestant 'Ellenville' continued to function as an information centre while the actual printing was done in the West with Childers occasionally coming and going on the only safe route remaining, the south of the lakes route by Inchigeela and Ballingeary. Though he was a great cyclist, Father Treacy's pony-trap was sometimes used to transport him (cf. *Magill* magazine, May, 1989). After the fall of Macroom to the 'Staters', and then Ballyvourney, the route was no longer feasible, and when Dev took to the bike on Sunday, 20 August, Childers, instead of being in Moneygave for the aforementioned conference, was on his way to the eternal hills. According to Calton Younger (*Ireland's Civil War*), quoting Seán Hendrick (p.486), Childers' last issue of *War News* was at Coolmountain, Inchigeela, or, as the Australian put it — 'the Coole Mountains'!

Finally, the Langford problem! Dick Langford of Kerry was no relation. Riobárd Langford was, indeed, a brother of Séamus Lankford (the one who really married Siobhán Creedon). The 'g' and 'k' problem arose early in life and the family are at the moment looking into the legal implications of the discrepancy, while Mrs. Riobárd Langford assures me (December, 1989) that her husband never, to her knowledge, printed in Moneygave but in Ballingeary! Which brings us back to Childers. Meda Ryan continues: 'Erskine Childers and Riobárd Lankford were known to be producing *An Phoblacht*, the anti-Treaty paper . . . in the home of Richard Woods at Moneygave (Note: This Moneygave is a mile south from Coppeen village) . . . De Valera was taken by Paddy O'Sullivan (this Paddy was from Drimoleague, and presently Commandant of the Fifth Battalion, Third Cork Brigade, according to Deasy, and not the Ballyvourney Vice-Commandant as implied elsewhere) in a pony-trap and reached Moneygave by mid-afternoon (but not on Monday, the twenty-first, as stated, but on Sunday evening, the twentieth). Here Seán Hyde, publicity officer for the Republicans, had joined Childers . . . that evening Liam Deasy arrived. 'They all gathered in the parlour and remained talking for the rest of the evening', said Maggie Sheehan, who was employed by the Woods family'. For the average reader this is a simple statement of fact. For the historian it is erroneous and misleading indicating sample visions of a country woman — what are called 'subliminal cuts' — culled from an extended experience and at a half-century remove. The writer who resorts to such is guilty of the fallacy of 'Petitio Principii', or 'begging the question'. Deasy wrote (in *Brother Against Brother*: 'I spent the next few days with Tom Crofts (his Adjutant) at Divisional Headquarters at Coppeen . . . a dispatch arrived from Erskine Childers (from Moneygave in mid-October) informing us that he was returning to Dublin and would be contacting us at Coppeen that evening'. Deasy tells how he conveyed Childers to Shanacashel, near Kilmichael, on the following day, sent him on his way to Ahadillane, Mallow (that would be Walsh's of Glashabee), and so on to Wicklow where he was captured on 11 November, tried and executed at Beggar's Bush Barracks on the twenty-fourth. On 15 July he had come from Dublin to Clonmel where Lynch and De Valera were established. They all left for Fermoy the next day, with assistants Kathleen O'Connell, Kathleen Barry (sister of Kevin Barry), and Dorothy Macardle. Childers continued on into Cork City to further his printing and counter-propaganda and was there when Major General Emmet Dalton landed by sea and captured the city from the Republicans on August 8-12, when he was seen by Seán Hendrick 'crouched on a running board' of a lorry in flight in Macroom, like Aeneas fleeing before the flames of Troy!

And back to Eamon de Valera! We left him needing a bed for the night (Sunday, 20 August 1922). He found same in Moneygave. Battalion Commandant Paddy O'Sullivan (to be distinguished from Vice-Commandant Paddy O'Sullivan of

Ballyvourney) intercepted him at Terelton and escorted him in a pony-trap the five miles to 'Ellenville' where he spent the night (according to Meda) 'on the settle in the parlour behind the door'. Late the following morning or in the early afternoon he was driven in the same outfit to Gurranereagh about two miles away by the famous pair, John 'Flyer' Nyhan and Jim 'Spud' Murphy, from Clonakilty, not on the dangerous 'Bantry Line' (as the author claims) but around by Barnageeha ('the top of the wind') where the Bride rises and where he had one of the most beautiful all-round views in Ireland. They stopped for a meal at O'Donoghue's of Renacahera, stabled and gave some oats to the pony, so the family say. Pro-Treaty Mrs. O'Donoghue received them with a bad grace. Her three sons still rememeber her disgruntled attitude. The Civil War had come to her door. She did not like its face. Just down the road Nemesis, the vengeful goddess who laid an egg, was gathering her forces for the idol, Michael Collins. And so to Gurranereagh. The same pony-trap conveyed Dev to Béalnabláth on the following morning, this time driven by Liam Deasy. It belonged to the local (Crookstown) parish priest and when it was eventually returned (according to Edward O'Mahony — nephew of Shawno Galvin — in *Magill* magazine, May, 1989) the poor beast was only skin and bones but a rebel hero forever. No wonder Fr. Treacy, P.P., lambasted Dev and his Irregulars off the altar and in the oft-quoted letter to the Press, a good five years later!

Commanant General Tom Barry made the first mention ever of 'Gurranereagh'. It appears in his book, *Guerilla Days in Ireland*. (The secondary spelling of 'guerrilla' is his own preference). It was after the extensive and sensational battle at Crossbarry, twelve miles from Cork City, when (19 March, 1921) several hundred British soldiers were dispersed by a hundred and four West Cork Irregulars. Afterwards they 'retired to billets at Gurranereagh'. Billets at Gurranereagh was Joe Sullivan's. It was, according to Barry, 'a large farmhouse . . . Joe was over seventy years of age, a dignified and patriarchal old gentleman . . . a Fenian, and in 1867 waited with his gun for the call'. (The word 'Fenian' first appeared in 1789, in Charlotte Brooke's *Reliques of Irish Poetry*. Fenianism, with its spirit of republican uprising, started in Skibbereen, Co. Cork, in 1858. It became a world-wide force not entirely quelled after abortive outbreaks in 1867. Its leaders took an imaginative line through the ancient 'national' army of Finn McCool [Fionn Mac Cumhaill]. Its natural successor was the I.R.B. [Irish Republican Brotherhood, of which Collins in his time was 'Head-Centre'], somewhat distinct in its philosophy from 'Sinn Féin' [Ourselves Alone] and the I.R.A.). Fenianism and die-hard Republicanism were all the one to old Joe Sullivan. His house was the final venue, the ultimate position from which to plan the last stand of the Third (West Cork) Brigade. The conference was set for Tuesday, 22 August. Time of day was not stipulated in dispatches. Delegates would be coming from far and wide. The clearance house for transport was four miles away, almost but not quite in Béalnabláth village. In charge was Tom Hales, Brigade Commander, released from incarceration in England. Tom's brother, Seán, was C/O of the Free State troops in Bandon, just arrived on Saturday. Strange arrangement! Sad situation! Pawns in the History game! One sheds a tear, but what of it! Each could logically retort - Am I my brother's keeper? Tom Hales had been in Pentonville Prison, in London, from July, 1920, until the Treaty. He was making up for lost time.

No one knows quite what transpired at the conference at Gurranereagh, nor much of what happened afterwards. General Liam Deasy, O/C First Southern Division, tells that 'towards evening De Valera arrived' and 'we discussed the War situation far into the night'. Then Deasy declares: 'Next morning, 22 August . . . I conveyed De Valera to Béalnabláth Cross, about three miles away. We arrived there around 9.30 a.m.' Dev himself says that he was driven from O'Sullivan's to Béalnabláth early in the morning in a motor car, accompanied by James O'Flynn, but more likely he meant from Béalnabláth to

Macroom. From Béalnabláth, Deasy continues, 'I had arranged that he (Dev) would be conducted by Dinny Crowley
(his own trusted driver from Coppeen) to Ahadillane on his
return journey to Liam Lynch in Glanworth'; while Edward
O'Mahony (in *Magill*, 1989) says that Fr. Treacy's 'commandeered' pony-trap brought Dev and Deasy to Béalnabláth
on that historic morning. Other 'authoritative' accounts have
the 'Long Fellow' spending that night of the twenty-first at
Long's public house (now the 'Diamond Bar') in Béalnabláth
village, and they continue that he heard the army convoy arrive,
decided that he was about to be captured and grabbed a
revolver as he jumped out of bed. Others again say that Liam
Deasy was with him in the room and drew his revolver. A final
story (definitely from the political hand-to-ear) is that De
Valera's pair of 'malevolent eyes' could be seen staring out of
the window at Michael Collins, as he moved onto the Bandon
road, while two gunmen with him held their weapons at the
ready; and this version even had clerical authority. Poor Dev! it
is no wonder that he wished to obscure himself in an aura of
religious asceticism as he left for Macroom at four in the afternoon. By a curious quirk of fate his fine motor car for the occasion represented the political last straw for Collins' Provisional Government. It was one of the fourteen new 'Sports'
models seized in Dublin, on 26 June, by members of the Four
Courts garrison for the purpose of a motorized attack on the
North of Ireland. A Dublin firm named Ferguson had recently
imported them from Belfast contrary to regulations. During
the operation an officer of the Four Courts was arrested by
Government forces. In response the Four Courts Executive arrested a Free State officer. As a consequence the decision was
taken to attack the Four Courts — and so the Civil War began!
On the day Michael Collins left Dublin for the last time four
men left the city in a new model motor car. They were
Republican members of the Dublin Brigade. The fact was
reported to the authorities at Beggar's Bush Barracks, the National Army H.Q. The matter reached Collins in Cork City and

he was advised to avoid his old family home during his inspection in West Cork. It was assumed they were an assassination group. His old home was (and is) at Woodfield, about three miles from Clonakilty and in the general direction of Rosscarbery. Just beside it his brother John had built a fine two-storey house some years previously. Both this and the old place had been burned down by the British Army. There is a good photograph of Collins standing at the miserable front door of the old place during the Truce period. A quarter of a mile away, at Sam's Cross, stood the old home of his mother, Ellen O'Brien, whose brother resided there. His son, first cousin of Michael Collins, had built a house next door identical with Johnny's. It was untouched and still stands. It is now occupied by Mr. James O'Brien of the third generation. It was here Mick was directed for safety and in the parlour (dominated by an enormous picture of the Commander-in-Chief), as Jimmy O'Brien proudly points out, he met his brother, John, and not in the pub across the road as is so often stated. But there was no danger. The Dublin 'hit men' did not go to Woodfield. They went instead to Béalnabláth (or Gurranereagh) and left the car, as a temporary convenience, to Mr. De Valera. (Note One: The particular motor car was clearly remembered by Mrs. Ellen Allen. cf. 'Five Local People'. It was an Armstrong-Siddeley, a model the present writer can still remember, with its high power-weight ratio and high efficiency six-cylinder engine. Mrs. Allen cleverly remembered it as a 'Siddeley-Armstrong' and told me that 'it went up the hill [Murray's] without a gurgle!' Note Two: James O'Flynn has been mentioned in two publications. T.P. O'Neill, in his Irish language life of Eamon de Valera [written in collaboration with Fr. Pádraig Ó Fiannachta of Maynooth College] mentions how Dev left Gurranereagh 'agus é a ghiollaíocht ag Séamas Ó Floinn' i.e. accompanied by James O'Flynn. Dev always referred to him as 'Séamas'. Meda Ryan says: 'With his aide, Jimmy Flynn, he took the Cloughduv and minor roads (by-passing Cork city) and on to Mourne Abbey near Mallow'. Jimmy O'Flynn was from Fethard, Co. Tipperary. According to his family he was Dev's adjutant for six months almost continuously from the abandoning of Clonmel, frequently sleeping in the same bed as the leader. He had been to Rockwell College and could type and do shorthand. Like Dev's shadow he is recorded as having been at Gougane Barra, at Béalnabláth and at Glashabee where he noted the shock on Dev's face at the news of Collins' death. He was a tailor by trade and in the Seventies, when business became depressed, even planned to emigrate and had a letter of recommendation 'to whom it may concern', now hanging framed on the wall, stating that he had fought gallantly for the continuing ideal of an all-Ireland Republic, penned by the President of Ireland himself. Was it a belated joke from two old, old comrades on the times that were? Or were they still fighting the old fight on the threshold of Europe?

In terms of Irish Republican Army organization, Béalnabláth (Pullerick) district was technically No. 1 Section, 'G' (Crookstown) Company, Seventh (Macroom) Battalion, First (Cork) Brigade. It was probably the most highly organized battalion anywhere, Macroom itself having two companies of four sections each. Traditionally a good business town (confluence of three important valleys), it was bound to have a divided allegiance with regard to the Treaty, but a mere handful actually joined the Free State Army. One in particular did so for swank, Denis J. ('Mutty') O'Brien, and such was the incongruity of the times drove about in a 'Whippet' armoured car showing off to his friends. The two O'Sullivan sisters of Kilnamartyra, whose brothers were prominent on the Republican side, were out for a stroll one evening when he pulled up in his 'Rolls-Royce' and swung out onto the road with a breezy 'Hello, Girls!' . . . Early in the Trouble times the Seventh became overcrowded and the Eighth (Ballyvourney) was hived off; but the Seventh still stretched all the way from Carriganimma, near Millstreet, to Bellmount on the far side of Crookstown. The Béalnabláth section comprised: Denis D. Long (Section commander), Patrick Desmond, Thomas

Bradfield, Matt Long, Denis Murphy, Thomas Taylor, Tim Murphy, Michael Holland, Daniel Long, John Murphy, John Taylor, William Bradfield, Jerh. Collins, Patrick Murphy and John Murphy. Its later allegiance was divided to some extent, and still is politically, but it remained mostly Republican. Two of those men, on the orders of Tom Hales and under the direction of his Brigade engineer, Michael Crowley of Kilbrittain, laid the barricade landmine at Béalnabláth and removed it later. Their names are known but are not for publication 'because their families still live in the place'. Two landmines (the second one from the bridge position) were said to have reposed in a house near the village (cf. 'Five Local People'), having been removed from the roadway late that evening. Still. . . 'The mine itself, defused, remained in the road until about twenty years ago (i.e. 1960) when it was dug up by (County) Council workers on repair duty'. (John Feehan in *The Shooting of Michael Collins*). And the contradictions proliferate!

Dev, in fact, did not take 'the Cloughduv and minor roads, by-passing Cork City'. He went in the opposite direction and had quite an eventful itinerary before reaching Mourne Abbey at two o'clock on the following morning, when Collins was long dead. And Meda continues: 'De Valera had reached Clashbee, near Mallow, by this time . . .'. The time of the ambush is what she refers to. At that moment (7.30 p.m., Summer Time) Dev was standing at the bar of the Hibernian Hotel, Ballymakeera (Ballyvourney) talking to Sandow. He reached Glashabee at eleven o'clock . . . 'Siobhán Creedon was in bed . . .' — not there but eight miles away at Clogheen, beyond the main Mallow-Cork road. Siobhán Lankford takes up the story at Walsh's of Glashabee, by the hillside village of Bweeng, and leads us to her home in Clogheen where, on the following day, she saw Dev off on his sad and cumbrous onward trail to Araglen, on the Cork-Tipperary-Waterford borders, and so to Dublin. Meda continues: 'De Valera was having a meal with Liam Lynch . . .' i.e. at Walsh's of

Glashabee. But in fact Lynch and Deasy had been in O'Connor's of Glashabee, a neighbour's house, for an important Republican G.H.Q. meeting some days before (cf. Lankford, p.242), and had left to go their separate ways, Lynch to Glanworth and Deasy to Cork and eventually to Béalnabláth. With Deasy went Vincent O'Doherty from Derry. Then Meda says: 'Michael Collins . . . had passed through the nearby area of Whitechurch (ten miles as the crow flies!) a few days previously . . . on his way to Cork'. Mrs. Lankford says it was the day before. It was, indeed, two days exactly i.e. Sunday the twentieth. Also, 'The ambush that had been set up in the Ballyvourney/Ballingeary area . . .'. These two important places in the mid-Cork 'Gaeltacht' should not be confused. They are quite distinct and separated by a mountain range. 'The news from the Ballyvourney/Ballingeary area was brought by De Valera; he also told them about the decision . . . to lay an ambush at Béalnabláth!' On the contrary, as is evident from Mrs. Lankford and from Dev's diary, the 'Long Fellow' sang dumb about the whole affair! Siobhán Lankford (Creedon) may have the last word (from her beautifully written *The Hope and the Sadness*): 'Later . . . Erskine Childers came through the same safe route. He arrived at Walsh's one evening with Liam Manahan and David Robinson (his cousin). They had cycled from Ballyvourney . . . Five Republican cyclists accompanied them to Killavullen . . . As they said good-bye . . . she (Mrs. Walsh) thought the revolver Childers carried was obvious, and might attract attention to him. "Mr. Childers", she said, "please give me the revolver — I will keep it safely for you". "Thank you, Mrs. Walsh, thank you, but I got that gun from Collins — I would hate to part with it" . . . that same gun was made the excuse for taking the life of that gallant man'.

* * *

Mr. De Valera was in reasonably safe hands with the Seventh Battalion. With sportscar and driver he retraced the 'steps' of Michael Collins from Section to Section to the outskirts of

Macroom (actually the partly demolished 'Two-Mile' Bridge) where an apparently miraculous transformation took place. He was seen driving through the town in a small pony-trap sitting enormously tall 'like a stalk', as a bystander said, and dressed as a nun! . . . John Lynch was a 'bootman' in Main Street, Macroom. His shoe shop was next to Mescal's stationery establishment and a short distance from Williams' Hotel. His wife liked to stand at the door watching the world go by on the street outside, and talk to her neighbour and friend. She was doing so in the early evening of 22 August 1922, and had just spotted the pony-trap with its strange passenger coming 'from the railway station direction' at the lower end of town. Suddenly the neighbour's child, little Nellie McCarthy, started to jump about with excitement. 'Oh, Mammy, Mammy', she screamed, 'look at that ugly nun!' The 'nun' was easily recognizable and ever after when Mrs. Lynch told the story she stamped her foot in indignation saying, 'And to think that he always denied being in the region on the day Michael Collins was killed!' Well, he didn't! Not really! He put the essentials in his diary, his essentials; and I have no doubt that he said, going through Macroom, the home town of gallant Art O'Leary, 'Needs must when the devil drives!' It is easier, even in wartime, to stand in doorways and gossip. Twenty four hours previously Michael Collins had stood a few yards away, at the door of Williams' Hotel. This time it was a young boy (now an aged cleric) who watched and admired 'the magnificent looking man in uniform'. Collins was approached by a poor old woman from Sleaveen Road, named Lehane, who was unkindly known as 'Mag the Ram'. She offered him a bunch of wild flowers, to present or possibly to sell. Collins declined the bouquet and handed her a ten-shilling note, a workman's weekly wage!

And so to Ballyvourney! Wonderful and interesting places to see from a pony-trap on a fine, early Autumn evening! The Sullane river, noted in song and story, flowing gently along to the foot of the Castle and on to the River Lee, nurtured the greatest body of Gaelic 'cottage' poetry in Ireland, with its soon to be established (1924) 'Dámh-Scoil Mhúscraí Uí Fhloinn' (the 'bardic school of Muskerry-Flynn'), the last of its kind in the country; then Raleigh Cross and the home of Art O'Leary whose wife, Eibhlín Dubh Ní Chonaill ('Dark Eileen O'Connell'), aunt of Daniel O'Connell, the Liberator, composed for her soldier-husband the touching and powerful 'Caoine Airt Uí Laoire' ('Lament for Art O'Leary'); then 'Fairyland' (where later would live the daughter of John Galsworthy, a practising vet and the first woman to appear in trousers in the whole district), and Carrigaphooka Castle sitting on the 'Rock of the Sprite' beside the bridge whose Civil War tragedy (cf. 'The Tom Daly Story') was still in the future; and the 'Half-Way House', a pub waiting to be noted in Literature 'half-way between Cork and Killarney, half-way between Cork and Bantry, half-way between Macroom and Ballyvourney, and half-way between any other two places that are equidistant from it' (Robert Gibbings in *Sweet Cork of Thee*); the little Coolavokig schoolhouse, up on the rocks, where I went to school, and the 'Master' who told his stories of Irish History as no one else could, but with a sniff and a tear, correlating them with superb analysis to the domestic, sociological and religious condition of that Gaelic land since before dreamers had dreams; just beyond then to 'Geata Bawn', the 'White Gate', scene of an ambush in 1920:

> At Geata Bawn, that fateful day, it was in mid-July,
> When Captain Airey was shot dead and his men were forced to fly;

and the great, rock-bound battle site of Coolnacahera where

> Major Grant and thirty Tans,
> Their bodies were laid low!;

and the 'Master' who really paid for Coolnacahera by having his house burned down and by being incarcerated and tried for his life in the Castle; and just off to the right, the 'Slippery Rock' ambush location where Catholic Lieutenant Sharman and his cycle patrol of British soldiers died; and S/L Bill

Hegarty who paid with his life for Sharman's at the entrance to Ballymakeera village. Patrick Pearse had cycled that road, at the beginning of the century, to see for himself what had become known in Dublin Gaelic circles at the end of the previous century as 'The Capital of Irish Ireland'.

*   *   *

Mr. Eamon de Valera was received by Mr. Daniel O'Donovan in the 'Hibernian Hotel'. In common speech that translates as — Dev met Sandow in Danny Arthur's. Sandow was a character. He was an outstanding fighting man from Cork City, previously from Kinsale. During the Black-and-Tan War he had been commander of the A.S.U. (Active Service Unit), the 'Flying Column', of the First Cork Brigade and of which Seán Hegarty, the Brigadier himself, was just a member. Sandow knew no fear. At Coolnacahera (25 February 1921) he had exposed himself impetuously, had been trapped by enemy fire, and had to be extricated by rapid rifle fire laid on by local officers Captain Patsy Lynch and Vice-Commandant Paddy O'Sullivan. His nickname needs explaining. Eugene Sandow, the 'World's Strongest Man', visited Cork early in the nineteen-hundreds. In Murphy's brewery he performed the dramatic feat of lifting a Clydesdale dray-horse off the ground with one hand. It became the symbol of 'Murphy Stout'. He was powerful, swarthy, black haired and moustachioed. Dan Donovan was like that. He became to one and all simply 'Sandow'. He never talked about his exploits, and ended his days as manager of the extensive limestone works at historic Ballybeg near Buttevant. But one evening, towards the end of his career (about 1960), he sat in his office at Ballybeg with his assistant, Dónal O'Donoghue, and a local curate. The priest showed interest in the map on the wall which indicated the many delivery spots for the quarry products throughout the county. The mention of places opened, as it were, the floodgates. Sandow talked for an hour. Dev, he said, had come to him with a project in mind, a 'last token stand in Ballyvourney'. Sandow was now

O/C of the First Cork Brigade, Brigadier Seán Hegarty having opted for neutrality. Sandow had his troubles. He did not want 'Private' De Valera to add to them. (Before Dev came South he had re-enlisted in the Republican Army as a private). By strange coincidence a man from Béalnabláth walked into the hotel and to his great surprise saw Eamon de Valera standing at the bar. He was the schoolmaster, Pádraig Fleming, a Kerryman, who was on his way home to Béalnabláth by bicycle having attended an Irish language Summer course in Ballyvourney national school under the auspices of the Gaelic League. (In fact later on the village of Ballymakeera changed hands twice and on one of those occasions the *Slievenamon* armoured car, then in Republican hands, was the catalyst; indeed Ballyvourney was the only place in the country, as a veteran proudly but incongruously pointed out, that was never conquered by the Free State and is still therefore, the only authentic segment remaining of the old Republic for which they all had fought together). Sandow decided to send De Valera on his way to Liam Lynch wherever he might be, a decision which brought relief to all concerned. Dev's strange conscience was such that it was good to have the action taken out of his hands. He would be moving on. The 'Dáil' (Parliament) in Dublin was finally going to assemble on Saturday, 26 August, having been postponed unnecessarily for several weeks past. He was still technically a member. He thought to be the uninvited guest, the Ancient Mariner, holding them 'with his glittering eye' — hopefully! But thirty miles further on his road, at Walsh's of Glashabee near Mallow (cf. Mrs. Lankford, *The Hope and the Sadness*), he heard that Collins was dead. Forevermore . . . instead of the Cross the Albatross about his neck was hung!

*   *   *

'Good-night, Eamon!'
'Good-night, Mick!'

*   *   *

Back to Ballybeg and the revelation of the century! Sandow declared to his two attentive listeners, Donie Donoghue and Fr. Pat Sheehan (now Canon Sheehan, P.P., V.F., Mitchelstown), that Dev had told him in the Hibernian Hotel that he had, that morning, seen Michael Collins in person. He was upstairs in the public-house at Béalnabláth when the convoy arrived and stopped at the crossroads. He decided that 'he was finished, jumped out of bed and grabbed his gun', but the military contingent passed on. Was this the 'about a hundred yards away' he mentioned late that night? Did Collins spot him through the window and decide to return? Is it fortunate or unfortunate that Sandow kept a closed mind, except for this once, even to his own family? That Deasy and Dev kept silent is understandable; and Dev's further travels, his incredible 'Bloomsday' journey, his agenbite of inwit, Sandow certainly had no way of knowing about, but recent research has provided the details.

On a fine Sunday evening of August, 1989, I stood on a by-road near Carriganimma with John O'Sullivan, farmer. Just behind us was his new house, in front ran the Keel river beside the Macroom-Millstreet road and three hundred yards to the left, on the S-bend, stood Pike Bridge over the Keel. I said -'Did you ever hear of De Valera passing this way during the Civil War?' 'Of course I did', said the honest fellow - 'Didn't he walk up across the "ray" there to this very gap'; and the extraordinary story began to emerge.

Dev left Ballymakeera village around eight o'clock in the evening of 22 August 1922. He travelled in a pony-trap driven by Vice-Commandant Paddy O'Sullivan, and in the company of Captain Patsy Lynch. Half an hour later he arrived at the Keel river in a big, red Buick motor car driven by Jim Grey and in the company of the aforementioned Republican officers. Magic? Not at all! At Ullanes, two miles from Ballymakeera, the famous automobile (it had featured largely in the Tan War) had been stashed, as well as an equally famous Crossley tender which had been wrested from the Millstreet contingent of the Black and Tans at Keimcarrige during (and contrary to) the

Truce terms of the previous year (cf. M. O'Sullivan, *Where Mountainy Men Have Sown*). Both vehicles have now vanished, the only bit remaining is one hub of the Crossley (in possession of the present writer) which had been used over the years as a dinner gong and is now badly pock-marked by the weather. The Buick was in safe keeping in the home of Patsy Lynch at Ullanes. They changed transport and travelled on through Liscarrigane, by the birthplace of Gaelic scholar Canon Peter O'Leary, down the steep, narrow glen known as 'Katy Bawn's Hill' and onto the Millstreet road. Pike bridge had been demolished but traffic, including motor vehicles, managed to cross the old river ford, emerging on the by-road at the gap in the dry stone wall. At the river bank Dev dismounted, navigated the ford and walked on up the 'ray' alone. The car followed but the gap proved too narrow for the massive body. Lieutenant Stephen Roche (whose son, Liam, still lives at the old home a mile onwards on the road to Mushera Mountain), who met Dev at the water's edge and directed his footsteps, began to move some rocks in the gap out of the car's way. 'Mind your feet, boy!', said the tall, gaunt ex-President of the Irish Republic. Further on the road still lives old Batt Moriarty. He had been Intelligence Officer attached to the Millstreet Battalion and has latterly been making some notes, mostly undecipherable . . . 'Do you remember, Batt, when De Valera passed through in the Civil War?' 'Oh, indeed, I do', he said; 'and when he reviewed the troops in Kilcorney I was there' — a prideful statement from an old man, but more especially an old soldier, on the eve of the Collins centenary. But, he admitted, that was an early morning review and their section had marched seven miles from Kilmeedy Castle at dawn in order to be there. The discrepancy in the time factor bothered him and I explained that Dev had held many reviews, including Kilcorney, during and since the Truce period.

The big, red Buick resumed its journey towards Mushera Mountain, but only for a short while. A trench and barricade effectively cut the little mountain road and once again the ubiquitous pony-trap (or 'tub' trap) made its appearance and Dev moved onwards to destiny accompanied by a squad of horsemen, with Lieutenant Stephen Roche handling the honoured reins for the length of his jurisdiction. The little winding road followed the rising contours of Musherabeg and then Musheramore embellished with several megalithic remains in the form of stone circles, one, 'Knocknakilla', so important as to be sign-posted in modern times; then 'St. John's Well', for contrast, its origin also an ancient pagan festival of light become christianized, with its fantastic views, devotional and relaxing air and arguably the finest spring water in Ireland — good stuff, all of it, for an Irish revolutionary leader on the run. Shortly afterwards they met an old coach road from Kerry to Cork (via Millstreet and Rylane) with beside it the rock formation known as the 'Kerryman's Table' where travellers of old paused a while to refresh themselves. And then Kilcorney. Kilcorney, for Dev, meant Michael Howard's 'Brookpark House', one of his most favourite 'safe houses' in the country, 'where', he said, 'you were well fed and never asked where you were going'. The old mansion is presently uninhabited but still boasts of 'Dev's Room' and, curiously, the barred windows harking back to the other troubled times of the 'Whiteboys'. Regretfully they were unable to pause for refreshment of mind or body but pushed on down and around to the little hamlets of Lyre and Nadd, crossed the dangerous Cork-Kanturk road, then upwards once again on the scenic French's Road (newly constructed and named for its builder) to Bweeng and 'home' for the nonce.

Siobhán Lankford wrote: 'I was scarcely settled in bed when a dispatch rider arrived. He carried a letter from Liam Deasy, asking that I would go at once to Batt Walsh's home in Glashabee, and bring some conveyance — Mr. De Valera would be there. I was to see to his accommodation for that night. A blue car would come along on the following day to take him over the Tipperary border. He was on his return journey to Dublin.' She and her brother, Michael, made the journey to Glashabee by pony-trap, arriving at eleven. Dev was already there. Half an hour later they were about to convey him to her home at Clogheen, Mourne Abbey, when a man named Con Healy brought news that Michael Collins had been killed that evening in West Cork. Through the stunned silence Dev was heard to say: 'My God, it is too bad! There's no hope for it now!' Glashabee is a mile from Bweeng village and Batt Walsh's house was three-quarters of a mile into a boreen which circled onwards to emerge on the 'Rock Road', a quarter of a mile further. Turning left and then right at Carrigcleena they made their way to Ballynamona. Walsh's house was crowded with Republican Army personnel when they left and a lorry load of Irregulars cruised the little back roads on the watch for a warning light from Castle Barrett that they were going by. Ten-day-old memories of Kilpaddder, a short distance away, briefly ebbed and flowed. It seemed such a long time. The world had turned completely over. The pony trotted on down the incline from the Castle, across the little Clyda bridge, under the still useless railway, up by Ballynamona cemetery and Protestant church, over the 'New' and 'Old' Cork-Mallow roads (the newest is a mighty thoroughfare no pony would dare to venture on, which rated twenty-eight motor accidents on this spot alone in the first couple of years since its inauguration), and a short mile to Clogheen and relative safety at two in the morning.

The 'blue' motor car arrived at midday on the twenty-third. It was driven by Jimmy Brennock from Rathcormack, the regular Republican driver for that region. He was to ensure Mr. De Valera's safe conduct to his own native Araglen on the Kilworth Mountains. (Brennock, pronounced 'Brunnick', was later to become one of Sandow's trusted truck drivers at Ballybeg). At Clogheen he found the 'Long Fellow' incongruously trying wing shots with his 'Peter the Painter', within easy Mauser sound of Mallow. They left at one o'clock, Pat Creedon, the father, travelling in the motor car as guide and Michael following with the pony-trap. A short distance from the entrance gate was the spot where young Eamon had been killed by the Black-and-Tans on the morning of the failed Mourne Abbey ambush. Michael, working with him in the potato field, had taken five bullets but survived. Just another Eamon and Mick and the worst of the killing still to come, the killing of neighbours and brothers! From the V-cross at Ballinvuskig to the Monee crossroads is half a mile. On the previous Sunday Michael Collins had traversed it. Now Eamon de Valera followed his tracks but while Collins, weighted with armour, slipped down, down, down to the flat of Cork City, Dev turned up into the Nagles mountains between great banks of scarlet and purple fuschia. Strange it is to think that Collins should also have gone that way as he was expected to meet Dan Breen, the Tipperary stalwart, for a peace conference at Hickey's, an old haunt by the Mass Rock just out of Glenville. At Beenaskehy, the 'Top of the Bush', Killavullen called because Glanworth was just a few miles beyond where Liam Lynch was last reported to be resting. Liam Deasy thought so (cf. *Brother Against Brother*) but apparently Jimmy Brennock knew better, so they turned sharply by the old school of the Bush (now just peering through the jungle like the palace of the Sleeping Beauty) and went over the hill to Glenville. 'Callhouses' (Mrs. Lankford's expression) were now few and far between. Hickey's was on the approach road to the village but Hegarty's, of Ardrour, was beyond and nearer to Rathcormack. They went on up the steep incline to Hegarty's.

*   *   *

He drove into the yard in the early afternoon and alighted from his motor car. He stood and took stock of the great two-storey dwelling house high on the hill above the village, the 'safe house' he knew so well. And then he took stock of the new stone and mortar wall just being completed around the front of the house. The later gravel and cement terrace in between was still in the future, but the wall took his fancy. The erstwhile professor of Mathematics, the man whom Einstein had stated to have been the first to fully understand his new Theory of

Relativity, looked over the dimensions of the wall. He took in the oddly positioned gate pillars, square and prismatically capped, perfectly formed but set edgeways to the gateway rather than square, and the perfectly shaped ridging of the wall itself, and he spoke. What he said was - 'It's all wrong! You haven't done it right!' To their amazement he proceeded - 'You should have it slotted for rifles!' Collins was dead, and the elderly academic, who was later to become the renowned elder statesman of Europe, President of the League of Nations, was thinking in terms of continued and more intensive Civil War; thinking perhaps of the Great House at Bawnard, near Castlelyons, a few miles away, quite familiar to him then and later, where the Kent family, men and women, had made their historic and tragic stand against the might of Empire in 1916. Theory of Relativity!

*   *   *

Four days, he wrote in his diary, it took him to travel from Clogheen, Mallow, to Nurney in Co. Carlow, four days of imminent peril when sometimes truck loads of Free State soldiers were only yards away and the Dublin Squad were commissioned to shoot him on sight. Four days would be Sunday, 27 August. The Dáil, which was his objective, had been convened for Saturday, the twenty-sixth, but following the now familiar pattern had been prorogued once again until September the ninth. Leaving Glenville in the early morning they crossed the northern Bride at the Old Bride Bridge and coasted down to Rathcormack, five miles from Fermoy. The dangerous Cork-Dublin road was crossed without incident. Castlelyons was only a short distance but Kent's, of Bawnard, was too risky even for a brief visit. John Kent, of neighbouring Ballyhampshire, a cousin, informs me that the only information locally was that De Valera crossed the Ballyduff bridge over the Blackwater. The direction is right, the route immaterial. At Ballyduff they did a dangerous thing, some kind of calculated risk with a purpose. Instead of going directly over the mountain to Araglen they headed on the main road towards Fermoy and only took to by-roads once again three miles away at Raspberry Hill. They were making for Dr. David Barry's of Kilworth, via Araglen bridge. Just beneath them was cosy Leitrim House, bereft of its Major Reeves who had sturdily gone off to war to fight for king, empire and 'small nations' and died muddily and miserably in the trenches. Now his widow had Irish Republicans helping her to work the land. Irony of ironies!

Dr. David Barry, of Kilalley, Kilworth, was succeeded at his death by Dr. Seán O'Flynn but his 'boy', Davey Sweeney, stayed on. He told the story of De Valera to Dr. O'Flynn (corroborated by Davey's sister, Bridgie, who still lives locally, May McCormack of Araglen bridge and Mikey Fox of Leitrim, friends of Jack Clancy, while old Joe Lomasney, of Kilworth village, gave the Free State side of the story). It is the story of the only known occasion when Dev was actually shot at by Free State troops . . . Jimmy Brennock returned to Rathcormack having delivered his charge to Dr. Barry and having arranged a driver for the following day. The driver was Jack 'Ducky' Clancy of Leitrim townland. Ducky Clancy was practically illiterate but was a genius with motor cars to the extent that his uncle had bought him a grey, hoodless Model-T Ford. Dev's life was literally in his hands as they headed down Kilalley hill the half-mile into Kilworth village early in the morning of Friday, 25 August. On Thursday Davey Sweeney had delivered the *Cork Examiner* to Dr. Barry's and Dev had read the sad story of the death of Michael Collins. The Free State Army was in occupation of the village, mainly in the vacant R.I.C. barracks. It was like the old days once again. The village square was sandbagged and barricaded on all sides but on the previous day the barricade by the Market House cross had been moved back a few yards for more security. This was the saver. In charge of the troops was Sergeant Jack Herlihy of Fermoy (who later defected to the Republican side). The soldiers failed to spot the speeding car in time and Ducky Clancy took his Model-T around the Market House corner 'on two wheels', onto the old

Dublin coach-road, and headed for the Kilworth mountains like the hammers of hell while rifles banged and bullets whizzed all about them. A year or so before it would not have been possible. British guns were then lining the high wall of Moore Park just across the way. On the previous Monday Michael Collins had written from Cork to President Cosgrave in Dublin - 'We need to do something about Moore Park!' The fugitives took a sharp right at the 'Mountain Barrack' and raced down to the safety of Commandant Con Leddy's house at Gortnaskehy, Araglen, where Dev put up for the night of the twenty-fifth. (Though the family were not aware of it, Con Leddy told this to Dr. Seán O'Flynn shortly before his death). The Free State forces, like the British, had reason to fear the forbidding highlands and secret lowlands of the Araglen river. Many of the prominent families had provided, in about equal parts, some able Republican leaders and monks for the monastery of Mount Melleray. From Gortnaskehy to the Tipperary border is just a mile and early on Saturday morning, 26 August, Eamon de Valera was escorted quietly down into Ballyporeen. From here onwards his itinerary is rather hypothetical. He has left no record. However, from the military situation, the terrain and the balance of political feeling, one may make an educated guess. No one knows if he caught up with Liam Lynch in Araglen. Lynch was out of sympathy and may have taken steps to avoid such a meeting while keeping on the move himself. Since the folding of the Republican front line (which Calton Younger refers to disparagingly and not very realistically as 'a bit of a joke') between the cities of Limerick and Waterford, there were Free State held barracks in Carrick-on-Suir, Clonmel and even Clogheen. On the morning of Sunday, the twenty-seventh, De Valera appeared in the town of Nurney, Co. Carlow. He wrote that it had taken him four days from Mallow. A straight line on a map goes by Fethard and Mullinahone, in Co. Tipperary, and Gowran, in Co. Kilkenny, all strong Republican places. Three miles south east of Mullinahone was the invisible hide-out, the

famous 'Katmandu', in fact the tail-end of a cow-shed at
Poulacapple. He must have called there. Republican leaders
were in residence. He would stay there himself in the Spring of
1923 when, at the invitation of Liam Lynch (who now regarded
him as the President of the newly formed Republic), he would
travel south from Dublin for his once ever attendance at a con-
clave of the Republican Army Executive in the Nire Valley
below Clonmel, the last such meeting ever. He wore a beard on
the occasion and travelling with him as his 'daughter' was Kitty
Teehan of Shipton, near Kilkenny City. The Egan family of
Poulacapple were strong supporters of his, and Stasia Egan
(Mrs. Brett) still lives hale and hearty in Mullinahone. The
Poulacapple people moved him safely on over the Kilkenny
border. Fifty years later he was to tell Lord Longford simply
that he was 'travelling by side roads and avoiding the towns' as
he 'continued his hazardous journey to Dublin'. History still
lives around the regions of Gowran and Nurney. Common conversation centres around not only the Tan War and the Civil
War but the Rising of Ninety-Eight, seasoned with the exploits
of Myles Keogh in the American Civil War. Eamon de Valera,
the political idealist, was in good company. He called for tea to
the Teehans of Shipton. He was now wearing a volunteer
uniform and carried a rifle. Somewhere along the way he had
decided that if it came to a fight he would acquit himself correctly. But at Teehan's came a change of attitude. Dublin was
calling. He borrowed a suit of clothes from one of the Teehan
boys and discarded the trappings of war. The two Teehan girls
were regular couriers for the Republican cause, Kitty (Mrs.
Bennett) and Molly (Mrs. Foley). They still live locally and time
has not dimmed the pride they take in their achievements of the
past. Kitty was the favoured messenger who carried the cease-
fire order from Dublin to Cork after the death of Liam Lynch,
10 April 1923. She recalls that the paper was signed in the home
of the Cassidy family on the outskirts of the city. At the time the
Cassidy girls ran a 'silk shop' in O'Connell Street. Kitty travelled alone and handed the paper to Tom Crofts acting on

behalf of Liam Deasy who was in prison and under sentence of death. The Civil War was over.

. . . Dev moved on to Murphy's of Mountruth, between Paulstown and Gowran, where he stayed the night and on the morning of Sunday, 27 August, he was driven into the town of Nurney by Maggie Walsh (Mrs. Prendergast) in a pony-trap. Two miles out of town was Michael Doorley's, of Clooneen. Here he remained until Monday morning. His chances of getting to Dublin with any degree of safety, and making his grand entrance to Dáil Éireann in due time, one would think depended even still on the significance of this town's name in the Gaelic - 'An Urnaí', the Prayer!

The Michael Collins Story: The Itinerary

Oliver St. John Gogarty was a doctor of medicine and a surgeon. He went to the best schools in Ireland and England. Friend of Arthur Griffith and James Joyce, he is referred to in *Ulysses* as 'stately plump Buck Mulligan' whose final departure from the Martello tower was due in about equal parts to the too free use of blasphemous obscenity and a revolver. Gogarty was a writer, an erudite classical scholar and had that kind of Irish wit that can be harmful if unfettered. He was an iconoclast and scarifier of the great, as witness his books of reminiscences, both fictional-factional and autobiographical. He tended to despise the simple people of Ireland. He seemed to regard the poet, Patrick Kavanagh, as a country 'cawbogue', an unlettered lout. In his strangely construed autobiography, *As I was Going Down Sackville Street* (which involved him in a libel suit in 1937, and eventual exile), he scurrilously vilified Eamon de Valera (for whom he developed an obsessive detestation amounting almost to hatred) and his 'Irregulars', and obsequiously venerated Michael Collins. He made friends and enemies with equal and facile disdain. All in all, Gogarty was a good surgeon, a good writer, a good poet, a clever and dangerous liar, a Brendan Behan of the operating table. Ironically he has become more relevant to the Collins Story than almost anyone else. He is on record as contradicting himself about the extent of Collins' head injuries, and he should know!

* * *

"Visitors to our country", (said George William Russell, known as 'Æ', editor of *The Irish Homestead*), "should know that revolution is De Valera's idea of evolution . . .''. "General Collins!'' (was announced). He marched into the room in front of his name. Everyone stood up . . . he was a burly man whose burliness hid his height. He was a smooth, burly man. You could see it in the unlined face and the beautiful, womanly hands. His skin was like undiscoloured ivory . . . Low forehead, but what was seen over the clear-cut brow was straight. The hair grew down and his head tilted forward as if his chin sought repose on his chest. Napoleonic! But a bigger and more comely specimen of manhood than Napoleon. In his newly acquired position (i.e. Commander-in-Chief), he kept his distance by an aggressive and good-natured abruptness . . . the countenance in all its swiftness of the quickest intellect and nerve Ireland bred . . . A few weeks later Emmet Dalton sent that key (a donated latch-key to Gogarty's house in Ely Place) back from the bloodstained tunic of a murdered man''. (From *As I was Going Down Sackville Street*). And Collins said to 'Æ' that night, 'Blaze away! Don't mind me!'. It could have been an epitaph for Béalnabláth!

From his appointment to the highest office in the Army the career of Michael Collins has been well documented. Much is made of his return from the original planned tour of the South for the funeral of Arthur Griffith, the then President of the newly named but still not official 'Free State'. His picture as he walked in the funeral cortège to historic Glasnevin Cemetery, in Dublin, shows a man of robust health for whom a military uniform was 'made', and for whom the plaudits of the crowd were a necessity. Much is made of the head cold he was suffering from at the time. Much is made of the shattering effect on him of the death of the man on whom he now depended, hoping against hope. And a rather elusive but intriguing point of view has been proposed that he was adroitly cajoled into the position so as to have him out of the way in Dublin — the 'kicked upstairs' procedure (Feehan, *The Shooting of Michael Collins*). It just may have been the truth. Others state that he claimed, or appropriated, the job and from that moment he seemed too eager to get back to his roots and the estimable fellows he knew who 'blew fight' at all comers down there in rebel Cork.

'Collins went to the Curragh and there inspected the army units. From the Curragh he proceeded to Limerick. From there he set out for Mallow in Co. Cork. It was the beginning of the end of the journey of his life' (Rex Taylor, *Michael Collins*). We take him up in Limerick, with a couple of qualifications. He had left Portobello Barracks, Dublin, where he had temporarily taken residence, early on Sunday morning. Portobello (now 'Cathal Brugha') Barracks is off the Rathmines Road and a short distance from the Grand Canal. Rather too much is made by writers and oral memoirs of his deterioration in physical and mental health, 'when pain and anguish wring the brow', as it were. The contrast of his too energetic plunge into the business of high-level soldiering is passing strange. In fact he was neither soldier nor politician. The charade had begun to please him much as the hobbies of a successful business managing director. The hindsight and the tragedy have imbued his every motion with a surrealism more awesome than the pathetic fallacy of howling church bells and silently flitting worshippers. In Limerick he simply went to Mass in St. John's Cathedral. The announcement said that it was being offered for the happy repose of the soul of Arthur Griffith. A certain Mrs. Gleeson saw him there in earnest prayer. Her son William (later Willie 'Whack' Gleeson of the *Limerick Leader* newspaper), as a young Free State soldier, was to have a strange encounter with the Commander-in-Chief later in the day. Lacking the intense concentration of his cloak-and-dagger days in Dublin, the country boy was getting lost. His whirlwind drive from Dublin to Cork, through Limerick, seemed to imply that he sought to 'bestride the narrow world like a Colossus'. If he wanted peace, as they say he did, it must have been on the lines of the old classical dictum — Si vis pacem, para bellum! If you wish for peace, prepare for war! Limerick, the 'City of the Broken Treaty', was the key to the South, to what was optimistically called the 'Munster Republic'. But the South had been beaten in the great campaign of the 'Kilmallock Triangle', referred to as the 'Fourteen-day Battle' (Eoin Neeson, *The Civil War in Ireland*), after the fall of Limerick to the National Army. The 'Nihil Obstat' of the neophyte Commander-in-Chief needed to be stamped on the lintel of every barrack-door, every cleared strong point, every newly won fortification. Limerick was once again a city of a broken treaty — two in fact. High-ranking officers of both factions of the Army had signed them on 4 and 7 July in a spirit of old comradeship, but they had been immediately repudiated by Dublin. And so, on Sunday, 20 August 1922, at 5 p.m., General Michael Collins moved out of the city of broken treaties to inspect his military stepping-stones on the way to his native Cork . . . On 8 April 1989, the *Limerick Leader* quaintly reported: 'We reproduce here St. George's account of his encounter with Michael Collins', as if they had finally decided to turn the 'Big Fellow' into a dragon; but it was merely a reference to Charlie St. George, the gentle giant of Limerick rugby of the past, who claimed to have been one of the last people in the city to have seen Collins alive as he departed the Henry Street headquarters with Eoin O'Duffy, G.O.C. Southern Command, and a large convoy. According to Charlie (whose once-off sideline view of everything from the start of the Great War to the end of the Civil War has to be one of the best pieces ever in cryptic journalism) the convoy was parked kerb-wise along Henry Street, facing uphill to the Redemptorist Church of St. Alphonsus. Commandant-General Michael Brennan, commanding the First Western Division, had his H.Q. at 104 Henry Street, erstwhile palace of

Protestant Bishop Austin. The inspection ended here. It had encompassed all strong points in the city from O'Duffy's stately sandbagged Staff Offices, in Cruise's Hotel, to the local school house at Patrickswell, decreeing prisoner accommodation and a location (in William Street) for a detachment of the new paramilitary Civic Guard already in training in the Curragh. 'The headquarters', said Charlie,

were alongside Despard's coal-yard, where the present 'Bord na gCon' (i.e. the National Greyhound Association) offices are now, alongside the old St. Munchin's College (now Garda Síochána H.Q.). I was standing on the road in front of the headquarters, close to a small armoured car in front of which were two motor bikes, standing on their props and facing up the road. Behind them were three big touring cars, standing around which were six drivers in all. There were no visible signs of arms of any description, with the exception of the muzzle of a machine-gun, pointing out from the slot at the front of the turret of the 'Whippet'. Occasionally the muzzle moved, indicating there was another soldier in there, like as if he were settling the inside or that he was uncomfortable inside. There were no pressmen or photographers to be seen. After about twenty minutes, Collins appeared at the door of the headquarters. He moved forward slowly, followed by six or seven officers, including Timmie Murphy (a local man just made Brigadier-General commanding the Limerick area). Collins wore a long, green overcoat, buttoned up to the neck, and he wore a peaked, round military-style cap. He had his two arms across his chest, as he stood at the top of the steps, at the entrance. He looked straight ahead. There were a number of groups of people standing round in curiosity, and Collins looked at them and then looked left and right. Collins' group moved to the cars with the drivers now in position. Suddenly Collins turned round to his right, stretched out his hand and shook hands with Murphy. Then the group broke up, Collins taking his seat alongside the driver of the first car, the other officers divided up between the other two cars. As I stood looking at the convoy moving off, in the general direction of the Redemptorists' church, I felt happy that I had seen 'The Chief' in person. Later that week, when the news came

1. Michael Collins pictured at Arthur Griffith's funeral.

2. The Owen Hickey snapshot at Garrienderk Bridge, Kilmallock.

3a. Collins' personal motor car, the spectacular 'Leyland-Eight'.

3b. The 'Slievenamon' as it is today. (*Photo: Pat Deasy*)

4a, b & 5a. Retreat from Kilmallock: Dan Breen, Seán Moylan,
Paddy O'Brien and Jim Brislane negotiating a culvert.
Driver unknown.

5b. Crucial conference in Kilkenny, May, 1922, with Dan
Breen, Seán Moylan and Jim Brislane facing Gearóid
O'Sullivan, Adjutant General of the Free State Army.

6a. The old O'Connell Home (now vanished) at Kilpadder, Mallow, where Dev had a room, and where he and Liam Lynch finally agreed to differ on the promotion of the Civil War.

6b. 'Clydaville' in the early Twenties.

a.

b.

7a. Brigadier-General Gibbs Ross;   b. 'Scottie';   c. Bobs
Doherty;   d. Mike Donoghue.

c.

d.

8a. Childers' cottage in Renaniree. (*Photo: Fr. G. Casey*).

8b. Historic Walsh's, of Glashabee, no longer inhabited.

through of the ambush, and that Michael Collins had been killed, I found it hard to believe.

Mr. St. George continued that he inquired of Brigadier-General Murphy for some information. He hadn't any. 'It was over a week before we met again, when he gave me the following account. Some local I.R.A. boys, on hearing that there was a convoy of Free State soldiers travelling in the area (i.e. in West Cork), decided to set up an ambush. Fire had been exchanged, and when the locals were running out of ammunition they decided to call off the engagement. In the course of pulling out — these were Murphy's own words to me — one f------"óinseach" turned round and took a pot-shot in the direction of Collins. This was believed to be the shot that killed him.'

Leaving Limerick City at five o'clock in the evening of 20 August, Michael Collins moved out on the Tipperary road eastwards. With him was Eoin O'Duffy. Was he thinking merely of 'promises to keep, and miles to go before I sleep', or the tedious chore of inspecting new military positions? Was he possibly thinking of Patrick Sarsfield, that bellicose Earl of Lucan, who had galloped that way to blow up King William's siege train at nearby Ballyneety during the first siege of Limerick in August, 1690? A fleeting thought of 'Collins the word, and Collins the man!', perhaps? Or was he thinking, which is more likely, that he was heading into the biggest and most significant battlefield of the Civil War where so many Irishmen had fought and died for him and against him, just three weeks ago? Eight miles out of the city the convoy took a right turn to the complex road junction at Caherconlish where they stopped and had refreshments at the roadside inn now known as 'The Big Tree'. At Caherconlish (pronounced locally as 'Carrick-in-Lish') Collins unknowingly came upon the first of those strange coincidences that went to make up the pattern of his curious death two days later. In mid-July the city of Limerick was being daily and nightly disputed by pro- and anti-Treaty (Eoin Neeson's distinction) forces, and in an effort to halt reinforcements coming to the National Army from the North-East, Comdt. Peter Kearney, of the Third (West) Cork Brigade, made a sortie to Caherconlish, established a salient there and held out until recalled by his superiors in the city just before the withdrawal of the I.R.A. on July the twenty-first. Now Collins and his Free State Army convoy briefly occupied the position before heading on to Bruff. It was only a tea break. Pete Kearney is significant. With regard to the death of Collins at Béalnabláth he said (to Eoin Neeson): 'Apart from the heavy fire on our positions (he admitted to being "one of the ambush party"), the dusk alone made it virtually impossible to get off an aimed shot'. There was one thing, however, he did not reveal at that time. He went to the end of his life fully convinced that it was he who had shot Michael Collins, and he heartily regretted same. The combination public house and shop at Caherconlish, then, as now, owned by the O'Connell family, had been burned down by the Black and Tans and rebuilt. Dick, one of the three sons, had been Brigadier in the mid-Limerick Brigade and was now in charge of the Army post at Castleconnell, a few miles up-river on the Shannon, where the Commander-in-Chief had paid a brief visit earlier in the day. Dick had now joined the convoy and would convey them to Bruff. (He was later a Commandant in the National Army stationed in the Curragh). Sister Josie provided the tea on this auspicious occasion and the great man turned at the door to remark - 'Josie, those scones were beautiful!'

One wonders, as Collins entered the town of Bruff, which became a sort of field hospital and clearance station for the big battle and changed hands several times, what details he had of the life-and-death struggle which had taken place in the region out before him. Whatever may have been the individual military reports (and Gen. O'Duffy's at least were far too sanguine), the details of the battlefield have been extensively winkled out by Eoin Neeson (1966) and Calton Younger (1968). The personal agony of the Republican soldier has been portrayed by Peter O'Farrell (Brooklyn, N.Y.), and writer Frank O'Connor (in his first volume of autobiography, *An Only Child*) contributes his own battle experience with the Republican forces. In the long ago people preferred not to know. In this, the Collins Centenary year, not many, even in high places, seem to care. As for the man himself, leaving Bruff and heading for Bruree, the feelings of the people concerned him, the destruction of property bothered him, the killing of men had become too facile to notice . . .

William Gleeson of Limerick and member of D Company, Mid-Limerick Brigade, Southern Command, at the formation of the Free State Army, 1922, stood guard at Cleeves' condensed milk factory in Bruree, on the right bank of the Maigue river and at the junction of the Charleville road. He was in army uniform and stood with rifle in proper sentry position across the yard facing the closed double gates. All five-foot-seven of him, Willie 'Whack' stood alone, but the danger was minimal. The Republicans were now presumably far away in the hills of West Cork and Kerry. There was just one aggravation (he still vividly remembers), the stench of milk that had been left to rot for three weeks. Suddenly the gates were burst open with a mighty kick and a strange man in high-rank uniform stood powerfully revealed. Willie yelled for the guard and came to the ready all in one. Two soldiers turned out followed by Lieut. Tom Carmody who was straightening his tunic. Carmody was in charge deputizing for Capt. Tom Costelloe . . .

I shouted to the two relief sentries, Volunteers Paddy Morrissey and Mickey Bowman, 'Guard turn out!'. Almost immediately an officer whom I recognized as Commandant Donncha O'Hannigan — since he never wore a cap in the army and, at the same time, carried a .45 Smith and Wesson automatic pistol held tightly in his hand — came into the yard. (Note: There never was a Smith and Wesson automatic. A notable feature of all writings, even the most reputable, on the subject of our Civil War, and especially Béalnabláth, is the treatment of weaponry with small expertise and wild abandon!). He was followed (Willie Gleeson continues) by a very high-ranking officer, whom I did not recognize, with gold braid on peak of cap and shoulders not-withstanding. Immediately he (i.e. the high-ranking officer) approached me and asked: 'Who is in charge here?' 'Captain Costelloe, Sir, but not here today, he being absent on official army business in Dublin'. 'Who, then, is acting during his absence', he quipped. 'Lieutenant Carmody, Sir', I replied. Scarcely had I finished when the lieutenant, who was in the office nearby, met his superior officer. They both moved towards the fence overlooking the Maigue river and after a brief conversation the matter ended. Next Lieutenant Carmody, who appeared to be smiling as he approached me, said: 'Did you know who the high-ranking officer was?' 'No', I said, 'I never saw him before!' 'Well', he said, 'that was General Michael Collins!' Most unusually I was lost for words. Anyway, what transpired from both officers' conversation was something like this:

1. Get any mode of available transport and go at once to Rockbarton, get a change of washing — shirt, socks, cardigan, jacket — and distribute same among the seventeen of the unit. (Note: Rockbarton House was some three miles beyond Bruff and near to Holy Cross and historic Lough Gur. It is now a stud farm).

2. Get away from this building no later than tomorrow (Note: The building no longer exists), and proceed to Galbally (i.e. sixteen miles away near the Glen of Aherlow), 'where the unit will be billeted in Lowtown schoolhouse', to quote the General. Three days later (it was actually eight), we, the unit, were firing three volleys in the local graveyard as a mark of respect to our late Chief, at the same time as he was being laid to rest in Glasnevin. (From: 'Collins, the Hero Limerick Forgot', *Limerick Leader*, 27 August 1988).

The town of Bruree (Ir. 'Brú Rí', the palace of kings) deserves more than a passing note of military activity. It is particularly associated with 'The Revolt of the Bottom Dogs', the very much neglected part of Irish History — the contribution of the ongoing Labour Movement to the ending of British imperial authority. The Cleeve family of Limerick owned major factories, bakeries and creameries throughout the city and county and even further afield. In all of these work places labour conditions were said to be poor. Taking its cue from Dublin, 1916, and Russia, 1917, the labour movement began its quiet revolt, extending right through the 'Trouble' times and the Civil War. Workers took over the factories from management and established temporary 'Soviets', sometimes improving not only pay and conditions of workers but efficiency and output. From factories the movement spread to railways (cf. 'The Tom Daly Story'), and harbours. Bruree was one of the first of the 'Soviets'. It happened at the Cleeve mill and bakery on the other side of town on the bank of the Maigue. 'We Make Bread Not Profits' was the motto placed over the entrance. During the Civil War the mill was occupied alternatively by both Republicans and Free Staters, and it is rather amusing that, during a counter-attack by Republicans, on 2 August, the officer in charge of the mill ordered his men to 'bake bread in preparation for a lengthy siege'. Even more amusing is the fact that during the interim Dáil between the Truce and the Treaty, in 1921, the Countess Markievicz, Minister for Labour and later anti-Treaty, summoned the Bruree 'Soviet' to Dublin (2 September) and ordered them out of the factory immediately or she would expedite their departure with the aid of Republican troops. They went. Note: The Cleeve Experience is of great interest. Forerunner of the Industrial Development Association and its continuing determined efforts to bring business, and therefore employment, to this country on a speculative-accumulative principle, the Cleeve phenomenon is worthy of attention rather than the oblivion to which it has been relegated. The first Cleeve, Thomas, came on a visit from Canada round about 1850, saw an opportunity for speculation and stayed on. Importing a newfangled hay-baler from his homeland, he began by collecting hay from farmers in the Limerick region and supplying same to the British Army. From headquarters in Limerick City the business gradually spread to the building of creameries and condensed milk factories. In 1924 the vast operation was nationalized by the new Free State government, with very little compensation, and the family fortune was dissipated almost overnight. Then the creameries were organized on a co-operative basis and unemployed German engineers from the Great War were brought over to build new ones. Our man in Coolavokig was Hans Neiss, and the set question was: 'Hans, do you like German Sausage?', and the answer, 'Oh, if I haff him I vud ate haff off him!' After nationalization the Cleeve family business became the Condensed Milk Company of Ireland, but the name was retained in the toffee factory of Limerick. The famous 'Cleeves toffees' were a major factor in my growing up and the change of format, when the ten-a-penny became five-a-penny, seemed a major disaster in the life of a nine-year-old. One wonders if the long arm and all-seeing eye of the dead Collins cast a posthumous blight on this apparently imperialistic form of profiteering! If Gogarty is to be believed, the 'General' was an ardent admirer of agrico-op's 'Æ'.

Michael Collins went from Bruree and the revolt of the bottom dogs with a wry curl of the famous upper lip, which had probably been there since his passing by Dev's childhood cottage shortly before and just a mile out of town. Five miles to the east lay the decisive Kilmallock, ancient town of the White Knights of Desmond, the approach to it controlled by the hotly disputed Kilmallock Hill and Quarry Hill (where Gilpin, the intrepid Kerry Republican machine-gunner, from Castleisland, held his own for an incredible three weeks in rain and shine and young Danny Murphy, from Liscarroll, was 'cut in half' by a burst from a Lewis-gun fired by a neighbour on the Free State side. The neighbour, a farmer, had been a special 'Collins man' and bond seller all through and naturally joined the Army. O'Farrell rather needlessly gives his name. He still lives alone in San Francisco with his fading memories). Kilmallock was the Gettysburg of Ireland's Civil War. It was definitely the 'high-water mark' of Republicanism just as Gettysburg was to the Confederacy. When it fell to the relentlessly advancing Free State Army, on 5 August, the Republican headquarters in the vast military barracks in Buttevant (vacated by the East Lancashire Regiment after the Treaty) was prepared for evacuation and fire.

*   *   *

'While we were there (i.e. on Quarry Hill) a Bishop Turner from Buffalo, N.Y., a relative of the house (behind the hill) came to see us in action. He took photos of us, told us how great we were, and said he would send us the photos when they were ready. When the S.O.B. got back to Buffalo he cut us to pieces. I later wrote to him asking for the pictures he had promised. I never received an answer'. What O'Farrell did not know was that the good bishop had already roasted them while 'preaching in the Church of St. Alphonsus last night (Monday, 7 August) to the men of the Arch-Confraternity of the Holy Family' as reported in the Protestant-run (now defunct) *Limerick Chronicle*, which then went on to out-Herod Herod with 'When the troops arrived in the town (i.e. Kilmallock) they received a tumultuous reception by the inhabitants, who expressed their sincere delight to be rid of the Irregulars, whom they described as being "worse than the Black-and-Tans" '. The enemy, however, was kinder . . . 'We were received with courtesy by well-armed and well-disciplined men and, on our undertaking that the three men with the car (i.e. a Red Cross conveyance under a flag of truce) were unarmed, we were allowed to come forward. One of them conducted us to where they had laid out the bodies with their Rosary beads in their hands'. (Eoin Neeson, quoting from a Free State veteran of the battle). Anyone who ever knew Liam Deasy, Seán Moylan, and Commandants Paddy O'Brien and Jim Brislane, of Liscarroll, would have expected no less.

*   *   *

With Collins it was just in one gate and out the other, both rather impressive remains of the medieval fortifications of Kilmallock. Even the mansion of Ashill Towers, with its great stables and newly captured field headquarters, he brushed aside. He was in a hurry. But he did stop the convoy, just out of town, to piss against the fence. (The picture of same is said to be in the most secret archives of R.T.E.). Gesture or otherwise, Abe Lincoln's effort on Cemetery Ridge was considerably more historic. At Thomastown, three miles away, County Cork was almost in sight. He had said - 'They won't shoot me in my own county!' No one asked him who he thought they were. 'Spur' Brien's farmhouse, with its unusual looking cut-stone walls, was an indication of what he might still expect. A premature probe by his men from Limerick had come to grief there, early on Monday morning, 24 July. On the previous evening they had reached the Charleville-Kilmallock road, captured an I.R.A. staff car heading from Buttevant Barracks to Ashill Towers, with three men in it. The three prisoners were kept overnight at 'Spur' Brien's. (As a child this O'Brien had ridden a donkey to school and had contrived a pair of spurs to make him go. The Royal Irish Constabulary, who were notoriously concerned for animal welfare, came to his father and threatened to take action unless he desisted from this 'cruelty to animals' activity. The name stuck). The Free Staters had some lorries for transport parked in the backyard and early in the morning had just started one up when they were suddenly surrounded and the battle began. The engine continued to run all through the fight until the Staters surrendered. During the battle a Republican armoured car toured up and down the road spraying the house with bullets. The pock marks are still visible. (Just recently I discovered a clip of live .303 ammunition on the site). By that time an army sergeant named Denis O'Mahony, from Cork City, had been killed and Mossie O'Brien from Charleville, the officer in charge, had been injured by a grenade. (He later defected to the Republican side). Young Mickey Donovan, from almost the same street as the dead sergeant, had been one of the prisoners taken in the Republican staff car. Some days later he wrote an 'Eye Witness' account for the *Cork Examiner*. He did more. He wrote the well known biography of Collins, called *The Big Fellow*. He was, in fact, writer Frank O'Connor. General Michael Collins might have shivered as he passed 'Spur' Brien's in Thomastown. A vast army of words had already begun to march over his grave. And so to Garrienderk, the broken railway bridge and Owen Hickey's camera!

*   *   *

'We held these positions for approximately a week, and then received orders to break the lines and to return to our local units "on the run" to form local columns. We blew up Garrienderk bridge, which had been prepared since the previous November. This later bogged down armoured cars and lorries, forcing them to go through Morty Foley's fields in the mud. On 20 August, I had just arrived home when three armoured cars from Kilmallock breezed past the house, with four or five Crossley lorries, escorting Michael Collins on his trip to West Cork' (Peter O'Farrell: *Memoirs of Irish Volunteer Activity, 1917-1924*).

*   *   *

Michael Collins left Limerick City for Cork City but had made a significant detour (which seems to have been overlooked by the various writers) via Kilmallock, an important road junction near the Cork county border, and thence to Charleville across that border. 'The *Slievenamon* went rolling on', as the old rebel Ballyvourney song went in the long ago; until, that is, she came to Garrienderk bridge. Then she stopped. There was no bridge. The Garrienderk railway bridge is two miles out of Charleville on the road to Kilmallock. It is still extremely hump-backed and dangerous and it still shows the same rough wall stones on which Collins leaned his 'beautiful and womanly hands' while he watched his convoy take to the fields to circumvent the broken arch. He still wore the long military overcoat. A crowd of locals began to gather round. One of them, Owen Hickey, had an idea. He slipped home for his 'Kodak' folding pocket-camera. Back at the bridge he pulled out the concertina-type lens compartment on its rails and clicked it into place. Collins spun round instantly and reached for the gun strapped to his thigh. Then understanding he stood a moment for the photograph with a poor grace, the bleak look on his face far different from the bland smile of a week ago at Griffith's funeral in Dublin. 'Can I take your photo, Sir?', said Owen Hickey. 'You can if you're quick', said General Collins. He had climbed down into the rubble of the bridge and out again on the Charleville side. 'Such destruction!', he said to Commandant Seán O'Connell as he looked into the void. Half a mile back towards Thomastown a small culvert over a stream had also been blown but only partly damaged. There he had dismounted and lent a hand at moving some rocks to make the stream passable. Then he took from his pocket a large, red silk handkerchief, wiped his hands in it and cast it aside as if he were discarding the frumpery of Dublin and London society in the approach to his native countryside. The culvert was known as 'Reardon's Bridge', or the 'Half-Way'. Near it lived old Mrs. Patrick O'Gorman, better remembered as Bridgie Quinn, with her husband. She picked up the handkerchief and took it to her cottage nearby where she kept it until her death many years later. There is now no trace of it. Forty yards from Garrienderk bridge, on the Kilmallock side, a five-bar gate gave entrance to a field and a track to a farmhouse beyond the railway line. Similar gates stood on either side of the track which was merely a branch line from Charleville Station to Limerick via Bruree, Croom and Patrickswell. Through this passage-way the convoy struggled, the *Slievenamon* alone having trouble with the rails while the Commander-in-Chief watched from high overhead. What a way to run a railroad! What a way to run a country! (Owen Hickey was now neutral but had been the first captain of the Garrienderk company of Volunteers when they had been affiliated to the movement in Bruree by the Countess Markievicz and Con Collins in September, 1917, both of whom had just been released from internment in England. Peter O'Farrell boasts that their company had been the first in Ireland to be so enrolled, which, he claims, is still in 'Records').

Michael Collins 'crossed the Rubicon' at the Pike Cross by the Effin road. There was no symbolic stream or river, as in the old Italian Civil War, when Julius Caesar left Celtic Cisalpine Gaul, in 49 B.C., to challenge Pompey and the Roman Republic. There was just two hundred yards of roadway where the county boundary trailed along from the Pike Cross (which

used to have a toll-gate in the distant past) to Ballincolly Cross
on the road to Bruree. Just half a mile away lay Charleville. It
was well and truly occupied by the Free State. Troops were
everywhere, even in the parochial hall. An 'alea jacta est' was
unnecessary. The die was already cast. The 'Cataline Conspiracy' of the Treaty was a long way behind. For Caesar it was
still a troubled five years to assassination, for Collins — just
two days!

Charleville was a contentious town. Charleville was a divided
town. Charleville still demurs at the authenticity of its own
name. Originally outright Republican, it was now intensely for
and against the Treaty, for and against Michael Collins, the
man (according to Mick Donovan, late porter at the Bank of
Ireland, Cobh, and once Seán Hales' gunner) 'you either loved
or hated'. The town had rapidly filled up with Free State
troops . . .

> 'Twas England gave the orders,
> 'Twas England gave the guns;
> 'Twas Collins dressed the boys in green
> To shoot our darling sons!

This kind of doggerel could only be matched on the other side
by the convoluted mind and poison pen of Oliver St. John
Gogarty. Still they were everywhere, two thousand of them.
Recruitment to the National Army was now at one thousand a
day. Collins apparently intended to win by sheer weight of
numbers, as did the Persian king Xerxes (said to be the first
military leader ever to put a million men in the field) against the
ancient Greeks. Failing a Lord Byron, the country balladeer
would have to do for the underdog. In Charleville the Free State
troops invested St. Patrick's Hall (locals removed the piano
and the billiard table) in Chapel Street, Coleman's (Royal)
Hotel, Madden's (Imperial) Hotel — Lord Kenmare's Lisnagry
House had been burned by the retreating Republicans — and
Dr. Magner's Block (a later title but then three large buildings
of an old endowed Protestant school at the corner of Chapel

Street and Clancy Terrace). This latter was occupied by the Cycle Corps who utilized a trick for convenience which they had learned from the Republican forces in Limerick City in July. They bored through the intervening walls to form a complex. Soldiers were also billeted in private houses. Colonel Dave Reynolds was in command and there were also some officers from the town itself, a sad mistake which was to have a bitter outcome in Kerry, especially in Kenmare, at a later stage. Peter O'Farrell naïvely puts down the local split in the Volunteers to an incident during the Truce (1921) when martial pride was all important. The Battalion had held an inter-company proficiency competition at Milltown. High honours went to companies with high-ranking Fourth Brigade officers. Garrienderk (his own) company got nowhere . . . 'The thing was rigged as usual and was very much responsible for the dissension that resulted with regard to Beggar's Bush (in Dublin) later on!' Collins held a brief review in Chapel Street before hurrying on. Captain Jack Phayer, of Nicholas Street, Limerick, was proudly in charge of the guard of honour. Even on his deathbed in 1988 he still mourned to his old friend and fellow soldier, Willie Gleeson, that it was 'only three days before he (Collins) was murdered!' The retroactive tragedy seemed to take all the good out of his guard of honour, just as it must have for Emmet Dalton after Béalnabláth. But — Murder! The harsh word and thought seem greatly misplaced after sixty-six years and 'sub specie aeternitatis'.

The Awbeg River, on the way from Charleville to Mallow, has a little valley all to itself. What of it? you say. Its name means just the 'little river'. It rises on the north side of the Ballyhoura mountains, flows westwards towards Charleville, then suddenly southwards under the portals of Castle Harrison to make its way into Literature and History. Only a mile wide at one point, the valley lies between the foothills of the Ballyhouras and a series of elevations from Charleville to Altamira House, Liscarroll, which might reasonably be considered representative of the distant massif of Mullaghareirk. The 'little river' is fed by many littler ones from both sides, one, in fact, from the Red Bog, Dromina, through the great Annagh boglands, being so prominent as to be likewise and confusedly known as the Awbeg. They meet at the delightful old three-arch bridge called 'Scairt', the 'Shout', at Aghaburn, and flow on quietly and peacefully to the historic town of Buttevant where the Awbeg finally comes into its own. At Mallow Michael Collins made a note in his personal notebook with regard to 'making good a passage over the Awbeg'. Significant, but not great literature — that had already been made! The significance lies in the fact that he had failed to do so himself. He had to turn back. The great literature was Edmund Spenser's *Faerie Queene*. From Kilcolman Castle, near Doneraile, the great Elizabethan poet had an unimpeded view of the Awbeg, his 'gentle Mulla', a short distance away and well within his three thousand acres:

> Strong Allo tombling from Slewlogher steep,
> And Mulla mine whose waves I whilom taught to weep.

Spenser also formulated the idea that 'Kilnemulla' (Buttevant) had been named in the Irish from his beloved Awbeg. This may have been because he had lived for a short while (1586) in Effin, Co. Limerick, and got to understand that the holy well of St. Mo Lua, near Ardpatrick, was the source of the Awbeg. Despite his love for the countryside and sympathy for the persecuted people of his time and place, his idea for the pacification of Munster was not unlike that of Collins: 'Let them (i.e. the English Parliament of the time) now bring over ten thousand foot and one thousand horse, plant these in six convenient garrisons, give the rebels twenty days in which to surrender, and then hunt down relentlessly all who stand out . . . and rebellion will be at an end'. (From Spenser's *Veue of the Present State of Ireland*). The present state of Ireland 300-400 years later is greatly unchanged! Spenser was burned out of his castle and Collins was stopped at the demolished Farran bridge three miles out of Charleville, where the Awbeg crossed the main road to Cork before wandering off under various other bridges only to join the main road again on the outskirts of Buttevant. It must have been known to the Army in Charleville that Farran bridge was down. There were two possible ways of circumventing it, to left and right a little way back at the second Pike Cross. (Note: The turnpike idea, which originated in England in the reign of Charles the Second, and is found to be so successful in the 'New World' as a means of on-the-spot payment by traffic for the maintenance of roads, was a failure in the Ireland of long ago. The first Limerick-Cork Turnpike Act of Parliament was passed in 1732, and the Abolition Act of same came one hundred and twenty-five years later, partly due to financial difficulties and partly because of the smashing of the toll-gates by unruly elements). Over on the left, and running parallel, was the old Cork road, but the Furze Fort bridge was down. On the right, and almost into Ballyhea village, was Ballynadrideen bridge. This too was found to be down, its name, 'the place of the little retreat', adequately summing up the dismay of the crestfallen Commander-in-Chief as he brought his convoy back to Charleville from where a wider sweep by Milford, Dromcollogher, Freemount, Kanturk, and the Navigation Road brought them into Mallow and the Royal (Railway) Hotel by 7.30 p.m. 'Making good a passage over the Awbeg' was more critical than even he had realized. Almost every bridge was down making motorized progress into North Cork virtually impossible. Likewise the guerrilla warfare, ordered by General Liam Lynch at Kilpadder as the only way, was to become most intense in this region and continued well into the following year and the end of the Civil War. Every field was contested. Every house became a potential battle site. (After his escape from prison, soon after the death of Collins, Commandant-General Tom Barry, cousin of Commandant Paddy O'Brien of Liscarroll, came north to mount a serious but abortive attack on Charleville. Liscarroll, with its great castle, site of many battles in the past, was also the home of 'Baby May' Corbett, college girl-friend of executed young Kevin

Barry, who became a Dominican nun and died only a few years ago).

Michael Collins would have known the value of Buttevant as a military base. He would have had details of the vast military barracks, the biggest in Cork, outside of the Victoria Barracks in the city. Brigadier-General H.R. Cumming, D.S.O., ventured out of Buttevant Barracks at the beginning of March, 1921, for a military inspection in Kerry only to have his brains blown out by Seán Moylan and Paddy O'Brien at Clonbanin, on the Killarney road, on his return, having shouted 'Give them the lead!' to his men. Buttevant (from 'Boutez-en-avant', the Norman-French war-cry of the Barrymores) was the H.Q. of the First Southern Division of the Republican Army during the battle for Limerick. Michael Collins missed the pleasure of inspecting the huge barracks (now appropriately a fine G.A.A. playing grounds). Every writer has also missed it, all, that is, except Peter O'Farrell who, in a bombastic, Irish-American and not quite literary style, has provided what is probably one of the most hilarious military records ever penned. As a kind of military policeman, with a special squad under his command, he roamed the town, barracks and even the Ballinvonear military camp, some miles away, trying to keep order in a worsening situation among civilians and fighting men alike. His main irritations were the wives and girlfriends of British soldiers still hanging around, and the tinkers gathering for the famous Cahirmee (Buttevant, 12 July) horse fair. The travelling people are said to be descended from Irish chieftain families dispossessed by Cromwell and others in the past. How they have persisted as a nation within a nation, all through the vicissitudes of Irish History, is a wonder in itself. They faithfully fight their own civil war every year at Cahirmee horse fair regardless of the passing scene. O'Farrell arrested the lot and not having room in his police station in the town herded them into the military barracks. When Paddy O'Brien arrived from Kilmallock he nearly had a fit. He rang the police station for O'Farrell:

'Get down here at once!'

'Yes, Sir!'

'Who gave you the authority?'

'The townspeople, Sir!'

'Get them to hell out of the military barracks — and never again!'

'O.K., Commandant O'Brien!'

'I opened the doors', said O'Farrell, 'and let the pigeons go!' The soldiers' women followed him about town chanting 'East Lancs are coming!', booing and throwing missiles as he escorted Free State prisoners from the Limerick region to the Cork train in Buttevant station. But Collins would not have missed much. The boys had burned the great barracks after the fall of Kilmallock. Even the burning has its curious side. It was organized by Quarter-Master Jimmy Winter of Aghaburn House near Churchtown, Protestant son of a landlord and convert to Catholicism and Republicanism all at once. Poor Peter O'Farrell, like the others, had to take to the hills once more — and to Annagh Bog where 'we were eaten by the largest fleas I have ever seen — but they were preferable to bullets!'

'At the Royal Hotel, then a military post, Collins listened to the troubles of the people of Mallow which were put to him by the Bishop of Cloyne, Dr. Roche, and Archdeacon Corbett' (Calton Younger). Errors abound with regard to literary detail on the present subject. The above paragraph is fairly typical. The causes of error are moot and immaterial, the correction necessary. The beautiful Georgian Royal Hotel on Annabella hill (still standing and well kept but now a block of County Council offices), beside the railway station, was not, as it happens, a military post of the Free State Army. The O'Meara family, who owned it at the time, are vehement on that. However, the story of Collins and the Royal Hotel persists. The presumption is that from the Navigation (Killarney) road the devastation of the great railway viaduct was clearly visible, the station and hotel were first in line and he pulled in to investigate. Commandant Tom Flood, of the dreaded Dublin

Guards, was in charge of the town. The man who had distinguished himself most in the Kilmallock arena had his H.Q. in the
military barracks on Barrack (now Emmet) Street. (He fought
against Irishmen with such energy and drive that it looked as if
he wanted to wreak vengeance on someone for the hanging of
his brother, Frank, by the British in March, 1921). Flood met
Collins in the Royal Hotel. The two clerics are also misrepresented. Archdeacon Corbett, as stated, was still and for some
years to come just plain Cornelius Canon Corbett, and Fr.
James Roche, C.C., became Bishop of Cloyne only in 1935.
(Mrs. Lankford waxes eloquent on the active hostility of the
local clergy to the Republican cause, with her own personal ex-
periences deeply etched in her rebel mind). Collins received the
two priests diplomatically but curtly. They wanted assurances
on the railway bridge. He promised a month. By now his self-
assurance was beginning to return. The old social magic may
have gone somewhat with his civilian attire, but the personal
charisma was still there. He was back in County Cork and was
still regarded as the power in, and perhaps the saviour of, the
country. From his present lowly position in the ecclesiastical
chain of authority, Fr. James Roche was to have a career not
unlike Collins' own. I carry with me a permanent fantasy of
those two big, strong, deliberate men standing eyeball to
eyeball, seeing mutual reflections with reserve but no embar-
rassment — Michael Collins with a long-standing head-cold
and political hang-over, and James Roche, with a kind of
chronic apoplexy as a means to an end. The cleric, as bishop,
conducted a personal vendetta against my lovely Maynooth
College on grounds now of scant interest, died accidently and,
contrary to appearances, a pauper; Collins more or less the
same. Sic transit gloria mundi!

Mallow is a fine place in which to study the transitory glories
of this world of ours. As Michael Collins stood on the steps of
the hotel the lovely building at his back would have been commonplace. He had been in many such, but the view before him
was something else. This was big landlord country, and the

lordly Blackwater, the 'Irish Rhine', had been given special attention by the settlers from source to sea. Over beyond, among those great groves on the rising ground, two houses in particular would have demanded attention: Park House, 'the most beautiful house in North Cork', and Clydaville, a quarter of a mile further on towards the village of Dromahane. Late eighteenth century Georgian architecture, though ascendency and therefore reprehensible, is still a thrill and pride in the past. The very recent activities in that particular pair, however, would have intrigued far more the most notable signatory of the Anglo-Irish Treaty, Chairman of the Provisional Government sworn to implement it, and Commander-in-Chief of the new Free State Army. Something was once again walking over his grave — not the old ghosts of the 'Rakes of Mallow' from the Jephsons' Mallow Castle hunt-balls or the evaporated spa waters, but the very leaders of the Republican opposition. One week before, those two great houses had given brief shelter to Liam Lynch, Eamon de Valera, Seán Hyde and Con Moloney. Because of the railway buildings he could not see those houses from where he stood and his attention would have been reserved for yet another of those bothersome Cleeves' 'milk factories' just beneath him (where the giant Ballyclough dairy system now dominates the town). But he might have seen them on the way in had he not been avidly watching the reserved ascendency salmon river and the rich rolling meadow land of the Blackwater. With the proper guide (who came later) he could have had pointed out to him those places beyond the river from Lombardstown through Brittas, Glantane, Dromahane and Quartertown. Oh, yes! They would have been of great interest. Just days before, those regions had housed the Staff of the First Southern Division and some of the highest ranking officers in the Republican Army. These men had now faded away leaving not a wrack behind. In fact, one might take a compass and inscribe a circle with Macroom as centre and Glantane as radius, enclosing thereby the still faintly beating heart of the old Irish Republic as visualized by Wolfe Tone, Robert Emmet and Patrick Pearse, extending from Gougane Barra to Blarney and from the Bandon river to the Blackwater. It was now being quickly invested, its would-be champions running helter-skelter, while a slight semblance of communication was being maintained by such intrepid dispatch riders as Jackie O'Brien, of Mallow, and Dinny Crowley, of Coppeen. Jackie writes:

Dublin, 11-4-'89 . . . With regard to the blowing up of the Mallow 'Ten-Arch' Bridge, I never knew who was responsible for pressing the lever until I read your letter. During that period I was attached to the First Southern Division, and also to G.H.Q. under Liam Lynch. Naturally that dispatch work brought me in touch with many of the Southern Brigades. On the day the bridge was blown (12 August 1922), I was returning from Fermoy, and I was held up on the road on the south side of the bridge a few minutes before it was actually blown. It was a sad moment for me to see it destroyed. As youths that was one of our favourite haunts. Anyway, when the all-clear was given I was first under the road arch which was still standing. I heard afterwards that it was the intention to blow one arch; but during the night the whole lot fell down. That is all I know . . . After spending a few days in Park House, in Quartertown, I was responsible for billeting De Valera, Liam Lynch, Seán Hyde and Con Moloney in R.F. O'Connor's (B.E.) house in Clydaville. Next day (12 August) we retreated with G.H.Q. to Danesfort, near Dromahane. While there a few days, Seán Hyde asked me — being local — would I ask a priest to hear Confession of the Boys, it being 15th of August (i.e. the Feast of the Assumption, a Holy-day of Obligation). I asked Fr. Dennehy who was the P.P. of Glantane. He came down that evening and we all received (i.e. Holy Communion) next morning at Mass (All except Dev! cf. Chapter Ten) . . . The next move was to Sweeney's, of Ahadillane. Here a large meeting was held before the different Brigades left for their own areas. While this meeting was taking place I was given a dispatch for Mulcahy's in Whitechurch, near Cork. After taking by-roads, as I could not travel on the main road for fear of being captured by the Free State Army, I arrived in Mulcahy's without incident. They gave me the *Examiner* with the details of poor Collins' death, which I brought back to the meeting. I can assure you it caused a gloom all over the place . . . On that day in August, 1922, De Valera was at Walsh's, Glashabee. Con Healy, locally known as the 'Gunner', rushed to Glashabee with the news . . .

(Note: Mr. O'Brien's account is here identical with Mrs. Lankford's. This Con Healy was actually quite famous as 'The One-Eyed Gunner', a native of Bweeng village. His exploits, as well as his fantastic tall stories, would fill a handy little volume. One story in particular was only too true! A little while back I held in my hand the Gunner's broken and corroded Short Webley revolver — 'the hope and the sadness', as Siobhán Lankford so beautifully said!). Jackie O'Brien has now died (1990). Before moving to Dublin he had been employed as rent collector for Mallow U.D.C. The man 'responsible for pressing the lever' on the Ten-Arch Bridge was Paddy Hawe of Lacka-roe, Liscarroll, who died at home last year having returned from the Canadian prairies. In his home was (and still is) a secret compartment where Republican officers often lay hidden, General Liam Lynch himself being in it on one occasion while the Staters ransacked the house without result.

*   *   *

I have now before me three small, flimsy slips of paper, authentic record of some faint but historic 'footprints on the sands of time'. Two of them are faintly lined pages culled from a loose-leaved notebook and embossed with: 'Clydaville, Mallow, Co. Cork'. They contain two autographs apiece. One has: 'Liam Lynch, C/S I.R.A., 12/8/22' and 'Seán Hyde, O/C Cavalry, 1st Southern div., I.R.A., 12-8-22'. The other has: 'Conn ua Maoldomnaig (Con Moloney), A/G I.R.A., 12/8/22', and simply 'Éamon de Valéra'. The third paper is an abbreviated octavo-size sheet made official with the bold heading: 'Óglaigh na h-Éireann, Headquarters, 1st southern Division, 11/8 . . . 1922'. It says:

To Mr. O'Connor, County Surveyor, Clydaville:
Dear Sir,
   Would you kindly give permission to have four Staff Officers billetted (sic) in your house to-night and oblige. Please reply by bearer.
                                                    E. Murphy,
                                              Col Com'dn't. on Staff.

The identical embossing appears on a further note dated 1973, which says: 'I was the bearer of the note signed E. Murphy, Staff Officer, 1st Southern Division. (Signed) Jackie O'Brien, Dispatch Rider, 1st Southern Division'. A similarly signed note, dated 7th Oct., 1977, states: 'I was the bearer of the dispatch requesting the billets' . . . Richard F. O'Connor, of Clydaville, was in his own right quite a remarkable man. Dev did him less than justice when he wrote in his diary for 12 August that he had spent the night in the home of an Assistant County Surveyor. In 1922 Richard O'Connor was one of the three Cork County surveyors and in 1929 became the only one. Bridge builder nonpareil, he constructed the famous 'Tim Healy Pass' (Cork . . . Kerry) with funds provided by his friend, the Governor-General (first in the new State, and named for him), after the Government had refused — so that the children of that remote and very scenic area might get to school. Also he unearthed and reset the ancient milestones between Cork and Mallow. An enthusiastic airman, he first broached and worked on the idea of a Cork airport, and he built the first ever wireless receiver in Mallow. His daughter, Madeleine, who still lives in the rather dilapidated old mansion, says that her father spent some hours, on the night of 11 August, trying to persuade De Valera to use his influence to prevent the Ten-Arch Bridge being blown up; but the Republicans were still involved in a life-and-death struggle and Dev's influence was on the wane. O'Connor's son, Dermot, a young railway engineer, was to supervise the rebuilding of the bridge in 1923 (with shabby steel girders provided by the Armstrong Construction Co. of London and Glasgow, and opened by President Liam T. Cosgrave). Across the little Clyda bridge from Clydaville, and half a mile nearer the town, was the magnificent Park House, now a burned out shell. Its incumbent in 1922 was Major J.S. ('Sherry') Sheppard, M.F.H. (Duhallow). It housed the G.H.Q. Staff of the Republican Army, possibly because of a friendly association with the flamboyant Seán Hyde and his cavalry. (Mrs. Lankford's story of the horse that died of a broken heart is a gem for all time). After the burning of the barracks in Fermoy (11 August), Liam Lynch, De Valera and Con Moloney (late Tipperary Third Brigade and now Adjutant-General in place of the neutral Major Florence O'Donoghue) came directly to Park House from where the notable dispatch was sent to Clydaville by Eamon Murphy of Newberry, Lombardstown. Dev was offered the principal guest room, top storey front, but refused saying it was too dangerous. The young boys of the family were ousted from the little room at the back and early next morning the girls as usual came tumbling in and leaped on the bed only to find an austere ex-professor of Mathematics. (From 1913-1916 Clydaville was home to Daniel O'Connell, bank manager, and his family. He was son of the Liberator). On 12 August Dev moved to O'Connell's of Kilpadder (cf. previous chapter), and on the fifteenth to Gougane Barra, and thence to O'Leary's of Gortafludig. Lynch went to O'Hanlon's of Brittas, Lombardstown. Their policies had become divergent. They were not to meet again until the Nire Valley conference shortly before the death of Lynch. Hyde and Moloney went to stay at Hunt's great house in Danesfort, at Kilpadder Cross (according to Jackie O'Brien), and a few days later Hyde went to Moneygave, near Béalnabláth, and the A/G went to the Glen of Aherlow with the C/S.

*   *   *

Many Great Houses throughout the country, apart from other buildings of prominence and military significance, were destroyed by the I.R.A. during those troubled times. By contrast Park House and Danesfort were burned maliciously at later dates. It is strange to note the prominence of Protestant families on the Republican side through the Tan and Civil Wars, as if the old pressure of absorption, the 'becoming more Irish than the Irish', was making itself felt on the Reformation and Plantation scene, while the new army seemed to be imbued with the spirit of the gallowglasses, the 'gallóglaigh', the foreign mercenaries. The Hunts of Danesfort have now disappeared except one aged member who, having lived 'the good life' to the full world-wide, is now being maintained locally by an old retainer family, as happened sometimes in England. Even under conversion, e.g. the Waters family (Ned Waters was shot by the British at Nadd in March, 1921), their in-laws, the O'Connors, both of Glashabee, and the Winters, of Churchtown, have completely vanished. West Cork records an amazing array of Protestant names of men who fought and died for 'the great ideal'. In Kerry one Protestant Republican is on record as having been tortured and killed by the Free State Army. Frank Aiken's Protestantism (he was O/C Fourth Northern Division, I.R.A., and later a cabinet minister) is never mentioned by historians as if Erskine Childers was being made to stand alone at the behest of the British Government (Arthur Griffith referred to him as 'that damned Englishman'). It was far from the reality. His being blamed by the Provisional Government in Dublin for the destruction of bridges in the South, including the Mallow railway bridge, is nothing short of ludicrous.

*   *   *

'The proper guide' (supra) was to be a valuable, though not wholly reliable, witness to the rest of Michael Collins' life. He was Mallow man John O'Connell. Discovered by Rex Taylor, bequeathed to Calton Younger, and adopted by Meda Ryan, it is nowhere certain whether he was an actual member of the Free State Army in Mallow or elsewhere. Referred to as 'Private', his public 'obiter dicta' have been allowed to infiltrate history rather more than was prudent. He made the canon an archdeacon (the present writer is uncertain as to what this signifies), the simple priest a doctor and eventually a bishop. He knew that Mourne Abbey, just a ways out on the Cork road, was impassable and he knew the alternative by-roads to Cork. He could have left things there. His geography of West Cork was faulty even in retrospect and his account of the battle of Béalnabláth, though useful, was contradictory. He served a temporary purpose from Mallow to Cork. He led the convoy across the Blackwater (Ballydaheen Bridge), then sharp left towards Kilavullen and right on Summer Hill and the Nagles mountains. It must have galled Collins having to be so circumspect but he did miss seeing the massive limestone blocks of the Ten-Arch lying about the river bed (as they still do!), like the ruins of Carthage. Meda Ryan mistakes the Ten-Arch for 'the Awbeg bridge' (the Awbeg meets the Blackwater only at Bridgetown Abbey, Castletownroche) . . . 'meant that the Cork/Dublin railway line was out of action' — but a couple of miles out towards Buttevant, at Two-Pot House, the Dublin line over the by-road was downed twice by old Paddy Doolan who still lives beside it and is proud of the action. Margery Forester compounds the bias by saying that the Ten-Arch job 'was probably the most effective ground operation of the Civil war'. Hardly! Siobhán Lankford is best. She has the local scene portrayed and the comic local 'efforts to "save" the bridge', by clergy and laity — i.e. the road bridge over the Blackwater which, she says, was fordable just there and had its own Desmond Castle to protect it in the past.

There are quite a few senior citizens still around and bubbling with the history of the times. Pat Sullivan of Knockbrack is one of them. So is his friend, John Riordan, who is nintey-three and now lives in Nazareth Home, Mallow. Pat is four years younger and resides alone in the old family stone-built farmhouse, which would be magnificent but for the devastation all about the place. Young Pat was at the Sunday evening outdoor dance (sometimes called a 'pattern') which has now become history, but he left early and joined his friend, John, who had been playing football. They walked home together from Knuttery Cross towards Knockbrack. Half-way there they encountered the Free State convoy . . . Knockbrack was not new to Collins. He had been there in 1919. Six high-ranking officers had come for a conference just as the War of Independence was hotting up all over. The conference was held in Mrs. Catherine O'Sullivan's. (Pat's father had been killed off a horse near Mallow). Dan Breen and Bryan Shanahan, from Tipperary, stayed one night in the house. Michael Collins and Seán Hales, from West Cork, were put up in John O'Leary's, of Gortaneelig, a quarter of a mile further down the by-road. Liam Lynch and George Power, from Fermoy, were above in Dan Linehan's. All six met on the following morning at O'Sullivan's. 'It was all guns and books, blue suits and soft hats!', says Pat. (Lynch had discarded his Volunteer uniform the previous year). Collins carried no gun, 'but I'm sure there was one there for him if he needed it. During the meeting two pony-traps arrived with the news that two lorries of soldiers had passed on the road above. They didn't seem to care'. Now Collins himself was 'the soldiers'. Did he remember? Or did he still not care? On that previous occasion he had taken young Pat to the gate across the road to show him 'the hills beyond Macroom'. 'Is it possible?', I asked. 'Oh, yes!', said Pat. 'From that hill above (Knockanannig, 'the hill of the marsh') you could sometimes see the town itself!' The map says twenty-two miles across and the intermediate terrain a hundred feet lower. It is just possible! The town and the hills beyond Macroom were still drawing the man on that fateful Sunday evening! And now to look at the interesting but confused trail from Mallow to Cork . . .

Taylor: From Mallow the convoy proceeded . . . by way of Whitechurch. En route they stopped at the farmhouse of Dan O'Keeffe . . . to replenish the car radiators.

Younger: The party travelled by mountain road to Whitechurch . . . *Slievenamon* . . . thundered along behind the yellow Leyland . . . Most of the escort travelled in a Crossley tender ahead of the Leyland . . . At Whitechurch an open air dance was in lively swing and the convoy stopped to search for arms.

Lankford: Michael Collins had gone to Cork . . . by a little frequented road over Monee to Burnfort Cross to Bottle Hill, through Whitechurch . . . Local men saw the convoy near Monee. It was stopped while a car was being examined . . .'.

Ryan: In Monee the convoy halted at Dan O'Keeffe's farmhouse to check the over-heated radiator of the Leyland . . . and headed towards Whitechurch where a gathering had assembled at the crossroads. The driver of the touring car became nervous and was on the point of pulling up when Collins shouted, 'Drive on, you fool. Don't you see it is only the usual Sunday evening cross-roads dancing'. (This unfortunate 'fool' motif comes from Piaras Béaslaí, 1926).

And the correct version . . .

Dan O'Keeffe's now deserted farmhouse is at the top of Knockaroura, two and a half miles out of Mallow. Monee crossroads is a further mile or more. Old Dan did not favour Collins. (He died shortly afterwards himself). Willie O'Keeffe, a nephew (who still lives in Mallow), was seven at the time. He was standing in the backyard. He can just remember a soldier with a can for water, and the greyness of the convoy in the distance. Half a mile further on, Ballinvuskig Cross brought a by-road to Clogheen and Mourne Abbey. To that point Dev came less than three days later on the now cold trail, which he followed for three miles, as arrangements were being made at Shanakiel Hospital for the transporting of Collins' body to the Cork City docks. At Monee crossroads stands a water pump-house. In 1922 there was just a pump, the village type with a long, curved arm. Here the convoy stopped once again for water supplies. From here comes Mrs. Lankford's caustic story about the indiscreet soldier. They carried on towards Knuttery Cross, two miles away. (That strange name is a corruption of the Irish 'Cnoc Eatarthu', the 'hill between the other two [hills]' i.e. Knockanannig and Bottle Hill, which is itself a corruption of Battle Hill, commemorating a skirmish there in 1691, during the Jacobite-Williamite War). The convoy went from Knuttery to Bottle Hill, three miles further on, and did not go to Burnfort. To do so they would have taken the Greenhill road. The dance was at Knuttery, on a movable wooden platform on the roadside facing the entrance to Lyons' farmhouse — and Whitechurch was eight miles away!

At Knuttery the two young men from Knockbrack met the convoy. A motor-cyclist was in the lead, followed by a Crossley tender. Pat Sullivan distinctly remembers ten soldiers seated five-a-side facing inwards. The little lorries are of great interest and are frequently mentioned in the context of Ireland's 'Troubles'. Brought over by the Auxiliary Division (the 'Auxies') in the Summer of 1920, they were originally designed for transporting R.A.F. personnel to and from the airfields in the Great War. They carried a movable hood and had an open cab, and approximated to the American 'Jeep' of World War Two. The Auxies changed the format to the extent of having a large bench down the centre of the body where they sat back to back and facing outwards and always on the ready, with strong, wooden, knee-high guards along both sides as floating barricades. (There was a story — probably apocryphal — from Rathcool ambush which said that a landmine blew a Crossley sky-high, which enabled the Auxies to see the I.R.A. hidden behind the fences of the road and fire on them downwards from the air!). It did not enhance the reputation of Michael Collins among Republicans to have inherited them from the British. After the Crossley came the Whippet armoured car. The Leyland was, in fact, at the back. Pat Sullivan recognized Collins on the left in the back seat. He did not know Commandant Seán O'Connell who sat with him, except that he was an officer. The dust on the vehicles was a notable feature, obliterating even the colour of the touring car. One wonders how and why Collins constrained himself to swallow all that dirt. He was a fastidious man. The dance was just a half-mile away. They came on it suddenly around a bend. The convoy halted. The men in the Crossley jumped down with guns at the ready. A couple of them started to search pockets. Some men, according to Pat Sullivan, actually had ammunition but dropped it surreptitiously on the ground. Collins, away at the back and out of sight, dismounted and came forward to investigate. His car remained stationary around the bend. He did not call his driver a fool. What he was heard to say to the soldiers was - 'Come away! It's only some people around enjoying themselves'.

Whitechurch* and Cork City.   At the Imperial Hotel, in the South Mall, General Michael Collins was glad to see

* See p. 152.

Major-General Emmet Dalton, but Dalton was not glad to see him. The conqueror of Cork cast a rueful eye on the scanty protection for the head of the Army while realizing that (as he said later) even if the ranks were reversed his view would still not prevail. However, Collins immediately proceeded to act like a political potentate rather than a soldier in dealing widely and freely with the commercial, financial, industrial and labour interests in the city. It was what he was good at. No one knew him as a soldier. Perhaps he did not see himself as such. The transition to liaison with the disaffected Republicans was simple. It became his objective. His double journey to Macroom, on Monday evening and Tuesday morning, poses a problem. He intended going to West Cork. He arrived in mid-Cork. He was apparently acting arbitrarily with the Army dancing to his tune. A Commander-in-Chief acting thus in real war would have courted disaster. The collection of documents and sundry papers, with further accumulation of same (Note: The typescript listing alone runs to many pages), bequeathed to the National Library by Major Florence O'Donoghue, was the one item of greatest interest awaiting the centenary of the birth of Michael Collins. Known as 'Florrie Donoghue's Papers', they were deposited at his death in safe keeping with instructions that they were not to be revealed until the year as stated. A time capsule of enormous import for humanity? Hardly likely! Revelations with regard to the dark secret of Béalnabláth? Scarcely possible! Confidential matter relayed to him by Collins in Macroom on the morning of the day he died? Of course! But what? An hour before his death Collins confided to John L. O'Sullivan, Free State officer in Bandon (who has just died, 1990), that he intended returning northwards once more in an effort to parley with the Republicans. Florrie Donoghue was a prodigious writer and thinker in a restricted field. In a little rate-collector's office in Cook Street, Cork, he rolled out the barrel. His material, serialized in a weekly newspaper in the Fifties, and later to some extent published in book form, was barely comprehensible in its intricacy and complexity, at that point in time, to the uninitiated. Friend of P.S. O'Hegarty, he performed an unique service for the well-known bookman and Treatyite who died in 1955 at variance with his Church, refusing all ministrations and Christian Burial. Florrie made a pilgrimage to Glasnevin on the day after the funeral and emptied a bottle of Holy Water on O'Hegarty's grave. (He told me so!). A good liaison man for here and hereafter, one would say. Collins thought so. They met in Macroom, 22 August 1922 . . . 'O'Donoghue related that he met Collins on the 22nd.' (Hopkinson, *Green Against Green*).

Florrie was a public and declared neutral in the Civil War. He was free to move about. In Macroom he was appointed by Collins, officially or unofficially, as a go-between with the Republican forces of the region. Had the life of the outstanding Mick Collins, Ireland's greatest revolutionary, become a matter of quiet desperation like Thoreau's 'mass of men'? Did Florrie confer with the Macroom Republicans as Collins had conferred with the Free Staters while in West Cork? Perhaps he went out to Ballyvourney to see Sandow! Maybe he saw Dev there at seven o'clock! Did the wing of the dying albatross sideswipe him too when Collins fell at Béalnabláth? All possible. All feasible. All to be revealed in 1990? Well, not quite. The National Library has placed an embargo on 'certain material relating to intelligence' (this in answer to a recent query). For another half-century? Perhaps the present writer's fantasy (cf. Chapter Eight: 'I Could a Tale Unfold') will one day be seen to be close to the actuality — if there is anybody left to care. The known doings and movements of Michael Collins in Macroom are fragmented and indecisive. The junior officer who made notes for him (cf. 'The Tom Daly Story') on the occasion has not been identified. His notes have not surfaced. Tom Daly, the ex-trooper from Clare, with the phenomenal memory, has contributed quite an amount. Tim Kelleher, the taxi-driver, presented material of immediate interest but his two published accounts (late in life) proved faulty and somewhat contradictory, and needed to be amended. Peadar Conlon, Free State officer from Ballinalee, Co. Longford, in charge of the Macroom post, never spoke on the matter, but his wife-to-be, who acted as Collins' secretary on the occasion, made notes which are still to be discovered. Nancy McCarthy, whose brother was married to Florrie Donoghue's sister, revealed a long standing family secret (1988) that Florrie was to have met Collins in Macroom on the evening of the twenty-second. (She told it to the present writer just before she died).

The Commander-in-Chief travelled in a special type of motor car, so special that it is now known only on paper and by repute. The 'Leyland Thomas Straight Eight' or simply the 'Leyland-Thomas' (as referred to by some writers) is totally inaccurate. The car is significant enough for an in-depth study. 'Leyland-Eight' was its correct title, 'Straight' by definition. It was a once-off effort from the British Leyland Company (now 'Austin-Rover'), but to its brilliant creator, J.G. Parry Thomas, it was to rival Rolls-Royce, which it did — and even surpassed — for a brief moment of glory (1920-1922). The car was first shown to the public at the 1920 Motor Show in London and was hailed by the Press as 'The Lion of Olympia'. (How apt for Collins!). 'It positively bristled with novel and logical solutions of problems which were then facing all motor car designers. Some of these solutions, unheard of at the time, are commonplace today' (Reid Ralton in *Parry Thomas, Designer-Driver*, 1959). Only eighteen cars were built in three years. They were grand and exclusive, with advanced 'straight eight' engines, and were geared to rival the Rolls-Royce. It was in 1923, when Parry Thomas (non-hyphenated) had left Leyland and started into motor-racing (which killed him), that the 'Leyland-Thomas' racing car was constructed on some unused chassis and from spare parts of the original models experimentally built for Leyland. Still, 1922 is the significant year in the history of this wonderful vehicle and regarded so by company archivists and motor museum people in Britain. Possibly like Collins himself, it was too far ahead of its time for its own good. How did he come to have one? Leyland presented it as a gesture to General Sir Nevil Macready, British Commander-in-Chief in Dublin. Winston Churchill had provided the Provisional Government with 'certain special stores in order that they might equip and organize . . .'. On the transfer of power the 'Big Fellow' put his eye on the magnificent motor car, which was duly noted by Macready and, in an 'eye-winking theft' manoeuvre, the unauthorized object changed hands and in a subsequent cover-up Leyland's Irish importer, Wilson and Co., formally presented the car to Collins. Immediately after his death it was returned to the famous Lancashire-based commercial vehicle builders, complete with bullet holes and blood stains. By this time Leyland were in trouble with a shady director and were defrauded of a million pounds. Both the director and Parry Thomas were fired and the historic motor car went with them. After refurbishing it continued to have a rather dramatic existence including being taken out to Africa by a big-game hunter and may still be there in some condition as it is not recorded as being in the hands of any vintage vehicle collector anywhere in the world. (For relevant information I am indebted to Mr. Bob Webster of Naas, Ms. Annice Collett of Beaulieu National Motor Museum, and Mr. Peter Mitchell and Mr. Anders Clausager of the British Motor Industry Heritage Trust who conclude that Leyland must have discarded the car in said condition as a matter of urgency as there is no record whatsoever of its return). The Leyland-Eight was not within the competence of the ordinary mechanic-driver. They had to train specifically under Parry Thomas himself, and when a car was sold (and they were more expensive than the Rolls-Royce), e.g. to a named Indian maharajah who took two, a skilled operator had to travel with them. Corry and Quinn, Collins' drivers of the moment, could have known little if anything about his new motor car, nor could Pat McCrea, his alternative Rolls-Royce driver in Dublin. It is highly probable that this accounts for some trouble with the car 'en route'. For example, a self-starter on the gear shaft would be a new and puzzling experience for routine 'crankers' of the time. Jim Wolfe, the driver of the armoured car, put down his own vehicle's trouble (according to Meda Ryan: *The Day Michael Collins was Shot*) to 'dirty petrol. The petrol tins had been refilled without being emptied and had thus accumulated sediment . . .'. My own information (cf. Chapter Four) and personal memories from the Twenties and early Thirties is that all petrol at that time was delivered in sealed cans and the empties were collected and returned to central depots. (The *Slievenamon* had a tank capacity of eighteen gallons with a subsidiary tank of four, assuring a continuous journey of possibly four hundred miles).

Timothy Kelleher of Macroom, taxi-driver and later extensive garage proprietor, has left two accounts of his contribution to Irish History. The first published (James Cooney, *Macroom: People and Places,* 1983) is dry, cryptic and to the point. The second (in *The Day Michael Collins was Shot*, 1989, from an interview in 1974) is essentially the same but much embellished. Why is he so important? He simply showed the Collins convoy the way from Macroom to Bandon. He did, indeed, lose the 'Big Fellow' on the way and got an inkling that something impressive was about to happen on the Republican side. In Chapter Seven of the present work his story is already given, highlighting the implication of certain features of his evidence. Here we need to deal with discrepancies, and trace (mainly with the aid of local traditions and family records) the trail he teased out for them from a maze of by-roads. The importance of the matter is that it involves the Florrie Donoghue theme — the reason which impelled Collins to return towards Macroom to his death, thus changing forever the course of Irish History. (Here is a small point which indicates the great experience of the man, Kelleher, and makes more surprising a large blunder attributed to him in old age. In *Macroom: People and Places* he is pictured holding his 1920 driver's licence, presumably his first, but at Easter, 1918, he drove my own parents from Kilbarry to the train in Macroom on their honeymoon. The 1920 licence was issued by the British authorities and such was his recognition that, during the Black and Tan

'Terror' of that year, he had freedom of movement to ferry supplies to the destitute and helpless nuns in the Convent of Mercy. His next licence was issued by the Free State) . . . Meda Ryan writes, 'A soldier was sent to get Kelleher . . .'. The man in question, in all humility, would have accepted the designation. He was — according to the Kelleher family — Major-General Emmet Dalton himself. 'When Kelleher arrived at the Castle barracks . . .' Macroom Castle had been burned down by the retreating Republicans, and young people of the time who are still alive (e.g. Jerry McSweeney of 'Mescals', John Ahern, ex-national teacher, and Canon John Warren of the Cloyne diocese) and who saw or even shook hands with Collins did so near the door of Williams' Hotel where the convoy reverse-parked on arrival from Cork City and from where it eventually departed. Some soldiers were encamped in the Castle precincts, some were billeted in the Victoria Hotel, some in the 'Union' (cf. 'The Tom Daly Story'), while the Commandant, Captain Peadar Conlon, had his H.Q. in the historic Town Hall in the centre of the Square, where his future wife, Nora Cremin from Lissyconnor, Rathmore, Co. Kerry, who had followed him from the Curragh (while he was madly battling the Republicans at Rochestown, near Cork Harbour), took charge of the secretarial work. Tim Kelleher told Meda Ryan, 'I . . . was aware that two of the bridges on this line (i.e. Macroom-Cork) were broken, so we took the Dooniskey Cross route'. In *Macroom: People and Places* he simply says 'Dooniskey'. There is a vast difference, an unbridgable gap. He omitted telling the lady that he sat between General Dalton and Captain Conroy, the driver, in the cab of the (leading?) Crossley. Varied accounts give one to three Crossleys. Kelleher's credibility breaks down further at this point (his family say that he had told and retold the story many times, and loved to do so, but by this time, fifty-odd years on, his mind had begun to wander). The two broken bridges were BETWEEN Macroom and Dooniskey Cross. They are now flooded by the E.S.B. hydro-electric scheme (1953-56). They were the Two-Mile Bridge over the

River Lee, and the Bunea (prn. 'Bing-ay') Bridge over the little tributary of that name, a mile further on. This latter was completely demolished, but the Two-Mile was only partly so. Just short of the Bunea bridge (at Ballytrasna) was a railway bridge known as 'Holland's' (from a family who lived there until the flooding). This was over the Macroom railway line and intact. At low water it still sticks up forlornly from the midst of the expanse, like 'the round towers of other days' in Lough Neagh. (De Valera returned by the Two-Mile bridge on that historic evening and changed his disguise and transport there, having retraced the Collins route through Kilmurry village from Béalnabláth). Two farmers who live beside Dooniskey Cross, Donal Lehane, a cousin of the present writer, and John Lehane, no relation, assure me that their fathers never mentioned the passing of the Collins convoy but always maintained that it came down on a by-road beside the Two-Mile bridge (i.e. Castleview Hill), and onto the extremity of the 'Beamish Line' on another by-road half a mile away near Dooniskey railway station. John Lehane's father, Mike, managed to cross the Bunea bridge, when necessary, with the use of planks. There was no possibility of heavy armour doing so. On the evening of 22 August 1922, Mike Lehane and his son Paddy were 'clearing the headlands' preparatory to reaping the harvest on the following day when a local Republican, Joe Murphy, came by on his bicycle and stopped. He said, 'Mickeen (i.e. Collins) got a 'plonk' at Béalnabláth!' Mike removed his cap and said: 'Ye could have left him alone!' Obviously it was still daylight, and Murphy had been at Béalnabláth himself. To continue with Meda, 'At the foot of the hill (i.e. Ballymichael, between Dooniskey and Kilmurry), opposite O'Mahony's, the Leyland stalled . . .'. Other writers have said that it was the armoured car. Also the banter shown here between the Commander-in-Chief and the soldiery is not evidenced elsewhere. A young boy of the O'Mahony household watched from an upper window with his mother. She was Bishop Galvin's sister and he was the future Fr. Donal O'Mahony of the Australian Mission. They saw 'the great Michael Collins' walk dourly up and down for a few minutes, his massive shoulders just showing above the high wall, impatiently waiting while someone tinkered with his tourer or with the armoured car or both.

When he left Macroom on his last journey Michael Collins was seated alone in the back seat of his 40 h.p. motor car. He could have had no misgivings about its ability to tackle any road conditions in its way. Identical models were just then in the process of breaking speed records and winning hill climbs. Emmet Dalton was in the cab of the Crossley tender (the best evidence is for one truck only) the better, presumably, to communicate with driver, guide and scout. When Dalton later described the Leyland as having 'a light racing body' it meant that he had been informed that it had the short 'speed model' chassis used for the open cars (Parry Thomas stripped them down for actual racing). The saloon versions had longer and heavier chassis . . . 'Another (Leyland Eight) was sold to Michael Collins and was used in Ireland during the troubles when in an ambush in August, 1921 [sic], it received through the windscreen the bullet that killed its owner'. (Hugh Tours in *Parry Thomas, Designer-Driver*). John Ahern, N.T., witnessed his departure from Macroom. John was then a lad of eight, just returning with his older sister from early Mass. He waved his hand at the famous personage as the Leyland moved away down the main street towards the railway end. The Rolls-Royce armoured car followed immediately . . . 'The only car which we consider worth while having as a sparring partner to the Leyland Eight is the Rolls-Royce' (Parry Thomas in *The Autocar*, 1921). He would have relished the deadly competition between the two on the roads of Cork. 'What (kind of) car was Collins in when his convoy was halted by the ambush? . . . Where did this controversial vehicle come from? . . . It is perhaps a small matter but if ever at this stage it can be clarified, further historical mistakes may be avoided. We may never know who killed Michael Collins; at least we should be able to establish what make of car he travelled in before his death!'

(Henry St.G. Smith in the *Irish Times,* 3 September 1981).

With the kind assistance of Mr. Finbarr O'Mahony, late of Ballymichael, who, though not born at the time, lived on the spot and is well versed in family and neighbourhood lore and the history of the period, I have made a careful analysis of the route followed by the convoy . . . Staking all on dangerous publicity, Michael Collins left Williams' Hotel, Macroom, to travel into West Cork, while Dalton, the soldier, now led from the front. It was ten miles to Béalnabláth Cross, with ten symbolic milestones. One mile brought them to the Inchigeela road. The Two-Mile bridge in front was down. They headed west. Macloneigh bridge crossed the 'Gaeragh', another mile away. (That famous ecological region is now covered with hydro-electrical water power). At Macloneigh House, just over the bridge, lived an aunt of Finbarr O'Mahony. The family are adamant about the Macloneigh crossing. Another mile and the motorcade had reached the Forge Cross where they took a left turn onto Castleview Hill and thus circumvented the broken Two-Mile to reach the main Cork road, a mile away, once again. Another mile and they had arrived at a sharply inclined by-road to Kilmurry. Over on the left was the demolished Bunea (Ballytrasna) bridge. They headed up to the right on 'Cnochán na Croiche' ('the little hill of the gallows'), and just another mile away, by 'Bóithrín na gCloch' ('the little rocky road'), lay the reverse side of the Dooniskey region and the 'Dooniskey Cross' the guide would have had in mind, close to Dooniskey railway station. One mile away was Ballymichael Hill and trouble. The trouble took the form of a big rock and a big, concrete water-tank, obstacles even an armoured car could not ignore. The *Slievenamon* stuck there. The rock and tank were in the angle of a sharp dog-leg, not quite a hairpin bend, fifty yards beyond O'Mahony's garden gate. It is strange that Jim Wolfe, driver of the *Slievenamon*, did not admit the mishap (he is now safely beyond question!) to Meda Ryan. He blamed the Leyland. Perhaps that had also stalled further up on that very sharp incline. The *Slievenamon* was presently at the rear of the convoy. By now young Donal O'Mahony had joined his father at the garden gate. He remembers what he thought was 'the back of a bread-van', a good figure as the delivery vans of the time were tall and narrow, and had apertures near the top of the twin back doors. Some soldiers were trying to push the 'bread-van' out of its predicament and young Donal saw the broad-shouldered man in uniform, who had been walking up and down, join them and get the thing going. Kilmurry village was one mile away. 'Lieutenant Smith . . . knocked on the doors of three different houses to shout the news, ''The Commander-in-Chief is coming'' . . . nobody emerged from any house to cheer' (Edward O'Mahony in *Magill* magazine, May, 1989). But note! 'Kelleher, the guide . . . remarked to Conroy, the driver of the tender, as they headed into Kilmurry Cross where some men were assembled: ''They're all Republicans over there. It looks as if there's an early morning gathering'' ' (Meda Ryan, *The Day Michael Collins Was Shot*). The family version is that Tim Kelleher saw some people he recognized standing about in Kilmurry village, made as if to wave to them, thought better of it, and said nothing. Come on, now, who has been spinning yarns? Perhaps the assembled Republicans cheered! Or did they stand to attention while an armoured convoy ground through their village? However, there were two more milestones — Currabeha Cross and Béalnabláth Cross. Both — whether one is an historian, a biased politician or just an interested onlooker — have had a vital import in Irish History. The question is: Where was Dev when Collins drove by? The cover-up, slander, or just plain lies have been virulent in this area of study . . . 'In the upper right hand window (i.e. of Long's pub in Béalnabláth) facing us, there was a man looking straight at us — it could have been anybody' (T. Kelleher to M. Ryan, 1974). 'There was a scowling face at a window, looking out over that lovely valley, and De Valera could tell who it was' (Canon Cohalan of Bandon, in a speech, September, 1927). 'In the morning of the murder, he (i.e. Dev) was seen superintending the arrangements (i.e. for the ambush) and about midday motored back to Ballyvourney' (Fr. P. Treacy, P.P., Crookstown, in a letter to the *Cork Examiner,* September, 1927). Local, political and Church opinion is still divisively for and against. To Siobhán Creedon (Mrs. Lankford), and her brother Michael, Dev said that he had seen the convoy a hundred yards away at a crossroads, but did not know who was in it. The crossroads had to be either Currabeha or Béalnabláth. Only in relatively modern times has the question been asked (and by foreigners): How could Collins have been so stupid as to get himself killed?

Timothy Hurley is eighty-five. He is a native of Lissarourke, Newcestown, where he has lived all his life. In the course of a quiet and uneventful career he had one sensational encounter that would be sufficient for anybody, even in a public capacity. He met and spoke with Michael Collins on the morning of Tuesday, 22 August 1922, just minutes after the Commander-in-Chief had passed over the spot where he was to die before the sun went down. At eighteen Tim Hurley was a 'creamery car' boy and transported the separated cream from Mossgrove creamery for churning into butter at the central station at Terelton, via Béalnabláth and the Bantry Line. Mossgrove creamery was two hundred yards from the vital Mossgrove crossroads. (It still exists but is now just a co-operative stores for the great Ballyclough Dairy system at Mallow). For his lawful purposes Tim Hurley drove what was known as 'a horse-and-car', which meant a cob drawing a farm cart or 'common-car'. Half-way between Mossgrove Cross and the creamery he met the military convoy. He was on the left going towards Béalnabláth. They were on his right. He sat as usual on the right extremity of the front cross-beam, with legs suspended, and close to the horse's tail. The convoy halted at a signal just as the open motor car was passing him by. On the right-hand side of the back seat, almost within arm's reach, sat a burly man in uniform whom he later recognized from pictures as Michael Collins. Collins spoke to him. What he said was, 'Can you tell us the way to Bandon?' More especially Collins is recognizable to him from the well-known posed photograph taken at Glasnevin Cemetery, after the burial of Arthur Griffith, in which the enormously large military man is seen looking sharply to his right with eyes slitted and askance as Jenghiz Khan, beneath the hard-brimmed military cap. The man now sitting beside him wore the soft-topped cap favoured by Emmet Dalton (the difference in caps was merely a circular steel spring), and Tim Hurley feels sure, from later pictures, that it was in fact Emmet Dalton (though more likely Comdt. Seán O'Connell). To the question Tim answered: 'Go straight through the next crossroads!', and, as if at an order, the convoy moved on without another glance or word. Tim Hurley then put the cat among the pigeons somewhat, and he may be right. He said that in front of the motor-car was just the motor-cyclist, who continued on and took the RIGHT-HAND TURN TO NEWCESTOWN. The car, to his surprise, followed. Tim is quite emphatic. A lorry of soldiers followed the car, and then the armoured car. These two went straight to Bandon. The road from the creamery to Mossgrove Cross is one long gentle swing and likewise the road to Newcestown. One vehicle a hundred yards behind another would have no idea where the first had gone to. I showed Tim Hurley photographs of the Leyland Eight as it was, and the *Slievenamon* as it is. He agreed that they were exactly as shown, but that the colour of the car in the original black and white seemed a shade too light. The colour, a trivial point until the recent R.T.E. documentary, 'The Shadow of Béalnabláth', has never given rise to controversy. John L. O'Sullivan, Free State veteran, told me last year that the colour was a light green. Trevor Roycroft of Belfast, late of Skibbereen (who, as a lad of fifteen, appears in the picture of Collins getting in his car at the Eldon Hotel), says it was 'a metallic silver-grey'. The Army maintain from their records that it was yellow, which is probably the one colour that has more variations than any other. The British experts say that the Leyland Eights were turned out in a variety of colours. Tim Hurley has still a clear vision of the colour. He said, paradoxically, that it was 'yellow, but not yellow'. We went through a variety, from light primrose through banana, lemon, orange, and variations, but nothing would do until we found the mustard pot. 'That's exactly it!', said Timothy Hurley of Lissarourke — 'Mustard!'

The 'creamery-car' went on its way to Béalnabláth and Terelton, and returned later in the day. The cart-barricade was already in position at the S-bend a few hundred yards out of the village. Some armed men were standing about. He did not know them. They moved the cart a little for him to pass. As he drove the one hundred and eighty yards to the first bridge (still known as 'Carroll's'), he plainly saw three large pipes, which he assumed to be explosive, lying on the fence of the road. One was near the barricade, one was centre-ways, and the third was near Carroll's (Glanarouge) bridge. Such clarity of vision and recall poses the problem of the convoy. Assuming that positions could have been changed according to the terrain (e.g. at Bally-michael Hill), and that Tim Kelleher knew what he was talking about, it must have been like this. The foremost lorry, with Kelleher, Dalton and Conroy in the cab, took a right at Béalnabláth and continued on to Bandon, until somewhere beyond Mossgrove they realized they were on their own and returned. Lieutenant Smith on his motor-cycle came into Béalnabláth Cross and stopped because he had no view of the tender. He leaned on the handlebars and waited for 'The Dane' to approach. When Long did so Smith revealed the 'Presence' at the back (cf. 'Five Local People'. Smith also must have been the 'indiscreet soldier' who earned Mrs. Lankford's censure at Monee Cross on the Sunday). When Smith turned his machine for Bandon the leading tender must have been far ahead. On the evidence of 'one just man', Timothy Hurley, there was a second tender in the convoy. What became of it is immaterial. It did not appear at the battle of Béalnabláth. General Emmet Dalton found General Michael Collins standing before the door of Newcestown church looking up at the stone-cut inscription. It was in Latin and commemorated the fact that the foundation stone of that church of St. John the Baptist was laid by the Reverend Jeremiah Cummins, parish priest, on Sunday, 23 June 1872. Collins seemed to have been waiting with the certainty of being found or the hope of being lost among his people. The inscription could have meant little to him except the satisfaction of interpretation which he probably could achieve seeing that his father (according to Rex Taylor, *Michael Collins*) 'from a schooling of the most meagre kind, the teaching of a wandering "hedge-schoolmaster", Diarmuid Ó Súilliobháin, a cousin on his mother's side, he had developed into a scholar of the "dead" languages, Latin and Greek' — a not unusual phenomenon in the days of the hedge schools of Ireland, likewise by no means a 'meagre' education! Collins went on to Bandon and points West, all newly captured to his apparent satisfaction from a coterie of old acquaintances by an admixture of new-found adherents and retainers. The motorcade reached Skibbereen in the middle of the afternoon. The returned West-Cork hero got a tumultuous reception. Eugene McCarthy, who now lives near Béalnabláth, was there. He was in a group of one hundred and fifty horsemen who rode into town to see Michael Collins. Mick was in powerful form among his own. There was a special greeting for the horsemen. Were they apocalyptic? For the townspeople there was a message of hope and promise. Eugene told it like this: ' "Skibbereen", he (Collins) said, "will be a prosperous town yet. I'll have ships coming in and out of that harbour". But the poor man . . . he didn't . . . well, you know . . .'. Then he returned to Bandon (the route is well documented, though sometimes in error). From Bandon Cork was north-east. He headed his motorcade north-west to Macroom to confer again with Florrie Donoghue. The 'Boys', he knew, would be at, or in the vicinity of, Gurranereagh. Of course he knew! He did not just direct the War of Independence — he invented that too! ('Myth!', said my friend, Canon Jim Corkery — 'This is part of the build up of Collins as a great hero and the vilification of the I.R.A. The War of Independence was planned by the "Volunteers" imprisoned in Britain after 1916. I have this from my father who was one of them. Hero-worship is among the greatest enemies of truth', the Canon said). Collins wished he had the 'Three Toms' on his side — Tom Malone, Tom Barry and Tom Hales. Two were in custody. The third, he guessed, would be at that conference at Gurranereagh. He had passed near enough to it twice that day, at Kilmurry and at Newcestown. He would do so a third time. The 'Boys', however, were not interested in 'Father Figures'. They replied with gunfire!

*   *   *

Macomber, as he fired, saw fragments fly like slate . . . He shot again; and he felt a sudden white-hot, blinding flash explode inside his head and that was all he ever felt. Mrs. Macomber had hit her husband about two inches up and a little to one side of the base of his skull. (Ernest Hemingway, *The Short Happy Life of Francis Macomber*).

*   *   *

The itinerary of the Collins cavalcade into West-Cork has been ignored by some writers, briefly referred to by others, gone into more or less in depth by a few, but all quite erroneously. Is it important? The subject matter is very important; therefore literary contradictions in detail would also appear to be so. Does it matter? To the extent that it tends to qualify or modify the stature of Collins among the people of the region, and so highlight the Civil War split in his own place, it should matter enormously . . .

Frank O'Connor: He simply says that they passed through Macroom, Bandon, Clonakilty, Rosscarbery, Skibbereen and Sam's Cross. According to Emmet Dalton's statement (quoted by Piaras Béaslaí), Sam's Cross was on the way out from Clonakilty to Rosscarbery rather than on the return journey.

Piaras Béaslaí: He leaves the narrative to Dalton . . . 'We halted at a hamlet in the vicinity of Sam's Cross'.

Rex Taylor: (Based on an interview with John O'Connell). He has the convoy to-ing and fro-ing hilariously . . . 'The route (from Cork) went by way of Skibbereen . . . to Bandon . . . in the direction of Clonakilty . . . over mountainous roads to Sam's Cross . . . re-entered Skibbereen . . . travelling by way of Bandon in the direction of Clonakilty . . . speeding along they came to the valley of Béal na mBláth'. Symptomatically he introduces the drinking theme.

Calton Younger: Following John O'Connell's somewhat amended narrative, he also dwells on some questionable themes, e.g. the drinking of the soldiery, some arbitrary conversation pieces (as favoured by Meda Ryan), and a wasteful hour, uncharacteristic of Collins, spent in hacking trees near Clonakilty (in Irish, 'the plain of the woods'), all in the interest of the pseudo-deification process (in which Margery Forester indulges enormously), which is not wholly Irish and is totally unhelpful to history.

Margery Forester: She takes in Sam's Cross on the way out west but omits Skibbereen and introduces the 'Five All' notion, in which significant error she is followed by León Ó Broin and Meda Ryan.

León Ó Broin: He has the proper order but omits Sam's Cross and also takes up (from a hint in Calton Younger) the Bantry idea, which would have involved a further twenty rugged miles to a totally different return journey into mid-Cork.

Michael Hopkinson: He just mentions Bandon and Rosscarbery *en passant*.

John Feehan: 'The convoy now left (Bandon) for Clonakilty . . . and moved to Skibbereen via Rosscarbery. Nearby Collins met his brother Seán and some relatives'. He makes no mention of Sam's Cross or Woodfield.

Meda Ryan: Having dealt otherwise with Bandon, she brings the convoy abruptly to 'the outskirts of Clonakilty . . . headed for Rosscarbery . . . headed for Skibbereen . . . back via Rosscarbery and on towards Sam's Cross . . . set out from Sam's Cross at 6.15'.

Note: As a further contribution to the itinerary, an interesting piece appeared in the *Southern Star* (February, 1988) from 'P.Ó.D.':

Although there were no Free State troops in Leap (i.e. between Rosscarbery and Skibbereen), his entourage stopped in the village. He was anxious to discuss the progress of Coláiste Chairbre, Glandore, with the late John O'Donovan, N.T., Woodview, who was then secretary of the Coláiste . . . The classes were for national teachers only, who were required to attend suitable Irish Colleges and secure a qualification for the 'new' language. (N.B. Irish was forbidden in schools under the British regime). Collins was keenly interested in the future of the Irish language . . . My father (John O'Donovan) had left earlier for Glandore and so missed the Big Man . . . On the return journey from Skibbereen, that evening, the entourage again halted briefly in Leap as Collins was hoping to meet my father, but he hadn't yet returned from Glandore.

The little crossroads commemorating Sam, the highwayman, shot to fame at the death of Collins. It is about three and a half miles from Clonakilty and is reached by a detour branching off one and a half miles out of town. The events associated with it on this occasion are likewise dubious and contradictory. The convoy left Clonakilty 'after lunch', and should have been at Sam's Cross between two and three in the afternoon. Jimmy O'Brien lives there, whose father, Michael, was a first cousin of Michael Collins. He tells it simply as his father had many times related it to him. The convoy, he says, arrived in the afternoon from Clonakilty. It pulled up in front of his house, just short of the public house. The touring car stood directly at the front gate, the armoured car just behind it closing the entrance to the backyard. A double file of soldiers stood to attention on the roadway. Through the kitchen window Michael O'Brien saw Michael Collins standing on the gravel in front of the public house. He went across to meet him. Collins asked him to fetch his brother, Johnny, from Woodfield, his home, a quarter of a mile away. Collins walked across to O'Brien's and had a cup of tea while sitting in the kitchen with some officers. Through the window he saw Johnny arrive at the front gate and jumped up to meet him at the front door. They went into the parlour across the hallway and talked there for about twenty minutes by themselves (Jimmy O'Brien keeps an enormous picture of Collins hanging on the parlour wall in memory). Then Collins left and sat into his car. As he was about to drive off Johnny said: 'You'd better put up that hood — you could be shot before night!' The advice was ignored and the convoy headed for Rosscarbery on the back road. 'I told all of this to that lady writer', says Jimmy O'Brien, 'but she would not listen!' The drinking theme has been very popular with writers and talkers alike. The convoy being drunk at Béalnabláth is a popular misconception. Probably Feehan alone has the thing correct. He says: 'The convoy had drinks in White's pub . . .'. White's pub was, and is, a mile away at the Pike Cross where they would have joined the Clonakilty-Rosscarbery road once again. The signal on the 'hit-gang' from Dublin was strong and reliable. It was talked about in his house, according to Jimmy O'Brien. Woodfield, or possibly Sam's Cross itself, would have been the obvious venue. The Dublin four, however, had gone to Béalnabláth for the conference instead . . .

Taylor: At the inn kept by his cousin, Jeremiah, Collins treated each member of the convoy to two pints of the 'Clonakilty Wrestler' . . . drank his last drink.

Younger: He . . . drank at the public house owned by his kinsman, Jeremiah . . . called his escort in to the pub and brought them a couple of pints of Clonakilty 'Wrestler'. (Note spelling in both references!).

Forester: In the Five Alls . . . he stood . . . his escort a pint of Clonakilty Wrastler (Note spelling!). But - 'Collins loathed the sight of porter' (p. 287).

Ó Broin: With him (Johnny) and other members of the family . . . Mick drank a pint of the Wrastler in the local pub, the Five Alls.

Ryan: The convoy wound its way 'back home' to his brother's place, to the Five Alls public house at Sam's Cross . . . today . . . he would sample a pint of the Clonakilty Wrastler.

Note One: The Deasy family, of Clonakilty, were recorded in 1770 as smugglers. In 1807-9 they built their brewery on the site of an older one and started to make stout. They used a good deal of promotional material, posters, mirrors, etc., showing the figure of a well-built man, in tights, and labelled 'The Wrestler'. Locally the word was pronounced 'wrastler', as spelt in Shakespeare, or colloquially, 'rashler'. The stout was mostly reserved for special occasions such as a threshing (prn. 'thrashing'), was declared to be 'poisonous' by some, but did earn a prize at the Chicago International Exhibition in 1893.

Note Two: Those writers who omitted the name of the Sam's Cross pub would appear to have been aware that there was no specific name for it at the time under advisement. It was referred to eponymously as 'Jerry Collins's' or 'The Cross' (according to old Brother Jerome Collins). It did have four cameo-type pictures over the door stating 'I rule all' (King), 'I pray for all' (Bishop), 'I fight for all' (Croppy Boy), 'But I pay for all' (Farmer). At a later date these four were made up as a sign and entitled 'The Four Alls', and placed on the roadside. Margery Forester first referred to the pub as 'Five Alls', indicating that this was a score in the popular Co. Cork (and Co. Armagh) game of roadway 'Bowling' (pronounced as in 'howl'), which is incorrect. It was a poignant theme from the Land League days.

Note Three: Woodfield has become famous as the birthplace of Michael Collins. All the more is it surprising that inaccuracy and contradiction have proliferated with regard to the burning theme, and as to which house was which. Just across the fence lived another Collins family. The last remaining member is Brother Jerome of the St. John of God Order, now invalided and retired in Dublin. His great-grandfather and Michael Collins' grandfather were brothers. (It was the typically Irish phenomenon of bad times — divided house, divided yard, divided friendship, divided property, but in this case an historic reunity). Brother Jerome met Collins twice — once when he was six, in 1919. Michael arrived by car while on the run. He was hatless and coatless, with just shirt and pants. He had the driver put the six-year-old into the motor car to show him the wonders of it. The second time was in 1922 while Jerome was living with an aunt (his family had broken up), Mrs. Margaret Beechinor, at Rossmore, northwards towards Ballineen.

Collins arrived at Rossmore to address an election gathering and was disappointed to find them dispersed. Br. Jerome was the 'gossoon', or 'garsún' (meaning 'little boy') of the six-penny handshake, a simple story which was given legs and sent careering through literature. Johnny's new house (he was to be known later as 'Seán' in Dublin when he was given a job in the Land Commission) and the old house were both burned down by the British in April, 1921. The house across the fence was untouched. Br. Jerome's other aunt now lived there alone. She kindly took them all in to her house, while blankets and other essentials were provided by the O'Brien family across the way. They stayed on until the family scattered and Johnny was remarried to his cousin, Nancy O'Brien, Collins' contact in the G.P.O., Dublin, during the Tan War. (I have in my possession a letter-card that Mick sent to Nancy on 23 December 1921 — Author). Br. Jerome adds that (despite what has been published) Jeremiah Collins of the Sam's Cross public house was no relation of the Big Fellow. He just wished he was. And why not!

*   *   *

Octogenarian Jerry Hurley is eking out his last days in St. Finbarr's Hospital, Cork City. He is the last surviving member of Tom Barry's famous West-Cork 'Flying Column', but he will not disclose what military actions he participated in. However, he has an even more significant niche in Irish History. He is the key to a further tragic coincidence of the many which contributed to the death of Michael Collins. (A native of Drinechnua, Bantry, he is not to be confused with Jerry Hurley, Dunmanway, of the 'Sam Maguire Cup' fame). Old Jerry was a Free State soldier. He was a member of a group of military from the Bantry Battalion, under Captain Denis Cronin of Borlin, who were at the Eldon Hotel, Skibbereen, 'on Army business'. They were in the lobby 'after dinner' when Collins 'blew in out of the blue'. He talked with them for a considerable length of time on the military situation in Bantry, and then left. He did not drink. Nobody drank. As a consequence of the meeting Collins decided not to proceed to Bantry and also arranged for the immediate transfer of their battalion to Tallow, Co. Waterford, so as not to have them facing their old comrades in that sadly divided town. In their place a battalion of 'strangers' was drafted in. It is almost too easy to speculate on the outcome of this chance meeting. Bantry would have given Collins a relatively easy access to Macroom through Ballingeary and Inchigeela, or Renaniree, and facilitated his projected meeting with Florrie O'Donoghue; and Béalnabláth would never have happened! At the end of the Civil War, Jerry Hurley left the Army and went to America, that grand and spacious happy hunting ground of Staters and Republicans alike. Too late for Collins! Too late for Ireland!

* Con Mulcahy still lives there. He and his brother, John Joe, saw the convoy sweep through, swing left on the 'Priest's Road' towards the 'Tank Cross' suburb while the soldiers shouted, 'General Collins is coming!' and the two officers primly saluted the assembled rustics.

12

The Michael Collins Story: The Battle

The blood of Michael Collins may still be seen as light and dark red stains on a woollen carriage rug. At Béalnabláth they saw his blood upon the road. It travelled in his personal automobile to Dublin and to England and, no doubt, a residue went to Africa where the animal hunter, with unconscious irony, set up a machine-gun and a spotlight on the car. His blood travelled widely as a blessing or a curse. In Glasnevin Cemetery a leaden missile rattles around in the empty casket of his skull, with the motions of the earth, or perhaps by now lies beside his head in a little heap of Gogarty's decorticated wax, while his dusty brain still stirs the futile passions of his people. He died in battle. Bernard Shaw said it was a good way and a good time to go. It was easy. There were seven men who might conceivably have killed him as an enemy on the spot. Two said they did. Two feared they might have. Two were in line to do so. And one was seen to fire the instant the big man fell. Then there was the machine-gunner who thought he might have accidentally done so, and the high-ranking officer who has been virtually accused of murdering him. The seven were a complete circle of Republicans on the hills. The other two were on the roadside fighting beside him for their lives. One way or the other he was dead when the battle ended. The rest is silence.

153

The ambush-battle is not peculiar to Ireland, though the term is much used in the context of the 'Troubles'. If it must be seen as having been invented, it was first used in recorded history as a weapon of inferior against superior forces by the Roman general, Q. Fabius Maximus, called 'Cunctator' i.e. 'the delayer', whose 'fabian tactics' in the war against Hannibal (218 B.C.) is still a text-book synonym for guerrilla-style fighting. In Irish History two staunch exponents of the art were Art MacMurrough Kavanagh (Fourteenth Century) and Fiach MacHugh O'Byrne (Sixteenth Century). The Irish 'Flying Column' was the additional dimension, copied by the Black and Tans as a necessity of means, and protracted by Lord Lovat's 'Commandos' in World War Two. Oddly enough the record of the ambush at Béalnabláth has suffered considerably from some curious tricks of logic: the fallacy of the apparent, the parallax dilemma and, indeed, the conviction of ignorance. To establish the position one needs to distinguish battle-scene and ambush-site. In 1924 a large monument was erected at the place, but not the spot, where he died. It stands on two roods of ground vested in perpetuity on the National Army. As evidenced by two photographs (from *Pathé Gazette*), identical but for a vanishing horse and cart, he did not die where the monument stands. He fell fatally wounded about forty yards further up the road to Bandon. A black X on the pictures marks the spot and also shows where someone had cut a cross on the roadside sod. This is just where local people still alive, or recently deceased, saw the largest splash of blood. It was, in fact, where his body was lifted onto the rear platform of the armoured car for transportation to his motor car, a hundred yards down the road towards Crookstown. Standing at the monument one is right in the battle scene. Despite undergrowth, overgrowth and general neglect, it is possible to see the main positions. One may be pardoned for concluding that it was an ideally chosen site for the ambush. That is the fallacy of the apparent. Add some salient features in the vicinity, and it needs but a mediocre imagination to set the machinery in motion. That is what writers have done. But one! One writer moved the battle scene six hundred yards (three-eighths of a mile) back towards Bandon. That is the parallax dilemma. It affected one participant, still living. The conviction of ignorance is more difficult to understand . . .

> He that complies against his will,
> Is of his own opinion still!

Samuel Butler's seventeenth century wisdom is highlighted in the twentieth when a plurality of freedoms allows one to take a stance on an issue, thesis it and publish with impunity, or compose a biography that is half-true, half-fiction and be hailed as the best to date. That has been Michael Collins' posthumous affliction. Even foreigners have come to 'speak a language that the strangers do not know', in the process of elucidation. It is a presumption and an irritation, and quite grotesque. It must be remembered that people lived on the battlefield of Béalnabláth, and all around. It was a dangerous time for all. They kept their minds to themselves. After some years revelation began to emerge. Cautious words at a pub or a fair became folklore. Parents' awesome confidences to children became tenuous memory. The fighting man had only a long bull's-eye view and for a twelve-month was running for his life, or had escaped abroad.

This is simply the situation. De Valera left Béalnabláth at 4 p.m., having agreed in principle to a token ambush. Liam Deasy and Tom Hales walked out the Bandon road from Béalnabláth 'about half a mile'. Deasy does not admit (in *Brother Against Brother*) to having been in the planning, but still he was, though not in the actual fight (cf. 'The Tom Foley Story'). Deasy states exactly the position. There are two bridges in the scene, Ahalarick Bridge and Glanarouge (or 'Carroll's') Bridge, over the Noneen brook. The bridges are half a mile apart, Ahalarick being on the Bandon side and Glanarouge towards Béalnabláth village. Between these two bridges, but more towards Glanarouge, the battle was fought. Between

Glanarouge bridge and Béalnabláth village the ambush was originally set, on an invisible old roadway about fifty yards across the little river. The horse-cart barricade was positioned in the middle of an S-bend and about one hundred and eighty yards from Glanarouge bridge towards the village. The usual Command Post was on 'The Rock' suspended above 'Jake's Pool', where Deasy placed a Lewis machine-gun and in a deadly position to enfilade the whole front from bridge to barricade. He had personally captured this gun at Crossbarry. 'The Rock' is thirty feet above the road and only twenty yards from it. Twenty-five men (Deasy said, but others say forty) were ranged along the fence of the old roadway, which was then only a cattle track and has now almost disappeared. A large landmine was sunk in the main road at Glanarouge bridge and slightly on the Béalnabláth side of it. A smaller one was placed in front of the barricade. How everybody has missed this is hard to say because the locals are adamant. The battle occurred on the Bandon side of Glanarouge bridge and away from all mines and barricades. Meda Ryan places the battle almost half a mile further back around Ahalarick bridge. She seems to have fallen lock, stock and barrel for an old man's persistent illusion, and contrary to all reports to date, official or otherwise. The trouble on the ground for an unwary observer is that there are actually six separate little L-shaped road-junctions that look almost exactly alike. Two of these are further complicated with little bridges, and that is where the illusion arises. Combine with this the fact that the ambush did not happen where it was planned or, rather, happened where it was not planned, and the fallacy of Illicit Major Premise sets everybody and everything at sixes and sevens. Apart from the above, every writer so far (and there are about two dozen books dealing with, or referring to, the 'Battle of Béalnabláth') has placed the intended ambush where it actually occurred to the extent of siting barricade and mine where one thought suitable. The general trend is to have the barricade slightly beyond — on the Bandon side of — Glanarouge bridge, with a landmine sunk strategically in front of it i.e. somewhere between it and the enemy. Lieutenant Smith, the motor cycle outrider, is said (by himself and others) to have seen the barricade, as well as the cables from the mine, in the nick of time. A careful perusal of his published statement will show that he was, at that moment, about one hundred and fifty yards further on towards Béalnabláth village and almost in sight of it; and the scene is totally changed. One other item of possible confusion is the fact that the entrance to the farm (Hennessy's) on the opposite side of the road (i.e. behind the backs of the Free State Army) was not as at present, but fifty yards or so nearer to Glanarouge bridge. The Ordnance Survey maps still retain the position. That was where the Crossley tender came to rest. The Leyland motor car was the regulation distance (roughly twenty-five yards) behind the tender, the armoured car a like span to the rear, its ultimate position, after reversing, being where the monument now stands, and the motor cycle scout was out of sight in front and well on his way to Béalnabláth village. Those who saw the barricade, and are still alive (November, 1989), were Ellen Long (Mrs. Ellen Allen), her sister, Maggie Long (Mrs. Margaret Shorten), Tom Murray of the conference house on the hill (referred to for some reason as 'Mrs. Murray's' rather than being named for her husband William), and — until just recently — Tom Foley, the intrepid cyclist, who helped in the transportation of two of the mines used, the laying of one and the positioning of the Lewis-gun on 'The Rock'. Moreover, Ellen Long with her first cousin, John Cronin, watched the removal of the barricade and its mine until they were put to flight by one of the guards on the spot. No statement made latterly by any of the participants deals with this feature of the affair, only with the subsequent action. If it had occurred as planned the outcome undoubtedly would have been the annihilation of a significant section of the National Army, including the Commander-in-Chief, the regional G.O.C., some high-ranking officers besides, and some soldiery. From the Republican point of view, acknowledging the position would have meant approving the design, and second-sight is always twenty-twenty, as they say.

At seven o'clock the fighting contingent dispersed. At seven-thirty four of them were attending to the barricade and its protecting landmine. Two had left the roadway at Carroll's (Glanarouge) bridge and were making their way up the 'boreen' (lit. 'little road', or etymol. 'the little way [on which] the cows come [home]'). Six men were at the other end of the same boreen, about a quarter of a mile away and proceeding at right-angles (i.e. westwards) on a further branch towards a farmyard. One of these saw the signal flag waving on the hill far away south towards Mossgrove, and directly afterwards the glint of armour. The six raced back and took positions along the fence of the boreen they had just left. The two men in the vicinity of the little bridge took their stance behind two gate pillars two hundred yards away. One of them fired a warning shot and the unplanned battle was on. The motor-cyclist was almost at the barricade. The lorry of troops was at the old entrance to the Hennessy farm and close to Carroll's (Glanarouge) bridge. The motor car was at the mid-point of a long curve and about where the new entrance to the Hennessy farm now lies. The armoured car, directly behind it, halted, opened fire and backed off to a final position slightly beyond and opposite to where the Collins monument now stands. All of these particulars are in accordance with personalized information throughout the present work and with reports of National Army personnel and Republican bodies who fought there.

*   *   *

THE BROKEN CIRCLE

Who shot Michael Collins?
1. Pete Kearney thought he did.
2. Shawno Galvin said he did.
3. Sonny O'Neill was reported to have said he did.
4. Mike Donoghue said he saw the man who did.
5. Jimmy Ormond fired directly at him and saw him fall.

6. Bobs Doherty heard (or fired) a shot and saw him fall.
7. Joe Murphy thought he might have.

The 'Broken Circle' illustrates their positions and the positions of other gunmen at the time he was killed. Michael Collins was titled 'Head-Centre' of the I.R.B. (Irish Republican Brotherhood, ineptly referred to by some foreign writers as 'The Brotherhood'), a secret, oath-bound society condemned by the domestic law of the Roman Catholic Church.

The action was neither battle nor ambush. The fighting 'became general' as the expression is. A running skirmish is what it turned out to be. The motor cycle scout, Lieutenant Smith, was thrown from his machine on the stream side of the roadway. He retraced his journey on hands and knees under cover of the fence. Beyond Carroll's bridge he took a squad of soldiers from the lorry and proceeded up the boreen from the bridge in the direction of the firing. Comdt. Seán O'Connell took a Thompson sub-machine gun and boldly crossed the open ground in the same direction and towards the gate pillars, being fired on and halted periodically as he went. Republican Jim Hurley held his gate pillar position while his companion, Tom Kelleher, moved back down to the bend in the boreen in order to prevent the soldiers advancing on them. As he did so he was fired on by the machine-gunner in the armoured car. The armoured car then reversed to engage the six Republicans at the other end of the boreen who were making their presence felt. Collins and Dalton, with the two drivers, had vacated the motor car and were firing from a prone position on the low fence of the roadway. The windscreen had been shattered by what Dalton later described as a burst of machine-gun fire. More likely it was a clip from Jim Hurley's 'Peter the Painter'. By now the men at the barricade had dashed across the stream to their original position on the old roadway and had moved quickly along it to where it joined the boreen at the bend between bridge and pillars, and continued on under good cover to where the six men were in position at the other end. Some of these were already beginning to make their escape. Two of them leaped over a fence at the junction and 'were seen to fall', according to one Army account. By this time other Republican groups had begun to converge. Liam Deasy made a rapid encircling movement from the village by way of the high places on the eastern side (i.e. opposite to the original ambush position), to arrive near the old (Hennessy) farmhouse and just where the new one now stands. He created some diversionary fire while the only things visible were the troop lorry and the turret of the armoured car. A shoulder of ground obscured the motor car. Mike Donoghue and the Kerry contingent dashed across Deasy's path and flung themselves down on a plateau with full view of the rising road to Bandon. Bobs Doherty and his companion travelled nearer to the precipitous brow and dropped down on the newly wet grass with full view of everything. Away over on the far (i.e. the western) side Peter Kearney had been leading a half-dozen men home towards Newcestown. The firing brought them back at the double. Jimmy Ormond and the Waterford group raced in from the south-west to join battle in the hope of capturing a truck. It happened all the time. Away to the north-west Shawno Galvin had been patrolling the hills on horseback. He galloped to the scene and was just in time to take a firing position before the end. He was close enough (he said) to hear the excited chatter of the soldiery as Collins fell.

*   *   *

THE MACABRE MILE

From Ahalarick bridge to Béalnabláth village is exactly one mile. Those were the limits of the action. An holistic view is necessary to grasp the scene. Perhaps 'bird's eye view' is more apt, or understandable. The mile may be conveniently divided in four sections that are roughly, rather than approximately, quarters. From Ahalarick (lit. 'the ford of the conflict') to the monument is the first quarter. One writer (Meda Ryan: *The Day Michael Collins was Shot*) places the battle in this sector, especially around the bridge itself and beyond towards

Mossgrove, which would be about six hundred yards (three-eighths of a mile) from the centre of activity: the Leyland motor car. How this error could have been conceived and elaborated is dealt with elsewhere.

The second significant sector lies between the monument and Carroll's (Glanarouge) bridge. Here the sad and undecided battle was fought for about three-quarters of an hour, with a sort of a Pyrrhic victory going to the National Army. On all sides they say — 'It should never have happened!'; and they mean different things.

The stretch from Carroll's bridge to the barricade is the third sector, extending to about one-eighth of a mile. Here is where the ambush was planned and laid. But for a little matter of time, Glanarouge ('the valley of the rout') and Pullerick ('the pool of the conflict') would have earned their dreadful and long forgotten reputations as never before.

The final sector, from the barricade to the village, is about seven hundred yards in length. Why the ambush should have been sited so near even to a tiny centre of population is difficult to visualize. There was nothing to defend. For a further three miles (i.e. to Crookstown) it is almost continuous defile. They could have placed the ambush almost anywhere along that route. Defending an ancient crossroads might have significance. A defiant gesture in the forefront of the location for an important conference might have meant something — a response to a challenge, perhaps. The outcome, at any rate, has had repercussions across the spectrum of Irish historical and political life, and will continue to do so. All brands of warfare carry the poison seed of repercussion. Fight now, pay later — or let somebody else do so!

13

The Michael Collins Story: The Aftermath

They buried him cleanly and clinically and ceremoniously, as one would expect from the Army. Potentates pontificated, women wept and men ground their teeth. But, by contrast, the aftermath of his death was a muddy, disorientated and blind scramble through the fields and boglands of mid-Cork, while his body jostled about on a crude and unworthy transport vehicle far away from historic Glasnevin Cemetery in the City of Dublin.

* * *

General Emmet Dalton moved his contingent out of Béalnabláth in a state of utter dejection. Commandant Seán O'Connell was in a towering rage. They had both seen death in the trenches of Flanders. This was different. Dalton still had sufficient 'savoir-faire' to think and concern himself about the man's immortal soul. He halted in the centre of Crookstown village. Macroom was to the left. Cork was to the right. Demolished bridges were everywhere. Over beyond the River Bride lay the parallel road to Cork. Beyond that again, in a great mansion high above the fertile valley, lived the Very Reverend John Treacy, critic and parish priest. He had heard the distant firing. He had his 'boy' tackle the pony-trap. The nearer bridge over

162

the river was impassable. He headed out towards Macroom but the railway bridge to the village of Crookstown was also down. He stood there waiting and just out of sight. Dalton spoke to a group of men standing at the corner public house. Among them was young Jack Murphy, thirteen years of age, now retired P.P. of the Cork diocese. Dalton asked for a priest. They directed him onwards to Cloughduv village, two miles away. The curate lived there beside the church.

On a somewhat higher road than the Bride valley Macroom-Cork line, roughly a mile away from it and running parallel, the Crookstown-Cork road harbours the villages of Cloughduv (two miles), Aherla (two miles), Kilumney (three miles), and Ballincollig (three miles). The book, *The Day Michael Collins was Shot*, has got the order changed about somewhat, but this is immaterial as the village that moved — Aherla — does not come into the picture. It is necessary to know this as the further historic happenings at Annesgrove, Srelane and Kilumney are relevant to the whole pathetic scene. Let us return to Crookstown. Young Jack Murphy was a native of the village. With some others he had stood around listening to the firing up along the Bride valley. It was, he says, 'a murky evening'. Presently the firing died away. After a few minutes there was a single shot. Curiously, 'that was the one that did the damage!' said a man named Buckley (from Aherla). He was still standing there, some short time later, when the Army convoy arrived at the T-cross of the village and stopped. ('They intended travelling to Crookstown . . . taking a right turn they wound their way until they arrived at the outskirts of a village which they thought was Crookstown but which in fact was Cloughduv . . .'. From *The Day Michael Collins was Shot*-interview with Bill Powell). When Dalton asked for a priest (Fr. Jack Murphy continued), Ted Murphy, local farmer and late of the London Metropolitan Police Force, went with them to Cloughduv to show the way . . . 'Murphy went on board the tender . . . on the way . . . a soldier said in a low voice, "This is a night that will be remembered!" ' Ted Murphy asked why and got the answer, ''The night Michael Collins was killed!'' ''. (Edward O'Mahony in *Magill* magazine). Then Murphy walked back the two miles to Crookstown and had the first historic message sent out by telegraph to Macroom (where American-Irish journalist, Peter Golden — *Impressions of Ireland* — saw the shopkeepers put up the window shutters, the usual mark of respect for the dead in that town. Apparently the shops were still open). The corner pub owned by Mrs. Horgan, a widow, was also the post office at the time. (Ted Murphy is of interest for another reason, an indirect association with the Irish 'Troubles' and particularly the ambush at Béalnabláth. As a policeman in London he had been involved in the famous 'Siege of Sidney Street', on 3 January 1911, at which Winston Churchill, as Home Secretary, was also present. It was there that the German Mauser automatic got its nickname of 'Peter the Painter', after Peter Piaktow, a Russian anarchist. Murphy received a Queen's Birthday medal for his part in the action). Fr. Jack Murphy continues: 'Fr. Tim Murphy (of Cloughduv) was a sick man, with a severe stomach ailment all his life. He was much maligned over this incident. I knew him. He gave the ''short-form'' Absolution (i.e. in case of urgency) to the body and mumbled that he was going in the house for the Oils (i.e. for anointing the dying. Note: In those days one hour was the canonical limit for anointing in cases of sudden or violent death — Author). This was apparently misunderstood and (by curious contradiction) one of the disturbed soldiers raised his rifle. (Dalton said he knocked down the gun.) While Fr. Tim was in the house a shot was fired ''in the air'' and they all drove off. Annie White (Fr. Murphy's housekeeper) had bandaged Collins' head with a (liturgical) linen towel. Later on she talked so much about the matter that she was taken away by the Republicans and had her head shaved'. Or so said Fr. Jack! A tradition in the village of Cloughduv still has it that the priest cursed the leading Republican family, as a consequence, saying that they would not see another generation in the place. Bluster or not, time has proved him right. He was by all accounts a proud, austere man who rode his horse as he walked, stiff and straight, and he always wore a 'tall hat', relic of a previous age. He was curate in Cloughduv from 1911-1925 and was transferred as P.P. to Watergrasshill where he died. Fr. Treacy remained on as parish priest of this vast (Kilmurry) parish until 1935.

Young Maggie Brennan (presently married to Florence O'Driscoll, fine old white-bearded West-Cork patriarch of 'De La Cour Villa' on the Beamish Line into Kilmurry) was standing by in Cloughduv, her native place. She saw the whole thing. She remembers the metallic glitter of the military vehicles in the failing light. She also remembers that an army officer (identifiable as Commandant Seán O'Connell) asked three men leaning against a wall for the way to Cork. They were slow in replying and he fired a revolver shot at their feet (she says 'between their legs'). He got his information that Aherla village was two miles further on. (Note: Comdt. O'Connell was very highly strung and particularly disturbed on this occasion. He eventually died in a mental hospital, as did Captain Peadar Conlon, Free State C/O in Macroom, who wrote a book on the subject of mental illness). The convoy did not go directly to Aherla, however. They turned into an avenue half a mile onwards and on the left. It led to the then unoccupied mansion still known as 'Annesgrove House'. Significantly the avenue was shown on the maps as the beginning of an old right-of-way through to the Macroom-Cork road beyond the River Bride and across an expanse of marshland . . . On a stone plaque in the hallway of Annesgrove House are carved the words: 'Annesgrove: Built by Mrs. Anne C. Barter, A.D. 1872. Every wise woman buildeth her house. Prov. XIV, v.1'. In the 'Sun Lounge' hangs a portrait of Michael Collins (by Tom Greany) with a brass plaque and the legend: 'General Michael Collins. Annesgrove, as a secluded house, was the resting place for his body en route to Shanakiel Hospital from Béal na mBláth, on 22 Aug. 1922. This historic fact has been authenticated by John Hickey, first sergeant (i.e. of the new 'Civic Guards') for the district of Farnanes'. Sergeant Hickey's first assignment in 1923 was to investigate the circumstances surrounding the death of Michael Collins. The Kenneally family (the present owners are Mrs. Kenneally, sister to Florence O'Driscoll, and her son, Colm, manager of Cruise's Hotel, Limerick) tell the story that the military contingent brought the body of Collins into the stone-flagged, four-hundred-year-old back kitchen simply 'to wash his face'. They then continued along the avenue through the yard and out onto a stoned cart-way across the marsh, which was frequented by horse traffic from the opposite side. Mid way in this marshland region ran the Cork-Macroom railway line, then temporarily out of commission due to enemy action, as they say, now long disused. All traffic had to cross over the vanished tracks — but the old safety gates still hang in place and one of them carried (until just recently) a rusty old sign with the poignant words: 'Beware of Trains'! It had swung through its ninety degrees to allow passage to the heedless body of the Commander-in-Chief. The widowed and charming Mrs. Kathleen Foley, whose late husband's parents lived on this farm at Aherlabeg at the time of the passing, presented the steel plate as a welcome souvenir to the present writer. Beyond Foley's farmhouse was a narrow girder and wood bridge over the Bride. The convoy managed to negotiate it and rocked its way the further few hundred yards onto the main road from Macroom to Cork . . .

John Crowley of Tullig, Coachford, was ten years and two months when the most momentous thing in his whole life happened to him. He saw the body of Michael Collins lying full length in the back of a Crossley tender. 'I thought he was the biggest man I ever saw', said John who is now (1990) a sprightly, lucid old chap of seventy-eight and lives in Ballinacurra village. He has thought long and clearly about his vision. He is in no doubt. 'Some soldiers', he says, 'came in the house looking for tea. One of them said to me - "Come out and I'll show you the greatest man that Ireland has ever produced". He was lying in the back of a lorry with his cap on his chest'. It was 'a soldier's cap, round on top, with a small hole in the back, ON THE LEFT HAND SIDE. The soldier pointed to a wound at the back of the head, ON THE LEFT HAND SIDE. There was no blood on his face and there was no bandage. The wound was only a small wound, a little hole about the size of a two-penny piece'. To the young lad the armoured car was a massive tower of steel reaching for the sky. He was on his Summer holidays with a family of O'Sullivans, relatives of his grandaunt, Mrs. Daniel Magner, then deceased, to whom she had left the house and farm. They lived next door, 'just across the wall'. It was the birthplace of Canon Magner who had been shot dead on 15 December 1920, by Auxiliary Cadets from Macroom Castle. (He was parish priest of Dunmanway. Cadet Harte, who actually killed him, was declared guilty but insane. His son, a Catholic priest, visited the town in the Fifties and said Mass for the murdered Canon). The place was Srelane, one mile from Ovens bridge. The convoy had gone on to the bridge, found it destroyed, with the road from there to Kilumney blocked off. They went back to Magner's and O'Sullivan's. Four fields separated them from Ovens church over beyond on the link-road to Kilumney. Some officers went down to inspect the fields. In the meantime the rank and file went into both houses and made themselves comfortable. They left the body by itself on the roadside with no one on guard. For once the 'Big Fellow' was going nowhere. 'It was still broad daylight', John Crowley says. The soldier who took him to see the body said they didn't have anything to eat all day. Nor did they on this occasion. They were just settled down when an officer came raging in to Magner's. 'He was a blocky fellow and in a desperate temper. He shouted at them to get out. I think he was Emmet Dalton'. He was not Dalton but the 'enfant terrible' once again, Seán O'Connell. Dalton was slim and tallish. The convoy entered the field just at the gable-end of the O'Sullivan farmhouse. The old gate and entrance are still there but the two houses are now unoccupied. Just inside the field the armoured car bogged down. (Note: There is an old local story that the *Slievenamon* then returned to Cork City by an amazing alternative route. At Srelane Cross, where stood an old coach inn, later known as the Bride Valley Bar and most recently the delightful and stylish hostelry, the 'Tatler Jak', ran the ancient Bandon-Mallow road over the hill and around by the now submerged Castle Inch to the River Lee where there was a usable ford just below Dripsey, then out by a steep incline through the O'Mahony farmyard to the Coachford-Cork road. At this ford about a year previously an I.R.A. contingent transporting a cart-load of munitions had come to grief in a flood). With or without (but probably with) the armoured car the convoy proceeded across the fields to Kilumney. The Bride bridge on the link-road into the village was also down. Their only chance was one of several river fords marked on the map between there and Kilcrea. The little river-road on the near side is still simply known as 'The Boreen'. It now carries an academic, sporting and domestic development that would have delighted the industrious heart of Michael Collins. Which ford carried his body across nobody knows — probably the first. It would have brought them out to the west of Kilumney village just about where the road bridge over the railway was demolished. The field they travelled on belonged to the Dennehy family who were also closely related to Canon Magner . . . 'My mother was Canon Magner's sister', says Miss Patricia Dennehy (who still lives there). 'She heard all the commotion, the noise and the shouting of men. She did not look out. Everyone at the time was afraid to do so. Anyway, all of the traffic at the time went in at that gate just beyond the broken bridge and across the field to the by-road at Cal's', she says. The lacuna in the heretofore unfinished Collins itinerary (which John Crowley has now filled in) is obviously authentic, but it raises some startling questions to be dealt with in due course . . .

The Leyland dashboard clock stopped at two minutes past seven-thirty p.m., Summer time. The firing lasted half-an-hour and ten minutes according to Tadhg O'Sullivan's watch (cf. 'The Tom Foley Story'). A Free State Army contingent from

Macroom scoured the highways and byways of Béalnabláth one hour later (cf. 'The Tom Daly Story'). But the book, *The Day Michael Collins was Shot,* has quite a large number of Republicans dashing or just wandering about the place for the remainder of the night, wondering about the possibility of a round-up, picking up various objects in the process and discussing the (hitherto unknown) course of events. The actual battle, across which the political divide is still all too painfully evident, is treated as a montage of varying degrees of folklore extended to half a mile, whereas the reality was a mere three hundred yards involving one hundred of a lay from Long's cross to the first bend with an outpost two hundred away at a couple of stone-built gate pillars, neither group being aware of the other's identity or position due to the swing of the boreen. So many names appear in the narrative, some identifiable, some not so! Liam Deasy and Pete Kearney are presented as participating fully from high ground behind (i.e. to the east of) the Free State Army position, but Deasy says (in *Brother Against Brother*): 'From where we were (he does not mention Kearney), some three hundred yards from the actual position, we could see very little...'. Peter (Pete) Kearney is of particular interest. A native of Dunmanway, he had been a medical student in University College, Cork, but left with three others (Jerh McCarthy, Dr. Eugene Callanan and Dr. Con Lucey) to join the fight for freedom. At Béalnabláth he was O/C Third (Dunmanway) Battalion. Afterwards Pete Kearney went to America, returned later and went into business in Dublin where he died a few years ago. Until his death he was tormented with the conviction that he himself had killed Michael Collins. He had left Béalnabláth in charge of six men (cf. Tom Kelleher's B.B.C. interview, and 'Five Local People'), and headed across country towards Newcestown. At the sound of gunfire they returned. Pete was impeded by the fact that he had broken his arm in the process of cranking a Model-T (a common occurrence at the time for the unwary), or so he told his family, but he managed to fire a single shot at a man facing him obliquely on the road far below. The man fell. He believed the bullet bounced off a rock or stone wall to the rear and returned hitting Collins in the back of the head. This he confided before his death to Fr. Jerome Hurley of the Dublin Diocese, parish priest of Avoca and a native of Enniskeane in Co. Cork . . .

Aherla village, had they arrived there, would have posed no problem for the distressed convoy but Kilumney clocked in with several. 'Kilumney Bridge', as mentioned in *The Day Michael Collins was Shot*, is in fact on another road, the cross-road by the church to Ovens bridge. It was down. Jim Carmody's 'three fields and a haggard' (he is unfortunately unidentified) rather understates the convoy's predicament on the ground, but his extended yarn of the press-gang-hostage-guide-at-gun-point vastly overstates it and appears to be the maudlin meandering of an old warrior, if not plain invention, fifty-odd years after the fact. An earlier work simply states that a man sitting on a broken wall (where the 'forty feet' is just fifteen!) warned the 'Staters' to watch out. They had plenty to watch out for. Kilumney had three bridges, one . . . river, two . . . railway. Bhíodar go léir ar lár — they were flattened one and all! The Bride bridge to Ovens has been rebuilt, the others no. Their magnificent cut-stone architecture still beams through the briars and bushes. The first (Aherla direction) railway bridge went under the road forward, the second, over a by-road. Dalton led his men and vehicles by torchlight around the first and across two fields to the by-road; but Cal's (McCarthy) Field had a difficult incline and the Leyland stuck and stayed, being abandoned until late the following day. The Crossley and (probably) the *Slievenamon* continued on into the 'haggard' and through a passage-way, coming to a halt at the front door of O'Connell's 'Kilumney House', a hundred or so yards from the roadway. P.J. O'Connell, grandfather of the present incumbent, was a Justice of the Peace and a Treatyite. His wife was a sister of Canon Magner. At Kilumney House the soldiers were well received and victualled. They left 'about two o'clock in the morning' the family still maintain, and contrary o other reports. The touring car had bogged down in Cal's Field and Michael Collins' body had been transferred to some other vehicle, the family say. On leaving they turned 'up' at the entrance gate to a workman's cottage (still there). O'Halloran, the farmhand, lived there. He led them back down and guided them as far as Grange Cross from where they continued on the back road, south of Ballincollig, to Dennehy's Cross in Cork City, and so on to the Western Road.

Jeremiah (Miah) O'Callaghan of Grange, Ovens, carpenter, saw the Leyland Eight in Cal's Field at seven-thirty, the following morning, on his way to work, (This is from a friend who knew him well). From the appearance of the back seat he thought the skull must have been badly damaged. He removed a small revolver and 'shammy' holster from a pocket of the car. (Note: This gun is now in the Clonakilty museum. It looks like a derringer but is in fact an odd-shaped five-cylinder revolver, about thirty-calibre, with no markings at all). Then the locals began to gather round. They were interested in souvenirs. Someone took a pincers (also in Clonakilty). Sis Walsh from the local public house (who later married John Forde, N.T., of Innishannon) found and retained an empty bullet case. Tim Bowen removed the fine brass dashboard clock (pictured elsewhere and in private hands), and another man (unremembered) picked up Dalton's magnificent long torch, held it a moment, put it back and regretted his punctiliousness ever afterwards. The cold light of dawn was a far remove from Mrs. Madge O'Connell's fainting in the night at the sight of Michael Collins' lifeless body in the light from her front door, at nearby Kilumney House. And it is passing strange (from an era of some quite strange stories) that the book, *The Day Michael Collins was Shot*, has the Leyland motor car arriving in Cork City around midnight with his body in the back seat, where, in a blaze of light and with guards standing to attention in front of the Imperial Hotel, South Mall, it was subjected to a medical and military inspection.

*   *   *

Professor Cormac Mac Carthaigh (McCarthy) of Glanmire Cork, died in the Autumn of 1989, aged eighty-three. He was a true 'Gaeilgeoir' i.e. a dyed-in-the-wool enthusiast for all things Irish. He founded an Irish language periodical (named *AGUS* and inaugurated a number of Irish-speaking schools for children. He was probably the last expert on Béalnabláth, having gained a national reputation for his research into the circumstances surrounding the death of Michael Collins, tending however, in the Irish way towards reading too much into too little. Just a fortnight before his death (October, 1989) the Irish language newspaper *ANOIS* published his review of *The Day Michael Collins was Shot*. Some excerpts herewith in translation:

It is hard to imagine why this book was ever written or published . . From page one to page two hundred (last page) the book is full of misinformation . . . Many of the people in the book were not present at all at the time, including Sonny O'Neill. We (that is, O'Neill's family and himself) have incontrovertible evidence that he was not there . . 'Fr. O'Brien' from the Sacred Heart church (in Cork City) did not anoint Collins — the church had no priest of that name. Nor did any other priest. The body was not taken as far as the Imperial Hotel. They had thrown it on the Crossley tender . . . and it was left on the side of the Western road . . . When Dalton arrived at the Imperial Hotel he ordered his aid, Frank O'Friel, to remove the body . . . and take it to Shanakiel which was being used (i.e. as a hospital) by British ex-soldiers. Dalton told me (later) that he had ordered the body to be taken to the Mercy Hospital (nearer the centre of the city), but O'Friel was certain that he had said Shanakiel . . . It is strange that only one of the photographs taken at Shanakiel was published — the one with the (new) bandage. Why were the ones which showed two holes in Collins' forehead (Note: There is no reference to this item anywhere else. Author.) not published? . . . With regard to the cap in the museum (i.e. the National Museum in Dublin), Dalton admitted to me that it was his but that (William T.) Cosgrave had asked for it to be put on display in his office . . . I asked him who tore the cap. He said he did not know but that it probably had been done in Cosgrave's office. Dalton admitted that he might have killed Collins by accident . . . I could continue on showing the inaccuracy from page to page but it is not worth it!

Well, perhaps there never was or will be an expert on Béalnabláth!

*   *   *

The old-time animosity, the for-or-against Dev: for-or-against Collins element though still felt and expressed, is of little concern any longer. Apart from one extraordinary coincidence (Michael Galvin, father of two and brother of Shawno, was killed at the nearby Lissarda ambush, 22 August 1920, and the event is still commemorated unnoticed on the evening of the much publicised Béalnabláth celebration every year), there are such glaring inconsistencies as Kilmichael (Ned Young, the last survivor of the famous battle died only last year) being celebrated only by die-hard Republicans while Béalnabláth is duly attended mostly by devotees of the Free State persuasion. Obviously the discrepancies encountered in Mrs. Ryan's book may still be of concern in the context of our country's history. A misreading of her own interview (1973) with 'Sando' [sic] has people and places in a state of almost inextricable topsy-turvydom. The two villages — ten cranky miles apart — of Ballingeary and Ballymakeera (Ballyvourney) become inter-changeable, as do the homes of James O'Leary of Gortafludig, Ballingeary, where Dev was residing, and Danny Arthur O'Leary's 'Hibernian Hotel', Ballymakeera, headquarters 'pro tem' of the First Cork Brigade under the command of Dan ('Sandow') O'Donovan (since Brigadier Seán O'Hegarty, brother of P.S. O'Hegarty, had opted for neutrality). The 'Paddy O'Sullivan' who becomes prominent in the interview (supra) was Paddy 'Donagh Owen' O'Sullivan, Vice-Commandant of the Eighth (Ballyvourney) Battalion. Paddy Donagh Owen was certainly 'on guard duty' outside the Hibernian Hotel for the Dev-Sandow conference on that Sunday morning of 20 August 1922, but he did not perform the virtually impossible task of driving De Valera in a pony-trap from Ballyvourney to Moneygave, near Béalnabláth, on Monday morning, 21 August. Dev (as related in Chapter Ten) actually left Ballingeary on a bicycle on the Sunday evening in the company of Séamus O'Flynn of Fethard, but on the Tuesday evening of the Béalnabláth ambush Paddy Donagh Owen and Captain Patrick ('Patsy Burrick') Lynch (both life-long friends of yours truly) conveyed Eamon de Valera in a pony-trap from Ballyvourney northwards to Carriganimma on the second leg of his long and dangerous journey from Béalnabláth to the next Dáil meeting in Dublin.

Before leaving the book, *The Day Michael Collins was Shot*, and Cormac Mac Carthaigh's tirade, it is well to indicate a macedoine of minor errors that appear in the text . . . 'On Saturday, 8 October 1921 . . . he (Collins) became unofficially engaged to . . . Kitty Kiernan . . .' — the two letters extant do not show this. She was at home in Granard, Co. Longford, while he was in Dublin on his way to London . . . 'Officer's uniform which he had worn for the first time . . . at the funeral of . . . Arthur Griffith (16 August)'; but cf. p.33: 'On 12 July . . . he donned his military uniform' . . . 'Close to the oak tree (p.31)' — it was a sycamore. One of the row still stands. Jim Kearney's latest version of the 'cap story' differs somewhat from that of 1973, lacking a good deal of the now familiar flamboyance . . . 'Lieutenant John Joseph Smith . . . had his bike engine running' — this was Portobello Barracks, Dublin; but Smith only joined the convoy later that day in Limerick . . . 'The Rolls Royce armoured car . . . called "Slieve na mBan" ' — its name was, and still is, 'Sliabh na mBan', or the anglicized 'Slievenamon', as in the mountain range, but not a combination . . . 'Portlaoise Barracks' — it was known then, and for long afterwards, as Maryborough . . . 'His nephew, Seán Collins-Powell . . . who had already fought in the War of Independence . . .' — Impossible! In 1922 he was only seventeen . . . 'Dalton, a twenty years old, slim built, active man' — he was twenty-four . . . 'He (Collins) expected to return to his duties as Minister of Finance . . .' — his sister, Mrs. Mary Collins-Powell, confided to her friend, Nancy McCarthy (who told me), that he said he intended going to America where he had a brother, a policeman, in Chicago, because he said he 'expected only trouble and bitterness in the future', and asked for her son, Seán (later Chief-of-Staff of the National Army) to accompany him . . . 'Deasy . . . Crofts . . . Tom Hales . . . gave thirty-seven other men their ambush positions . . . Liam Deasy gave this number . . .' (Interview, 1973) — but in *Brother Against Brother*(1974) Deasy gave the number as twenty-five and said Crofts and himself had returned to Gurranereagh . . . 'Smith, having dashed back to the tender, warned the driver . . .' — amazement turns to incredulity from here onwards as we witness the public utterances of Smith, Dalton, O'Connell, on the Free State side, and Kelleher, Deasy, Hales, on the Republican side, being apparently ignored in favour of one likeable old gentleman who still lives with his parallax dilemma and contrary memories. (John Feehan, in *The Shooting of Michael Collins*, 1987, says, 'I would like to record with regret the death of William McKenna of Athlone, the last remaining member of the Collins escort.' No! Andy Caverley still lives in San Francisco. He is the last. He hails from Kinsale) . . . 'Hales . . . jumped in beside the ditch . . .' — but Deasy said that Hales was with himself in the pub for ten minutes, and Maggie Long saw them emerge when the firing started . . . 'The armoured car settled over the disconnected mine . . .' - it was nowhere near a mine at any time. 'Wolfe (Feehan spells it 'Woulfe') . . . reversed the armoured car . . . past the Crossley tender, touring car and motor bike . . . to Ahalarick bridge' — this is in reverse order. The *Slievenamon* was already at the rear of the convoy . . . 'Dalton called out to McPeak' — they would now evidently be five hundred yards apart and out of sight of each other . . . 'Collins . . . to the right of O'Connell and Dalton . . . moved further north . . . behind the armoured car . . .' — but we just left it away to the south beyond Ahalarick bridge! Military reports give that he moved in the opposite direction i.e. south towards Bandon . . . 'Eight Republicans from Kerry were hiding . . . across from Bill Murray's laneway . . .' — actually they were walking the old Bandon road on the east side and about a mile away . . . 'Mike Donoghue and Bobs Doherty were among a group . . . Bobs Doherty was about to fire a shot in the air when Mike Donoghue grabbed his rifle . . .' — the truth is that the two men until they died never knew of each other's presence at Béalnabláth. This item is wrongly culled from newspaper references of 1985 and 1988 . . . 'Dalton, who was not far away . . .' — in his documentary (1978) he points to the spot. It is totally different from any of the positions as outlined in the centrefold map of the book under advisement . . . 'Dalton . . . beckoned to Wolfe to bring forward the armoured car' — in the documentary Dalton said that Collins 'moved to the back of the armoured car' and, when Collins had been hit, 'I called the armoured car back' i.e. to reverse. As he said these things on camera he was just across the road from where the monument now stands — not four hundred yards away! . . . 'Dalton remained . . . numbed in disbelief as bullets whistled and ripped the ground . . .' — he himself said, 'All action . . . had stopped because the firing had departed' . . . 'High up . . . near Coleman's Rock . . . Deasy had a view of the entire procedure' — he himself wrote that he could see practically nothing, and 'Coleman's Rock' is half a mile away, over the hill and well out of sight of this so important battlefield where General Michael Collins died . . . 'Deasy arrived . . . fuming. He held a revolver to Jim Kearney's forehead . . .' — concerned for this uncharacteristic and futile behaviour, I wrote to Mr. Kearney. His reply: 'I never said that! Meda and myself have had a big fight over it' . . . 'Seán O'Galvin told the men that . . . Anne White sent the information to him . . .' — the man was not O'Galvin, nor O'Galbhin, as Eoin Neeson has it, but Galvin, Seán (called 'Shawno'). According to his nephew, Ned O'Mahony (in *MAGILL*), he had been to the forge in Crookstown with his horse. Ted Murphy, ex-London policeman, was now a farmer living at Pound Cross between Crookstown and Cloughduv. He brought the news and sent it on its way . . . 'Because Collins had turned . . . the Kerrymen . . . could not have hit him in the back of the head . . . Therefore this theory can be ruled out' — alas for the days of the rule-of-thumb Syllogism! . . . 'The

position Collins was in when he was killed has been established'
— except that it contradicts two *Pathé Gazette* photographs
taken on the following day! . . . 'Jim Wolfe saw Collins a
distance in front of the armoured car . . . "He was down from
us . . ." ' — this is totally at variance with gunner McPeak's account. (cf. Ray Smith's articles in the *Irish Independent*, May,
1971) . . . 'He fired to kill' — in 1971 McPeak said he fired to
frighten. His bullets shattered the slates on a farmhouse roof
far away on the hillside . . . 'The total number of executions . . .
was seventy-nine' — it was, in fact, seventy-seven. The very
number itself was to become a bitter catch-cry in the serious
political disturbances of the Thirties . . . 'So the "Slieve na
mBan" was towed away to the Curragh minus gun and turret'
— it did not, however, arrive in the Curragh until the Fifties
when it was fortunately saved from the scrap-heap by the father
of Sergeant Pat Lynch, its recently retired keeper. The turret
had NOT been removed but the Vickers machine-gun had, as
well as the speedometer and other dashborad dials which remained hidden in wall niches of the Cronin cowshed, Derrinlunnig, Ballingeary (cf. 'The Slievenamon Story'), until they
were eventually bulldozed into oblivion.

*   *   *

Nora O'Donoghue of Waterville, Co. Kerry, went to England
as a young woman in 1922 and became an army nurse as a
member of Queen Alexandra's Imperial Nursing Service. Forty
years later she retired and returned to Ireland, living in Killarney with two sisters until her death in 1974. Her army nursing
experience, however, had begun in Ireland, at Shanakiel
Hospital in Cork City. It was there, in the early morning of 23
August 1922, she helped the matron, Eleanor Gordon, to lay
out the body of Michael Collins. A blood-stained and bullet-
holed carriage rug had been delivered with the body. The
matron told her to take it away and wash it. In some strange
fashion it remained in her possession until 1965 when, at a
political rally in Killarney, she put it into the hands of Cork

solicitor, Mr. Brendan O'Connell, for safe keeping. He presented this extraordinary souvenir to the present writer in 1990. Its history is as follows: It is of the type known as a 'knee rug' which was used extensively in pony-traps and motor cars in the long ago. It is of pure wool, unprocessed, and is woven in an intricate pattern of Green, White and Gold, the national colours of this country, worked with natural dyes from the local vegetation of Co. Mayo. It was a once-off job, the prime mover in its creation being Mother Mary Arsenius of the Irish Sisters of Charity, Providence Woollen Mills, Foxford. She was aided by Mr. Tom Turnbull, Scottish designer at the mills. The time was July, 1922, and the rug was meant as a present for Michael Collins, the newly appointed Commander-in-Chief of the National Army. Because of harassment by both sides in the incipient Civil War, Mother Arsenius decided to close the mills for six weeks. A skeleton staff was retained to complete an order of woollen goods for Dublin outlets. The rug was packaged separately (with no identification label), addressed simply to 'Michael Collins, c/o Dublin Castle', and included in the larger consignment sent to the capital. He must have been pleased. He took it with him on his tour of inspection to the South in August. (The original is now in the National Museum, Dublin, while the Foxford Mills have done some exact and beautifully executed reproductions, through the good graces of the resident Latvian designer, for the Collins Centenary). But the story has more to it than meets the eye. Mother Arsenius was born Agnes Morrogh-Bernard in Cheltenham, England, her father an absentee landlord with an estate in Kerry, her mother of an aristocratic English family named Blount. She had come to Dublin to join the Irish Sisters of Charity, went on to Mayo and founded the famous woollen mills in 1892 in a successful effort to help the particularly distressed population of the Foxford region (being mainly backed by a Protestant, North of Ireland mill owner, freemason and member of the Orange Order. In due course, by the use of influence in high places, she vanquished a high-ranking Black and Tan officer for local atrocities. Known locally as 'Mrs. Morrogh-Bernard', this deformed English lady — of whom the present President of Ireland, and the first lady President, Mrs Mary Robinson, is a descendant on a collateral line — was truly a valiant woman!). In 1921 she formulated plans for extending the mills and building a new chapel (her stated motto was 'Providence'), but was restrained by both civil and religious authorities. Soon after the signing of the Anglo-Irish Treaty (6 December 1921), however, she suddenly and unaccountably got complete clearance for her plans and by the Spring of 1922 was already in the process of going to work on the building scheme. One can detect the hidden hand of Collins who, at the signing of the Treaty, had set out immediately to revitalize the country's badly shaken industrial base. The rug was a gesture of thanks to the benefactor . . . At Summerhill, Foxford, eighty-eight-year-old (1990) Mrs. Mary Molloy (née Foy) still lives on serenely remembering the time when, as a privileged young woman, she had actually worked on the rug that was sent as a gift to General Michael Collins and which was in his motor car on the evening that he died in faraway Béalnabláth.

*   *   *

There was no inquest into the death of Michael Collins, nor was there much in the form of an autopsy, a fact which has exercised historians, agitated politicians and bemused the general populace ever since. There was, however, an inquiry on the spot. It was carried out by the new 'Civic Guards' on the orders of the new Government. Neither the report nor its findings was ever published, and its whereabouts have never been ascertained. This special inquiry was conducted by Sergeant John Hickey, Lixnaw, Co. Kerry, currently stationed in Crookstown. He was aided by Sergeant L.P. Clear, of Tipperary, and a third unnamed member of the Force. The investigation extended over a period of six months from January, 1924, and was sent to the Government through the usual police channels. A résumé from memory (by Hickey) appeared in the *Evening*

Herald, Dublin, in September, 1970, and more extensively in a series of three instalments in the now defunct *Limerick Echo* in August, 1972. To say that both accounts contradict everything and everybody to date is only a slight exaggeration, and John Hickey's (by then retired from the 'Garda Síochána') choice of candidate for the doubtful honour of shooting Michael Collins, not stated in the résumé though written, he said, into the original report, was obviously Tom Kelleher and not the by now (1990) much publicized Sonny O'Neill; and his reason for the return of the Collins party to the Crookstown region was in order to consult Canon Treacy, parish priest, on the urgent matter of peace negotiations — based mainly on a number of interviews with the priest's housekeeper. The 'Dark Secret' gains nothing, and there appears only an extension of the ever lengthening Shadow of Béalnabláth!

*   *   *

Yanna's Tale: She was christened Julianna Hurley. 'Yanna' came to her by 'second intention' as her mother had been a family governess in Vienna at the height of its glory and on one occasion had dinner with the Emperor Francis Joseph. She is now Mrs. O'Callaghan of Newcestown, a sprightly eighty-five-year old, to whom the battle at Béalnabláth is still a living memory, and whose husband had fought against the British at Crossbarry. 'Total recall' is how an American would term it. From her old home at Mallowgaton, on the road to Bandon, she, like so many others, heard the shooting on that historic evening. Moreover, she had seen the convoy pass, a few minutes previously, while she worked in the 'Barley Field' beside the road with her father and other family members. Her next-door neighbour was engineer John O'Callaghan, the only Republican casualty at Béalnabláth. He was wounded but did not die from his wound, a couple of years later, as has been said, but from an illness incurred in the hardship of the times. On the following day, around four o'clock in the afternoon, Yanna Hurley drove with her older sister, Aggie, and younger brother, Mossie, to Bellmount Mills, Crookstown. They travelled in a horse-cart and brought oats for milling. At Béalnabláth they stopped the horse and walked about to inspect the scene of battle. Aggie, who later became a teacher in England, was not only a rabid Republican but an avid photographer and happened to have the camera with her. One of her pictures in sepia, which is still in a family album, is of enormous historic import. Across the little road from where the monument now stands they found a large congealed bloodstain, 'like a bastable cake', and just beside it a white, starched linen collar standing upright and round. On the left side it had a bloodstained bullet hole. Having photographed the sad remains, Aggie took her sister and brother on a tour of the Republican position on the back road. On the one hundred yards stretch from Long's crossroads to the first bend they saw the impressions of the gunmen on the fence. They counted nine. They collected thirty-six empty rifle-bullet cases and brought them with the collar home to Mallowgaton. These mementoes remained in the house until 1941 when their mother got tired of seeing them around, buried the shells and burned the collar.

Yanna adds a further observation of her own. The convoy, she said, did not leave Bandon on the Convent Hill, as has been stated, but went back out on the Clonakilty road about three miles to Gaggin church, turned right there at the crossroads, continued on to Tinker's Cross on the Dunmanway road, crossed over to the 'Creamery Line' and continued on under Carhue Hill to meet the Crookstown road a short distance from Mallowgaton, and so on to Béalnabláth. That was, she remembers, the indisputable local version and there seems no reason to doubt it.

With regard to the photograph, her assumption is that Michael Collins wore a detachable collar and tie under his uniform, and in the effort to drag his body across the road to the armoured car position the collar had come away in the hand of Commandant Seán O'Connell. How it got a bullet hole in it in the left side is still, therefore, a matter for historical debate, and a further observation deepens the mystery because another brother, Jerry, a medical student (latterly Dr. Hurley of 'Mount Alvernia' Hospital, Mallow) was informed by Dr. Christy Kelly, who examined and photographed the remains at Shanakiel Hospital, that he had noticed a distinct singeing of the hair on the left side as if Collins had been shot at close range with a revolver. Perhaps one of the British officers in the convoy succeeded in 'getting the bastard' in the end!

14

The Michael Collins Story: 'In Great Haste'

Perhaps all our loves are merely hints and symbols; vagabond-language scrawled on gate-posts and paving-stones along the weary road that others have tramped before us; perhaps you and I are types, and this sadness which sometimes falls between us springs from disappointment in our search, each straining through and beyond the other, snatching a glimpse now and then of the shadow which turns the corner always a pace or two ahead of us. (Evelyn Waugh: *Brideshead Revisited*).

Those thought-provoking words were written by a master of the English language some twenty-two years after the death of Collins. They could not, I think, have been written by any other. Still, the complete import of that passage sears through the two hundred or so letters which passed between Michael Collins and Kitty Kiernan throughout one year (August 1921-August, 1922), a year which may fairly be judged as the most perilous and destiny-ridden in all of Irish History. Ireland, I think, may have suffered, may be suffering, as an indirect consequence of those letters.

That the letters were written at all is a source of amazement; but one looks in vain for any trace of elaborate or clever forgery. What then? It was a year of deadly confrontation at home and abroad — abroad, where the threat of immediate and

183

total war hung by a silken hair over the Treaty negotiations, at home, when brother ranged against brother, friend against friend, Irishman against Irishman, when death was the victory and eternity the sting. A principle was at stake, you say. What? Whose? A man of destiny, a man named Collins, in great haste dashed off, between events of enormous import, personal communications of the most trivial import while petulantly complaining that 'they', 'the other side', were taking an insane and unpatriotic stand against 'us', 'our side'.

And the lady . . . 'Larry met Harry in town. Harry said he was coming, but Larry doesn't know the day, I think. However, I didn't ask Larry. I forgot. It was Peg told me' . . . The intimate letters of Miss Catherine Brigid Kiernan, of Granard, Co. Longford, and Mr. Michael James Collins were edited by Professor León Ó Broin (d. 1990) and published in 1983 under the title, *In Great Haste*. To take them out of context is a temptation that is well nigh unbearable. They are so out of context one wonders why they were ever published, why, indeed, they were ever written. Collins was a type that generated devotion and hostility in about equal parts. He carried with him the seeds of civil war. All he needed was to meet a De Valera — and vice versa! His emotions were a turbulent underground stream hidden beneath the solid predictability and violence of his actions; his thoughts often lay too deep for tears, his tears too free for credibility. Did he protract his sweep to the South as an heroic gesture designed to impress the woman who held his mind in thrall? Was Kitty Kiernan the evil genius of Ireland's Civil War?

Letters about letters about letter-writing, about letters written, unwritten, post-crossed, misrepresented, misunderstood, hysterically re-understood, missed, lost, checked, re-checked, questioned, un-questioned. Words. Words. Words. A lifetime of words needed saying before life presently ended. What, one asks oneself, does it all mean? It was an age of social letter-writing when letters of thanks were written, and required to be written, for every single act or gesture of politeness or courtesy

and letters of thanks were frequently written in thanksgiving
for the letters of thanks themselves. Kitty Kiernan of Granard
emerges in print somehow as the age's champion of letters; in
History, with Constance Markievicz, Maud Gonne, Anne Dev-
lin, Betsy Gray, Grace O'Malley; in Literature, with Fionnuala
of the Swans and Deirdre of the Sorrows; in Drama, with Nora
Clitheroe and the Countess Cathleen. In any sense did she send
him to the South, his own place, with the Spartan mother's
directive to her son to come again to her bearing his shield or
laid upon it? The thought certainly crossed her mind. Did he
glimpse her pretty face, peeved, sickly and impatient, as he
leaped from his chariot at Béalnabláth to castigate his opponents? Daily and twice-daily letters (not to mention tele-
grams) for a year must have had some pathological issue while
Caitlín Ní hUalacháin, 'Kathleen, the daughter of Houlihan',
waited in vain for her man of destiny. Read in a vacuum, one
might be inclined to dismiss these letters as — young love! But
Collins was thirty-one and his Kitty was twenty-nine. For the
purpose of marriage accommodation, the Canon Law of the
time would have designated her as 'superadulta' i.e. beyond
marriageable age, said to be twenty-four. When one considers
that Kitty was five years beyond this margin and Collins himself
was actually beyond his prime, one sees the implication of what
one reviewer wrote on the publication of the book of letters in
1983: 'The book shows a new side to Collins interesting to all
students of the period and essential to a future biographer'.
(John Bowman in *The Sunday Tribune*).

A new side to Collins! He was not known as 'The Big Fellow'
for his height. He was five-eleven. Nor for his weight, though
he was sixteen stone at the end. That particular build, so ana-
tomically specified by Gogarty, is, in fact, a type. All of
humanity runs to types, such is the mystery of genetics, and not
merely among close blood relations. Back about the year 1943,
when the war was at its height, Mr. de Valera brought the Army
with him to visit Maynooth College. It was an emotional moment of time. The then 'Taoiseach' (i.e. Prime Minister,

literally 'Chief') had vanquished Mr. Winston Churchill on radio with regard to our neutrality, and Cardinal Spellman, of New York, who came to Maynooth in an ill-advised effort to whip up a bias in favour of the Allies at war, had been vanquished by the Bishop of Galway, the redoubtable Michael John Browne. The Number One Army Band played among the flower-beds in St. Joseph's Square and the Army treated us to a much appreciated and rare film show. In charge of such matters was a certain captain who added a film of his own making of the Army on Emergency manoeuvres. What struck me was that he fitted exactly the type as stated (I had read *The Big Fellow* by Frank O'Connor) and the rank-and-file, speaking with us students, freely agreed that he was 'the best looking man in the Army'. All well for its time, but at the present day a more complex world presumes to see into murky depths, to hear some strange and perplexing overtones. O'Connor wrote: 'Collins' love for men was so much greater than his love for ideas . . . Then he (a friend) noticed the old mischievous gleam in Collins' eye. "And now", said the Commander-in-Chief, "what about a bit of ear?" He pulled off his tunic with lightning glee. "I will not", said the other, scandalised. "What would the sentries do if they saw me wrestling with you?" "They'll do nothing at all", said Collins. In a moment the Commander-in-Chief and his friend were rolling on the floor'.

I have watched wrestling in Africa. I have seen a mighty champion laid low by a little man while the drums beat and the whistles blew in the sandy arena of a native village named Fulabantang, near Bathurst, in the Gambia. I have witnessed the physical struggles of big men and small men elsewhere throughout the world, and I invariably thought of the happy, exciting days when I too struggled vainly to ground an opponent in a little field beside Coolavokig schoolhouse. We called it 'rash-ling'. It was more than puppy-dog romps. It had an ancient lineage. It emanated from prehistoric pagan death-rites and, through the 'civilized' pagan Coliseum of Rome and other arenas, became perpetuated into the Christian wakes of the

ot-too-distant past. The physical touchability of the Celt was
n strong contrast to the psychological aloofness of the Anglo-
Saxon. So we find that in the native Irish ball games of hurling
nd football wrestling was an integral part. That is to say, until
he founding of the Gaelic Athletic Association in 1884 when
new rules were brought to bear to restrain the ferocity of prev-
ous encounters. Even so, the 'rashling' of those earlier games
had a set format and some recognized rules independent of the
play of the ball, or, as a member of the old Dublin Metropolitan
Players (quoted by Dagg from T.F. O'Sullivan) put it — 'There
were forty other players (teams were then twenty-one a side) to
ake care of it (i.e. the ball)!' More than anything, the sort of
thing that went on appears in the tactics of modern American
ootball. Furthermore, wrestling was commonplace in the
Ireland of long ago ... 'Wrestling was a recognized form of
public entertainment in the seventeenth century. It appears to
have provided a living for its successful exponents and to have
been governed by at least one or two accepted rules' (Edward
MacLysaght in *Irish Life in the Seventeenth Century*). Two
centuries later a high-ranking cleric had occasion to endorse the
varied physical sporting activities of the Irish countryside. In
his letter of acceptance (dated 18 December 1884) in response to
the invitation to become first patron to the new G.A.A., Most
Rev. T.W. Croke, Archbishop of Cashel and Emly, referred to
ball-playing, hurling, football-kicking according to Irish
rules, "casting", leaping in various ways, wrestling, handy-
grips, top-pegging, leap-frog, rounders, tip-in-the-hat, and all
such favourite exercises and amusements amongst men and
boys ...'.

What has this got to do with the life and death of Michael
Collins? Well ... he was born a few short years after the founding of the G.A.A. Into his youth and schooldays the old theme
of wrestling and 'falling' (i.e. felling or throwing down) by
foot-tripping entered largely as the only form of physical self-
expression and sometimes endured in the ball games themselves
despite the rules. (Two young West-Cork men, Dan O'Mahony

and Steve Casey, who were boys when Michael Collins was a man, became world-famous wrestlers in the Thirties). Bully boy tactics went hand in hand with physical strength and size and sometimes (as I remember from my own schooldays of the late Twenties and early Thirties), when the will was weak, the larger bodies became the butt of smaller and more aggressive opponents. In the Army of a later era (as I am authoritatively informed by a high-ranking personnel officer of the time, Lt Col. George McEnery), a state of perverted sexuality occasionally entered into this need for physical superiority. The same, they tell me, is to be found in the prisons of the U.S.A. Otherwise, homosexuality 'per se' (if one can visualize it as a positive phenomenon rather than a mere mental aberration) may be found in an over-refinement of the primitive. Half a century ago Dr. Halliday Sutherland found it so among the static hill dwellings and along the caravan routes of the Orient. Its concomitant is set in the decadence of civilization, in the over-breeding and under-producing (the philo- and miso-progenitive) activities of highly specialized living conditions. As a corollary, journalist Negley Farson, two decades previously, found collective masturbation as an occasional outbreak or epidemic in prisoner-of-war camps of 1918. But then he found the same in an indolent and suddenly agitated tribe of monkeys somewhere in the Amazon Basin, or so he said (from *The Way of a Transgressor*). Michael Collins was no pervert. His boyish yen for physical struggle in the form of wrestling was the ongoing flow of life that he had known, and kept pace with his intense interest in all things Irish, the Irishness of the country people he knew and loved. This propensity of his, this peculiar feature of his 'persona', as noted in some of the books, would, I think, have been glossed over or deleted nowadays in the light of the new tendency to make sex, in all its exaggeration and absurdity, the be-all and the end-all. Likewise, certain phrases frequently repeated in the exchange of letters as noted above, and which in his time would merely imply and be passed off as 'courting', would now be interpreted, are being interpreted, as overt sexual behaviour. We, here and now, are the perverts. Memento, Homo! . . . Michael Collins was a man of prayer. He prayed in Newcestown church on the morning of the day he died, as he had prayed, attended Mass and lit votive candles in the churches of Dublin and London, for his trials and tribulations, for his Kitty!

TIERCE DE PICARDIE: In musical terms it means a major idea to round off a minor theme. In Literature, as in conversation, it would correspond to 'name-dropping'. Let's try it a little!

a. *George Brent* was one of Hollywood's most popular actors and starred in over one hundred films. A 'Heavy' or 'Macho' type according to the needs of the film industry, he was married and divorced several times. Born in Dublin, he died in Los Angeles in 1979.

b. *Frank Duff* was a distinguished civil servant and an accomplished 'estimator' of his day. A member of the St. Vincent de Paul Society and the Pioneer Total Abstinence Association, he became the world-renowned founder of the Legion of Mary and may still be destined for higher honours in the Calendar of the Church. Born in Dublin, he died there in 1980.

c. *Coinneach Og MacKenzie* was an ardent Scottish nationalist who, in the early decades of this century, kept a bookshop in the Blythe Road in London. A distant relation of 'Scottie' (Ian MacKenzie-Kennedy, whose name in Gaelic read Ian Mac Coinnich Ulric. cf. Chapter Nine), he specialized in books of Irish interest.

d. *May Bellew-Usher,* of Drogheda, despite aristocratic lineage, was a fierce nationalist, member of the Gaelic League and enthusiastic student of the Irish language. She became a highly successful educator and founder of schools for girls. Tall, good-looking, oval-faced and stern, with autocratic bearing and piercing blue eyes, she was just the age of the century when she died in 1969.

*. *Philip Murphy* was an American Army sergeant who landed

in Normandy on D-Day in 1944. Noted for gallantry in action, he was one of the most decorated soldiers in the American Armed Forces. He was a native of Churchtown village (my village), and died in New York City in 1988.

f. *Marion Stewart,* of Rosslare, worked for the British Civil Service at Blythe Road General Post Office, in London, in the early years of the century. A member of Cumann na mBan, she managed to filter a great amount of information relative to the Irish cause as it was being passed through the Post Office system.

Those six notable people of divergent life styles — what could they have had in common? They all, in one capacity, and at one time, or another, 'belonged' to Michael Collins. George Brent was one of his dispatch riders and, later, a motorcycle scout in the Free State Army. Frank Duff was for just three days his private secretary and was the last man to shake hands with him as he left Portobello Barracks. Coinneach MacKenzie was a 'friendly Scotsman who admired the Irish boy, Michael Collins, who bought so many books from him' (John McCaffrey). Phil Murphy was in the Collins convoy and fought beside him at Béalnabláth. And the two ladies — girl friends of Collins, no less, whom nobody so far seems to have known about. Ivor Murphy (in a letter from Hounslow, England) vouches for the girl from his home town, Rosslare, with whom he worked in London. Finally, Sister Stephanie (May Bellew-Usher), of the Cross and Passion Convent, Kilcullen, fiercely Republican, who, in a rare moment of indiscretion in the early Forties, made the startling revelation to some of her more intimate girl students. What else!

15

The Larry Finnegan Story

Captain Lawrence Finnegan celebrated his twenty-fifth birthday on the Feast of the Assumption, 15 August 1922, having landed with a contingent of Free State soldiers at Union Hall, a little seaside village on the coast of West Cork. Despite the fact that its name in Gaelic is 'Bréantrá', the 'putrid strand', he had landed just the same. If he were religious-minded, which may be presumed he was, the coincidence of sailing by Adam's Island and Eve's Island on Sunday, August the Sixth, on his way into Glandore Harbour, one of the prettiest and most secure harbours in the world, he must have been suitably impressed and affected. His mind, however, was on war, Civil War in his own country, and the manoeuvre of circumventing the territory by sea was with a view to conquest. He is now ninety years old (1987), a retired Commandant (it is to be noted that this is an independent rank only in the Irish and French armies) and resides in an excellent nursing home 'in Dublin's fair city', likewise his town where he is quite at home with his thoughts and memories but for one small grievance that, following the death of his friend, Michael Collins, an undue preference was given to British officers over Irish in the new army of the new government of the new state. He left the Army in 1924 due to strange circumstances which have never quite been brought to light, the fact that a mutiny occurred among some Army officers of the time. It appears that General Richard Mulcahy, the new Commander-in-Chief after the death of Collins, had taken to a policy of replacing Irish officers with British. Larry Finnegan wryly admits that the policy was probably a right one because the amateurish soldiers of the new Free State, even hardened old guerrilla fighters, could not match the élan, the spit-and-polish, the battle wisdom of the traditional British officer class. The dog it was that died — Mulcahy himself fell victim! . . . 'On 7 March 1924, after the Civil War had finished, a small bloodless mutiny broke out in the army amongst members of the officer corps . . . a total of 115 officers absented themselves . . . "in such a manner as to show wilful defiance of authority", and a further 92 officers "resigned without having been absent since the crisis began". In the conclusion of the affair, the majority of the absconding officers were allowed to resign'. (Captain A.A. Quigley in *Green is my Sky*).

Larry Finnegan's memories of war begin largely with the burning of the Dublin Customs House. As a young boy I remember my father, in a mood of petulance, saying to his cousin, Captain Tadhg Twohig: 'Ah, it was a great pity — ye shouldn't have done it! Ye shouldn't have burned it down!'. For long afterwards I had thought that poor Tadhg (who had been involved to his regret in the execution of a famous spy in Cork City in the 'Tan' times and, for a country lad, had himself become a street fighter of renown) was personally responsible for one of the most regrettable events in Irish History, the destruction of the vital Customs House records. Far from it! The enormous — for its time and place — military operation was the work of the highly organized and active Dublin Brigade, later to be split so seriously in its divided allegiance.

*　　*　　*

'If it had been possible to strike effectively at the tyranny it represented without injury to the structure, the Customs House would have been spared. But it was not possible. The destruction was an unavoidable military necessity'. (From *The Irish* [Republican] *Bulletin*). It happened in the afternoon of 25 May 1921, just six weeks before the Truce. One hundred and twenty men took part in the actual operation, surrounding, evacuating and burning the building, but as many as two hundred and fifty were said to be variously involved in obstructing fire brigades and retaliatory military and police forces. Despite that 'Gandon's glorious Custom House still rises serenely above the river (Liffey) without any obvious concession to restoration' (Marese Murphy, *Travellers' Guide to Ireland*), the destruction was thorough and only the walls remained on the following morning. Two Dubliners, Larry Finnegan and Tom Ennis, had set fire to the top and ground floors respectively, and Larry was among the group of seventy-five Volunteers taken prisoner by the British as a result. Commandant Vincent (Vinnie) Byrne, still vigorous and vital and latterly a television personality, escaped capture by a ruse. He threw his revolver into the flames, stuck a stub of pencil over his ear and told the soldier who was searching him, back to the wall, that he was a timber merchant filling an order. As he did so he held out a slip of paper by way of evidence. The 'Tommy' said: 'Go on! Get out of it!', which he did. The paper was a list of weaponry in abbreviated form but the soldier did not bother to look. Vinnie is the best known of Michael Collins' personal active service unit, known as 'The Twelve Apostles'. His regular gun, now in an army museum, was a Mauser automatic which he used on 'Bloody Sunday', 21 November 1920, in eliminating two of the fourteen intelligence agents on the orders of Michael Collins. Vinnie's personal victims were American Lieutenant Ashley Aimes of Titusville, Pennsylvania, (referred to by General Crozier of the Auxiliary Division of the R.I.C. as 'Captain A'), prominent member of the notorious 'Cairo Gang', and a man named Bennett. (Note: The 'Cairo Gang', frequently referred to and whose demise was rejoiced in, is given variously as meeting in a pub of that name, meeting in a restaurant of that name, or as having been formed in the city of Cairo, Egypt, after the Great War and for the purpose of Intelligence work in Dublin. How the American got involved is impossible to say. His grave is still marked in Titusville). General Tom Ennis, who had been wounded and permanently lamed in the burning of the Customs House, in a strangely different cause fifteen months later handed over the command of the town of Bandon to General Seán Hales whose brother, Tom, was a brigadier on the Republican side and involved in the ambush setting at Béalnabláth which encompassed the death of Michael Collins.

*   *   *

'It was agreed that Major General Seán Hales and John L. (O'Sullivan) would set out by boat from Dublin with a number of men and land at Bantry Bay. According to John L., when the plan was put into practice, they had no difficulty in landing and capturing the town. Local men joined them and by the time they got to Skibbereen they had about 150 extra men'. (Meda Ryan, *The Day Michael Collins was Shot*). Such a passage, referring as it does to a vital sequence in the Civil War, causes difficulty for an historian with alternative information to hand. After the withdrawal of the British the Skibbereen barracks was occupied by pro-Treaty forces. On July the second, when the battle for O'Connell Street, Dublin, was at its height, these came under attack from the Republicans. 'In the early hours of Sunday morning a force of I.R.A. from Bandon H.Q., Cork No. 3 Brigade, entered Skibbereen in motor cars and lorries . . . The attack lasted until 7.00 p.m. on the evening of Tuesday, 4 July, when the barracks fell'. (From the *Cork Examiner*, 6 July 1922). The attack was carried through by Brigadiers Tom Hales (Third Brigade) and Gibbs Ross (Fifth Brigade). Tom's brother, Seán, was in Dublin interviewing Collins about the situation in West Cork. Gibbs Ross is of particular interest at this point. Catholic scion of a Scottish Presbyterian family, from Glendart, Bantry, he had replaced Ted O'Sullivan as brigadier of the Fifth. His committed republicanism encompassed his death while leading an attack on the

National Army occupied Post Office in Bantry within eight days of the death of Collins at Béalnabláth. There is a plaque to him and others who were killed with him. The bed in which he last slept is still preserved as a memorial. 'The anti-Treaty forces, or Republicans, were to control Skibbereen for one month. When news reached Skibbereen that 180 Free State troops had landed at Union Hall, the Republicans decided to withdraw. On Tuesday, 8 August, the barracks at Skibbereen were vacated and set on fire .. . At 3.00 a.m. on Wednesday morning the Free State troops marched into the town'. (Pat Cleary in the *Southern Star Centenary Supplement*, 1989). In the meantime John L. O'Sullivan was confined to his home at Carrigroe, five miles south west of Clonakilty. He had opted for the Treaty and 'when the division arose among the ranks of the Volunteers he was unable to travel openly to Skibbereen to join the National Army forces . . . because of the local strength of Republican forces, so he rowed from Rosscarbery around Galley Head to Glandore and walked the rest of the way'. (The *Cork Examiner,* 1 March 1990). 'We were devoted to Collins!', said the old man simply (to the present writer in 1989). Unfortunately there were others who were devoted to Ireland instead. They lay entrenched along the roadways.

Bandon was the ultimate objective when the Free State Army contingent, under Captain Larry Finnegan and Captain Paddy Kelly, landed at Union Hall quayside from the B & I boat, *Alexandria*. Larry said, 'We had with us about two hundred men comprising battalions from Dublin and Carlow'. On reaching the main road two prominent provincial towns, Skibbereen (5 miles) and Clonakilty (13 miles) lay to left and right of them respectively. They headed west. After vacating Skibbereen, the Republicans 'took up positions at Cork Road, and at Cullinagh and Smorane, on the hills commanding views of the main road', but the Staters marched in just the same. When John L. had joined them they headed for Clonakilty. Behind them Bantry was safe. Until the Collins visit (cf. Chapter Eleven) the town was in the hands of the pro-Treaty members of the local battalion under Captain Denis Cronin of Borlin. They marched eastwards. Bypassing Glandore they carried on and occupied Leap and Rosscarbery. Skirting the bay they made for Quaker's Cross on the way to Clonakilty. Trouble lay ahead, but the spirit of Collins was strong on the air of Woodfield. 'We had two fights on the way in', said John L., 'and General Seán Hales came out from the Bandon side to join forces with us'. In an afterthought (1989) — 'I could see the man next to me firing his rifle in the air when we could see them running'; and then, reflectively, 'Why did we have to start shooting each other!' In a pincers movement set up by Hales and O'Sullivan (whom Hales set up over the heads of the Dublin captains) they succeeded in taking Clonakilty. On the morning of Friday, 18 August, Hales had landed by boat from Dublin at Courtmacsherry, on the edge of the great headland formed by its own bay and that of Clonakilty. He had brought with him an eighteen-pounder cannon and a 'Lancia' armoured lorry. Just the day before, a special correspondent of the *Cork Examiner* had been on a motoring trip to Courtmacsherry with some friends. The town, he reported, was still in the hands of the 'Irregulars', but only just. Four of them marched nervously about the place with rifles on their shoulders. As the correspondent returned to Cork City through Bandon he estimated that about two hundred Republicans held the town . . . 'The complete destruction of the Military Barracks', he wrote, 'as well as the Devonshire Arms — a large hotel on Kilbrogan Hill, formerly used by the R.I.C. as a barracks — by the garrisons of these buildings seems to indicate that they will not defend the town'. On the way to Cork from Bandon the travellers noted that the Republicans were knocking trees and otherwise blocking roads as the troops (from Cork) were expected in a day or two. They took no notice whatsoever of the passers-by. Intense activity centred around Killeady bridge, just beyond Crossbarry on the way to Cork, which the men were attacking with pickaxes and crowbars. Their efforts were in vain. General Tom Ennis was to come that way from Cork within forty-eight hours and the Collins convoy could undoubtedly have gone that way three days later, had they so wished, instead of returning by Crookstown. Otherwise news ran late in the paper in those times, frequently up to four days. The *Cork Examiner* reported on Tuesday, 22 August: 'Bandon Captured ... A battle was fought on the outskirts of the town but the Irregulars did not resist for very long. They retreated to the country and the national troops entered the town on Saturday evening (19 August)'. They were led in by Tom Ennis. He had been first into Cork City on 10 August, but even at this late date a good deal of sniping and an occasional bomb blast was reported from the city itself.

Meanwhile Seán Hales had faced towards Timoleague and Clonakilty bringing with him the Lancia with the cannon on tow. In a state almost of urgent hysteria Emmet Dalton had sent a communiqué from Cork (from the 'Mulcahy Papers' for 14 August 1922) to Collins in Dublin for extra troops and equipment so that he might effectively hold the city and progress towards the towns throughout the county, which was his committment. A Lancia was particularly requested. (Note: The 'Lancia' armoured lorries were, strange to say, manufactured in Italy, in the Turin factory of Vincenzo Lancia, an Italian racing driver of the early years of the century who, like Parry Thomas, was an innovator of considerable talent. His 'Lancia' is frequently mentioned in the context of the 'Troubles' in this country as a heavy troop-carrier, stop-gap or floating barricade.) Marching north-west from Courtmacsherry the troops passed by the famous old monastery site of Timoleague which was brought into the mainstream of Irish 'cottage' poetry by the Gaelic poet of the late eighteenth century, Seán Ó Coileáin, another Collins, in his 'Aisling' or dream-sequence of ancient glory gone to decay, with strong overtones of Gray's 'Elegy in a Country Churchyard' and the paths of glory that lead but to the grave. They turned westwards to Clonakilty to help in taking the town, then northwards to Ballinascarty on the road to Bandon, 'walking, walking, walking', said Larry Finnegan —

the Irish expression, 'de shiúl na gcos' i.e. 'by means of the walking of the feet', seems very apt. At some point on the way Hales decided to mop up Kinsale, fifteen miles to the east across the estuary of the Bandon river. He sent John L. O'Sullivan with a squad to do the job. At any rate, John L. is the only one mentioned and that in two interviews given by himself, ten years apart, in the Sixties and Seventies, in which the way in and the way out appear to be confused. He told Calton Younger that he made the estuary crossing under fire 'with bits of boat flying' to get into Kinsale. He told Meda Ryan a somewhat different story that they took Kinsale on Sunday (the twentieth) but then found that all the bridges had been blown at their back and he had to ferry the men out again in boats. He had planned to rendezvous with Hales at Skeaf House on the Timoleague-Bandon road. But trouble lay ahead for both of them.

Bandon was a large centre and stronghold of Ascendency in times past. 'Even the pigs were Protestants', people used to say. The Earl of Bandon had been traditionally one of the leading 'Loyalists' in the country. Over his main gate in the remote past, supported by his mighty portals, was the brazen caption: 'All Hope Abandon, Ye Who Enter Here!' It was from Dante's *Inferno*. Consequently the river which flowed beneath these portals of Castle Bernard became the 'Bandon', and the bridge at the ford became the 'Bridge of the Bandon', Droichead na Bandan, the neat and sweet transmogrification of which only the Irish language is capable — a mellifluous adaptation far removed from the brutal 'official' Irish of our time which, like so many other things official and modern, has the look but not the mind of Ireland; and very much removed from Dante's 'Lasciate ogni speranza'. Bandon had been a garrison town during the Tan War, with three large enemy posts — the military barracks, the Devonshire Arms R.I.C. barracks, and the commandeered Munster Arms, then known as Lee's Hotel. Now the I.R.A. held the town but withdrew at the approach of the Free State Army on Saturday, and once again Lee's Hotel became the Military H.Q. for West Cork. But the Republicans still persisted in the southern fringes of the town and now on Monday, the twenty-first, a few miles out at Knockbrown, towards Timoleague, and at Farran Wood, towards Ballinascarty, they were entrenched across the paths of the marching soldiers. Hales cleared Farran Wood and made for Skeaf to join O'Sullivan and they both made for Bandon over the top of Knockbrown beside the old home of John L.'s father. Then they halted. At the far end of the decline was a strongly barricaded position. It was plainly in view. General Hales ordered up the eighteen-pounder, gave the gunners the range as half-a-mile and ordered them to load and prepare to fire. The gunners failed to respond. He turned to them and asked: 'What's the matter? I ordered you to load!' There were four gunners, all British. 'With what, Sir?', he was asked. 'There are three kinds of shot', they told him — 'High explosive shells, shrapnel and blanks!' Hales thought a moment. 'Use blanks!', he said at last — 'I don't want to kill the poor devils!' Two of the 'poor devils' were his own brothers, Tom and Bob. 'He was a great gentleman!', said John L. O'Sullivan in extenuation of his story. The blanks were used and apparently were as devastating in their ultimate effect as the high explosive or shrapnel would have been. Still, Eugene 'Nudge' Callanan, one of the medical students who joined the I.R.A. (later a doctor in Clonakilty) had a different story to tell. 'It was no blank', he said, 'that blew the hole in the road just beside where I was lying! It frightened the shit out of me!' And the road was clear to Bandon for the marching soldiers.

*   *   *

'When Seán Hales and his men arrived in Bandon they went first to barrack quarters in the Devonshire Arms . . . Hales sent John L. Sullivan . . . to Lee's Hotel where Michael Collins was expected to arrive on his return journey . . . the Collins convoy had already arrived'. (Meda Ryan in *The Day Michael Collins was Shot*). There follows a long, imaginative conversation piece construed between author and witness from 1974. This is difficult. First — the Devonshire Arms was no more. Second — Hales had been in Bandon to receive Collins on his way out on the morning of Tuesday, 22 August, according to other sources, having replaced Tom Ennis (who had gone on inspection to Kinsale). Third — if Collins had arrived before Hales from Clonakilty, it would mean that he had passed directly through the region held by the Republicans where barricades and cannon fire had just been experienced. Perhaps a friendly 'Caveat Ipse' to historians of the future would be in order!

*   *   *

Late in the evening of 22 August 1922, a large group of people congregated at the main door of Lee's Hotel. They were there to see off General Michael Collins, Commander-in-Chief of a few weeks of the newly formed National Army, known throughout the country as the Free State Army and in a divided Dublin as the Beggar's Bush Army. Among the onlookers was a group of Army officers. Captain (later Commandant) Lawrence Finnegan was there too. As it happened they were seeing Collins off on his last journey. Within an hour he would be dead. The time was approximately seven o'clock, 'New', or Summer, Time. The evening was fine but a heavy downpour (according to Larry Finnegan — others say just a 'Scotch mist') began quite soon. Some particulars relative to that sad but historic occasion are still (1987) clear in old Larry's mind. They have a certain drama, even comedy, which add to the poignancy of the moment. The news of Collins' death did not reach the West-Cork Command in Bandon until three o'clock on the following afternoon and was sent on to Kinsale where some officers, including Larry Finnegan, had gone on inspection. Hales and John L. rolled on to Dunmanway where they got the news a day later. The only communication with Cork City was by road. In Kinsale an immediate decision was taken. Fr. O'Neill, an Army chaplain, owned a powered boat in the harbour. In an effort to reach the Collins cortège before it left the city, General Tom Ennis and another prominent officer (who seems to be remembered only as 'Skeef' Murphy but was in fact Lieutenant James Murphy of Skeaf, near Timoleague) took the boat and started out for Cork by sea, the element by which they had arrived in the first place. It is a distance of twenty-five miles and it is not known what became of them. The cortège left at four. Larry Finnegan and another officer commandeered a second boat but all at sea they came to grief and had to abandon the effort.

Larry Finnegan's memory of the storied *Slievenamon* affair is not only dramatic in content but fraught with controversy in the light of current writings. Here is how he remembers it. John McPeak, the machine-gunner at Béalnabláth, was a member (according to Larry) of a nationalist splinter group in Scotland with I.R.A. affiliations. He came from Scotland to join the Free State Army as a mercenary and was assigned to the ex-British armoured car renamed the *Slievenamon* (after the famed 'Mountain of the fair or fairy women' in Tipperary. Calton Younger regularly refers to it as *Slievenamon*, without the definite article, as if it were an aristocratic title like 'Lord Bandon'). The car had escorted Michael Collins on his last journey and the Scotsman was credited by many (especially members of the National Army) with having performed the technically impossible feat of shooting his Commander-in-Chief in the back of the head with the Vickers machine-gun while engaged against the I.R.A. in the opposite direction. After the burial in Glasnevin Cemetery (Larry says) the car had been returned to Bandon even though it had come from Dublin in the first place. It was parked in the yard of Lee's Hotel with a second one known as *The Big Fellow*. (It may be that the *Slievenamon* belonged to Bandon originally as one of its kind appears in a frequently published photograph of a British 'Wireless Section' in Bandon at the time of the Truce). The two soldiers in charge of the *Slievenamon* bunked together in an attic of the hotel. For security purposes the driver was accustomed to bring with him to his room the float of the carburettor. McPeak (according to Larry) knew them both. Some months after the

ambush he arrived at Lee's Hotel accompanied by two Repub
lican fighters dressed like himself in Free State uniform
Managing to entice the two soldiers from their room he stole the
vital float, got the vehicle started and drove away unchallenged
even by a sentry. An alternative version, often told, is that he
got a permit to remove the car for repairs at a local garage and
then absconded. (Meda Ryan has an extended and highly
dramatized version of the same event and yet another will ap
pear in 'The Slievenamon Story' in the present work). There
were three well known drivers from Cork City on the
Republican side, a garage mechanic named Billy Barry and the
brothers Jim and Miah Grey (whose father had worked for the
British Army in Victoria Barracks), one or even two of whom
must have accompanied the Scotsman on this escapade which
greatly improved the Republican position in mid-Cork for a
brief period. All three are known to have driven the vehicle on
some daring attacks against the Staters while the only alter
native gunner to McPeak himself was Mick O'Sullivan of
Kilnamartyra (author of *Where Mountainy Men Have Sown*
. . . The now historic *Slievenamon* is permanently on view a
Plunkett Barracks, Curragh Military Camp, Co. Kildare, it
Rolls-Royce engine still in perfect working order. It has go
honourable mention in the records of the British (Inter
national) Rolls-Royce Society, one of whose members is in the
process of reconstructing an exact model on an extant chassis
The *Slievenamon* is presently valued for insurance purposes a
a massive quarter of a million pounds. The premium for one
day's hire (in the making of the recent R.T.E. documentary
'The Shadow of Béalnabláth') was a round thousand pound
On special military occasions the old warrior is led out or
parade like a captive rogue elephant . . .

Old Larry Finnegan is also adamant on another controver
sial matter closely associated with the death of Michael Collin
at Béalnabláth — the extent of the Collins escort. He says tha
about forty men left Bandon with the convoy. He should know
He was in charge of the assignment. This would mean that thre

of the light transport vehicles, known as 'Crossley Tenders', were in the convoy leaving Bandon. From one to three have been mentioned even by men who travelled in the convoy itself. The Crossley (originally constructed for the R.F.C. — later the R.A.F. — in the Great War) was accurately 'designed to seat eight mechanics inside, and three on the front seat' (From *The Autocar*, 1915). It had a 20-25 h.p. engine and the men were seated face to face. The 'Auxies' used a bench down the centre and extant photographs show them seated five a side. So if Larry is correct the forty men leaving Bandon with Michael Collins (exclusive of his drivers and the complement of the *Slievenamon*) could have more than filled three Crossleys. Perhaps two of the lorries swung back by Newcestown after reaching Mossgrove crossroads. Certainly Collins had an altercation with Seán Hales with regard to his security before leaving the town. The last remaining (1990) member of the convoy is Andy Caverley, a Kinsale man living with his ailing wife in Alameda, San Francisco. Even though he has admitted the fact, he has so far refused to speak on the matter. John Feehan (in *The Shooting of Michael Collins*) gives an Athlone man as the last survivor, whose name he was unable to divulge until the man's death a few years ago. And so the old soldier, Commandant (retd.) Lawrence Finnegan, reclines in his favourite chair in his neat little room somewhere in the Northside of Dublin, dreaming placidly of:

> Old, unhappy far-off things
> And battles long ago,

with nothing more fearful to disturb his well-earned and heartily enjoyed tranquility than a buxom and bustling Reverend Mother.

*   *   *

'No!', said sprightly old Mrs. Eileen O'Brien of O'Connell Street, Kinsale, emphatically — 'Father (Hugh) O'Neill was not an Army chaplain, nor did he own a boat!' He was,

however, a native of the town and was currently stationed i
Bandon. But he did help the Army in two matters — he foun
them a chaplain and he found them a boat. A priest of th
Southwark diocese (London) was presently staying with Fathe
Fitzgerald, the curate in Kinsale. He was under a cloud of som
kind, she said. The Army snapped him up. The boat belonge
to her brother, William Deasy. It was a rather large launch wit
an inboard motor and was named the *Diana*. The family used i
for taking friends on pleasure-trips on the river. It could ac
commodate up to twenty people. Mrs. O'Brien still treasures
picture of the *Diana* taken at the time, but the faces o
childhood friends in it have begun to fade from her memory.
local fisherman piloted the boat into Cork on Wednesday t
meet the Collins funeral cortege. Whether they succeeded o
not she cannot recall. The boat did return safely, howeve
because it was used once again on an historic occasion to carr
General Seán Hales into Cork Harbour in December. A
Queenstown (Cobh) he found a ship bound for Dublin where h
was soon to die by an assassin's bullet as he was investigatin
the death of Michael Collins.

16

The Tom Daly Story

Limerick, you're a Lady!', goes the song. Even so, she has had turmoil in her entrails with the sudden and overnight bringing forth of armed and hostile men as bent on conflict as any from the fabled Field of Ares. In March of 1922, while armed and motorized British troops still ranged the streets of that city despite the Truce of July, 1921, a serious confrontation developed between the pro-Treaty and anti-Treaty sections of the Irish Republican Army. Limerick naturally became a key issue in the festering dispute as it had been in historic times past and gone. Impetuous and die-hard Ernie O'Malley (author of *The Singing Flame*, inter al.) was Commandant of the newly formed Second Southern Division. Limerick City was part of his beat, a highly invidious part. The British troops were to move out on February 23. The 'Staters' moved in — and so did O'Malley. With him was Tom Barry. More Government troops were poured in. The British were still there. Republicans from the South and West were all over the place. In time this was to be the 'La Vendée' of the French Revolution, with investment from the sea as the threat and the fall of Napoleon as the significant outcome. A conference in Dublin, at what may be called the highest level, brought liaison and an uneasy peace, and the Republicans withdrew. Then the British left the city . . . At

4.07 a.m. on Wednesday, 28 July, the Civil War opened in Dublin with the shelling of the Four Courts, a request for surrender from Tom Ennis, on behalf of the Provisional Government, having gone unheeded. Ernie O'Malley, by now Commandant of the First Eastern Division, was inside. Tom Barry tried to get in and failed. Collins had made the strategic and stock error of seeking peace by ordeal. It was to cost him his life. Republican Chief-of-Staff Liam Lynch went to Limerick on July the First and occupied part of the city. Commandant Michael Brennan agreed to a truce and signed on behalf of the pro-Treaty sector, the first signing of its kind in that historic city since Patrick Sarsfield signed a treaty and marched out to lead his men into exile in 1691. The Government *pro tem* demurred. More troops were drafted in and the fight was on. It lasted less than a week. The Republicans withdrew and took to the hills.

* * *

Old Tom Daly, of Clare, resident temporarily in Fermoy Hospital, lifted his drooping shoulders, smiled at his daughter-in-law and said: 'He wants to hear my story!' It sounded like a favour. I felt it an honour. It was his eighty-eighth birthday, Sunday, 8 February 1987. He disregarded the switch of the recording machine, fondled his donated and favourite 'Mick McQuaid' pouch of pipe tobacco, and told it like this:

I was a private in the Free State Army from 1922 to 1929. I signed on in May of 1922 and re-enlisted about every two years thereafter. I had been a Volunteer and a member of the Republican Army before and during the Black-and-Tan War, and had engaged in 'cattle running' before the trouble really started. This period was known in Clare as the 'Eleven-months-grass' trouble. (Note: Patrick Kavanagh tells about it in *The Green Fool* but with a different slant). I am a native of Newmarket-on-Fergus, about three miles out of town. The Republicans objected to the big land-owners in the 'flat' lands so they drove the cattle off. There were about three hundred of us, with four R.I.C. in attendance. The R.I.C. were armed but took no action, just merely ooked on. Once I saw a policeman bend down to tie his shoe lace while we drove out the cattle. We drove out in two places in Clare and then went to Athea and Castlefergus. I got to know about guns while in the I.R.A. I went to England in 1920 and had no more to do with them, so when I came back I was free to go where I liked. In 1922, I returned from England with my sister on holidays. We both intended returning to England but there was a railway strike on which prevented us from doing so. (See Chapter Eleven for 'the revolt of the bottom-dogs'). We got as far as Limerick Junction but were sent back again and spent the night in the (railway) station. I don't know what the strike was about but they were allowing no one to go. That was before the Civil War, before any shot was fired. We returned home to wait . . . The trouble then started in Limerick. I was in Ennis. Major (Michael) Brennan had a recruiting station there for the Free State Army. He was a Clareman, from Meelick, and had been out in the Trouble. He was involved in the Haulbowline incident (referring to the seizure of the *Upnor*, the British munitions boat, off Cork Harbour), and had a price on his head. Then he joined the Army. Meelick is only a short distance from Limerick. I was from the parish of Newmarket-on-Fergus. I joined up in Ennis with Major Brennan just for something to do. He became a general later on. They formed a new column and a new battalion and then the First Western Division of men from Clare and (south) Galway. We also had a Captain Chambers, and a Lieutenant Donoghue who later had a chemist shop in Youghal. We were formed up and sent in to Limerick where the Republicans were in occupation. We surrounded the city. The Republicans started boring through the walls from house to house. They threatened to blow up the city. They were on one side of the main street while we were on the other. The Army authorities decided to save the city and withdrew from our side giving the Republicans a chance to withdraw (from the city). They headed for West Cork and Kerry.

In the meantime Major-General Emmet Dalton had come up the River Lee and had taken Cork City from the Republicans. I was only one night in Limerick and the next morning we were all put on board the *Garryowen*. She was a big boat but there was no cargo and no ballast to keep her steady and she was swaying back and forth. We were only at the mouth of the Shannon when the officer (captain?) radioed Limerick to say that all the men were getting sick. The officer was given orders to commandeer a cargo boat just coming in towards Limerick (up the Shannon estuary). It was coming from some foreign country with a cargo of cigarettes and drink of all descriptions. The decks were covered with barrels of beer (wine?). We were on the ocean on the fifteenth of August. We sailed the whole way up the river (Lee) and landed in Cork City itself. Some of the I.R.A. were still in the city when we arrived (Emmet Dalton had captured Cork City a few days previously). We were lucky. We slept in some club rooms down on the Quay. It was in the Square (Parnell Place?). There were about two hundred of us. We just lay on the floor. Then we came out the following morning on parade and had to head immediately for Macroom. We landed (in Cork) on the sixteenth and left on foot for Macroom on the seventeenth. There were no bridges on the way. They had all been blown up. The following morning another battalion arrived in Cork City by boat. They were called the 'First Midlands', from Athlone and thereabouts. They were not so lucky. When they paraded the morning after, the I.R.A. were waiting for them and fired on them from the rooftops and shot a couple of them. The Dublin Brigade were also in the city at the time.

Of my crowd only some of us had uniforms but we all had rifles. These were Lee-Enfield three-naught-threes. They had round-pointed bullets. (Lee-Enfield bullets were usually sharp-pointed and encased). We heard tell that the I.R.A. filed the points to expose the lead so as to cause more damage, because the lead bullet was covered in some metal like copper or nickel. They were called 'dum-dum' bullets. (N.B. Various forms of expanding bullets came to be referred to as 'dum-dum', from a town in India of that name where they had been originally manufactured for the British Army for the purpose of spreading on impact and stopping the charge of fanatical tribesmen. They were outlawed by international law, but in wartime have been the subject of mutual recrimination). So we set out to walk to Macroom. It took us a couple of days. The first place we got food was Coachford (i.e. on the northern road). We were divided up and sent into different houses and my group were sent to the Protestant minister. There were seven of us. We came out best of all. We got a big helping of bacon and eggs. I can't remember the minister's name. When we got to Macroom we were stationed in the 'Union' (i.e. the present 'Cottage Hospital' at the top of 'Pound Lane', or New Street, on the Ballyvourney road). Nothing happened until Michael Collins came to inspect us. He came twice (i.e. Monday and Tuesday, 21 and 22 August, 1922). He wanted to know what we needed. We had nothing. We hadn't a plate, a cup, a knife, a fork or a spoon. I didn't actually speak to him but I saw him close up. He was a big, strong man. He could be around the six foot and very broad. (The image of Collins as the 'Big Fellow' may have been due partly to the impact of his personality, but certainly he was a large man. His height is often put at six feet but that is so standard as to be a cliché. More likely he was five-eleven and Tom Barry, in his *Guerilla Days in Ireland*, says that Collins was sixteen stone in weight). He was wearing an overcoat. He had a bit of a cold but he was in very good form. We were in two ranks and he walked along between us. There was an officer with him making notes. Collins said he would have what we wanted sent out from Cork straight away, which he did, although he was killed on the way back.

When the report came to Macroom that Collins had been ambushed there were two lorries of us sent out. (Macroom post office got the message early in the night). We dropped the lorries and had to take to the hills. We didn't know if they were waiting for us or not. We stopped near Crookstown village and took to the hills. We had to surround the hills as best we could. We got no one. But I saw the cartridges and I knew that there were only a few rounds fired. The cartridges weren't there (meaning that they were scarce). There were no more than two or three men there, judging from where we found the cartridges. I saw one little heap of six or seven shells. The cross road was coming that way down (gesturing downwards with his hand) to the Bandon road, and this ditch was going away (swinging his hand upwards) in a kind of slant, and there was great cover in it. When they fired, the troops could not see where the shots were coming from (this was not subsequent information but personal observation on the spot). I was standing (later) in the position of the ambush (i.e. on the Bandon road) but nobody could point out where Collins fell. (This implies that he was hit while out of sight of Emmet Dalton and the line of troops, that he was beyond the armoured car and around the bend in the direction of Bandon while he ran to keep in view the three or more remaining ambushers fleeing over the hill in the direction of Kilmurry). Collins and his escort were gone by the time we got there but we knew already that he was dead. (Tom Daly seemed to have no bother with daylight the absence of which has been made into a distinct problem by historians!). In charge of our group was Captain Chambers from West Clare. He had been out during the whole Troubles, including the Black and Tan War. (The First Western Division, consisting of Clare and

South Galway, under Commandant Michael Brennan, had opted for the Treaty while the Second Western was against). I don't know what became of him afterwards. We were transferred here and there from time to time, but I was in Macroom for thirteen months overall except for a month's training in Youghal. After leaving Macroom I went to Rathmore, Co. Kerry. After 1929 I was on the Reserve which meant eleven months out and one month's training.

It was very rough in Macroom. There was a hill to the back of us, high up over the 'Union'. It was called Mount Massey. The I.R.A. had no bother firing down on us from there. We were out on patrol every day. There were no bridges. We used to have to walk across the rivers up to our waists in water. We would get a few minutes then to empty our boots and carry on all day with wet clothes on. There was a group blown up at Carrigaphooka (i.e. about two miles west of Macroom towards Ballyvourney). I knew them. They were all officers except one chap named Paddy O'Rourke. He belonged to us. He was driving a small lorry. We weren't there at the time. We were coming across from another area with one prisoner, and we were crossing a field about three hundred yards away when the mine went up. The Republicans put a mine in the road and fixed a grenade under it so that when the mine was lifted the grenade would go off and blow the mine as well. O'Rourke went into the hole and as soon as he lifted the mine the grenade went off. There were six officers and two privates killed. Some (parts) of the bodies weren't found for a fortnight. (Note: I remember hearing from locals when I was quite young that human flesh was hanging from the whitethorn bushes around the place. It happened eighty yards from the old Carrigaphooka bridge over the Foherish river, on the Macroom side. The monument erected on the spot has now been moved some hundreds of yards away to the edge of the new main thoroughfare, ill-advisedly, I would think, if for no other reason than to let the memory rest in peace in the quiet back-water. It gives the date as September 16, 1922, and the men who were killed are named as Col. Comdt. Thomas Keogh, Capt. Dan O'Brien, Sergt. William Murphy, Vol. Thomas Manning. Vol. John O'Riordan, Vol. Patrick O'Rourke, Vol. Ralph Conway. After sixty-five years old Tom Daly erred just a little). Then the Dublin Brigade took over the prisoner we had (he was James Buckley of Codrum) and shot him into the hole in revenge for the Dublin officers killed. As a consequence of this we grounded arms (the military equivalent of a strike) the following morning. Colonel (General?) Ennis came out from Cork and decided that we should go on leave in groups together, and he decided (i.e. fixed) it.

There was great excitement about the shooting of Michael Collins and we were out every night searching houses. We searched them on the way out and we searched them again on the way back. There was an eighteen-pounder gun at the Castle in Macroom. Sometimes it was fired from the Castle and sometimes it was taken about a mile out of the town to a hill called Codrum, to the west, but never beyond. The troops in the Castle (grounds) didn't know that some of us in the Union were still in civilian clothes, and once when we were marching along by the bank of the river (i.e. the Sullane), under Carrigaphooka Castle, they fired on us from Codrum but the shell exploded in the river and did no damage. We were at Renaniree (about seven miles from Macroom, on the road to Ballingeary) on a Sunday, at Lyons the egg merchant's, and the I.R.A. came above on the top of the hill and fired down on us. They had a barricade across the road. They also had the *Slievenamon* at that time. We knew that if we went beyond the barricade the *Slievenamon* would come on us and mow us down with its machine-gun. There was a man named 'Mac-Peak' (so articulated) who forged a pass in Bandon for to bring the *Slievenamon* out to the military garage and instead of going to Bandon, to the garage, he drove it away. We were on guard in Macroom, one night, and we could hear it far away tearing through the countryside. They had the *Slievenamon* for a good bit. There were eight lorries of troops left Macroom one morning and the orders were that there was no coming back until we got the *Slievenamon*. We went out by Inchigeela and into Ballingeary. So we stopped in Ballingeary that night and we put the lorries across the road so the *Slievenamon* could not attack us. We took to the hills the next day. Every house and wood was searched, and every haybarn. We had one man with a bayonet. He was the only one who had one. He used to poke with his bayonet in the haystacks and begor! he came to a reek of straw just above Gougane Barra, up in the hill there, and he poked the straw. 'Come here, lads!', he said, 'I've something here — 'tis very soft!' He poked away and we pulled out some of the straw and there was the armoured car inside under the straw in Gougane Barra. It was a farmhouse, just as you'd go up to the chapel, in there to the right. (It was, indeed, Cronin's of Derrinlunnig). The reek of straw was built over the armoured car. We all got spars and the next thing the reek of straw was gone. (Note: The Cronin family version of the incident will be given later in 'The Slievenamon Story'). There was only a narrow space between the house and the wall where the *Slievenamon* went down and the farmer's front door was beside it. The man said he never saw it going in. 'If you didn't', said Commandant Conlon, 'you'll damn well see it going out!' Mac-Peak's army tunic was in it. Well, we couldn't get it started. The principal part (rotor? float?) of the engine was gone. So we tackled it to the farmer's two horses, collar and all — some of us knew about horses — and pulled the armoured car up to the road and hitched it to a lorry and took it to Macroom, the lorry pulling it. The steel rope broke several times. The Macroom people were pleased to see it, because if it arrived there any time to attack us the eighteen-pounder would open up on the town. (Actually such an attack had been planned by the O'Sullivan brothers and Billy Barry!).

Commandant (Captain Peadar) Conlon was the commanding officer at the Union. He got married in 1923 and went to live in Rathmore (Co. Kerry). He refused to have a guard. He said he would deal with any trouble himself. I think he died last year, but I'm not sure. He was followed at the Union by Commandant Kearney. I remember once in Kilnamartyra the O'Sullivan girls made tea for us and delayed us with talk. We heard after that their brothers were carrying a cartload of rifles to Ballyvourney, covered in hay. They ran into the Dublin crowd and galloped the horse but the Dubliners shot the horse. The men got away but there were twenty-seven rifles in the cart.

(Signed) Thos Daly.

*   *   *

The old 'Union' still stands, or part of it, in its early Victorian eminence, its laboriously worked stone lying neat and colourful and true, with a large flower-bed where Michael Collins reviewed his troops early in the morning of the day he died and wondered, no doubt, about the great men who had fought with him and were now his enemies . . .

> In such a night
> Troilus methinks mounted the Troyan walls,
> And sighed his soul toward the Grecian tents,
> Where Cressid lay that night.

17

The 'Slievenamon' Story

The partnership of Rolls-Royce Ltd. began in 1906 with Mr. Rolls as the business man and Mr. Royce as the mechanical genius. They set up shop in Derby, England. Previously Royce had been interested in the construction of a more silent internal-combustion engine than heretofore. Rolls had a passion for aeroplanes, which hobby encompassed his death in a short time. The 'Silver Ghost' chassis-engine combination, 40-50 h.p., was the immediate result of their partnership. It endured to 1925. The armoured car version appeared late in 1914 but it is not clear if it endured as such. With frequent modifications a more perfected model was manufactured later in the 'Great War'. The latest models were built in 1920, in a batch of one hundred, and for some reason were designated 'One-Hundred-And-One' and upwards. For some other reason they were code-named 'Whippet'. One wonders if this latter were the result of some cynical turn in the mind of Sir Henry Royce who was a North-Country man. (Note: The whippet is a small sporting dog, in fact a miniature greyhound, and speedier, if one is to credit the enthusiast, over a relatively short distance than the standard hare-chaser, and has been used traditionally in the north of England by the tough coal-mining fraternity for chasing rabbits). Royce had become seriously ill and incapacitated but continued to design with true genius and aplomb. His famous motor car, with the correspondingly famous silver grill and red monogram, if not the absolutely most expensive automobile, is certainly the most prestigious of all time. The armour-plating and general 'décor' of the 'Whippet', while effective of its kind, seems certainly to have been unworthy of such exalted lineage.

The 'Whippet' armoured-car appeared in Ireland in 1916. At the end of 1920 the latest model followed the notorious 'Auxies', the Auxiliary Division of the Royal Irish Constabulary, and figured in many battles, its speedy and rather silent appearance being a rather frightening experience for the Republican element, as some of them have witnessed. On the cessation of hostilities thirteen of the cars were handed over to the Provisional Government by the British authorities and were individually named by their new handlers with a more endearing sense of humour and possession, e.g. *The Baby*, *The Big Fellow*, the names being inscribed in large white letters on the rounded front of the revolving turret. (A pleasant change from *Blast*, *Bulldog*, *Buzzard*, etc., as previously!). The most famous was, and is, the *Slievenamon*. Its designation, on front and rear licence-plates, was 'A.R.R.2', for Armoured Rolls-Royce No. 2. At the end of the Great War the Rolls-Royce 'Whippets' were sent to North Africa, and to the Middle-East to help Irish born General Allenby sweep the Turks out of Palestine. They were still operating in those desert regions in the late Twenties and early Thirties. Gradually becoming a substitute for Allenby's famous cavalry brigades, they were used in riots and other disturbances in association with the Egyptian struggle for independence, and in Palestine with regard to the heightening of stress between the new Zionism and Arab claims in what was essentially an Arab region even during the Turkish domination up to 1918. Under a mandate from the League of Nations, England endeavoured to administer that troublesome region for twenty-five years (1923-1948). The 'Whippets', appearing in many news-reels and photographs, would seem to have been very active in the early throes of the administration. Their motto in Arabic translated as 'In Every Place'. It is no wonder they were a terror in Ireland depending, of course, on which side one happened to be . . . Some days after the big battle of Coolnacahera (Ballyvourney, 25 February 1921) where the British suffered a defeat, a British soldier stood polishing a 'Whippet' just outside the gates of Victoria Barracks, high above the rebel city of Cork. Watched by a group of onlookers he fondled the shining metal, then stood back and surveyed the monster lovingly. 'Ah, you beauty', he said, 'If I only had you at Ballyvourney!'.

*   *   *

'During the war RRAC's played a part in subduing the Easter Rising in Ireland in 1916. Armoured car units remained in Ireland and, following partition in 1922, thirteen RRAC's were handed over to the Irish Army. One, *Slievenamon*, remains at the Curragh in Dublin (sic) — proudly maintained in excellent running order. In the early 1950s the armoured bodies were removed and the Rolls-Royce chassis sold with a considerable number of surplus vehicles. These chassis went for around £70 each and some were in almost new condition. One at least is suitably owned in the U.K. — its owner (garage proprietor John Malamatenios) is determined to rebuild it in its original armoured car form'. (Lt. Col. Eric Barrass in *The Rolls-Royce Armoured Car*). The machine would seem to be historically significant enough for some brief specifications. When this fighting vehicle, one of the most successful in history, came into being it was termed Admiralty Pattern 1914 Mark I Rolls-Royce Armoured Car. Its basis was the standard Rolls-Royce (Alpine) chassis. When fully operational and with crew aboard it weighed upwards of six tons. The familiar armoured hulls were designed and produced by Vickers in Sheffield and fitted by Vickers at Erith in Kent. The normal crew was driver, co-driver/gunner and commander, all trained to interchange. Winston Churchill, as First Lord of the Admiralty, was the instigator of the idea, aided and abetted by the flamboyant Duke of Westminster, the richest man in England. In 1915 Sir John French, the Commander-in-Chief, declared that he and the other generals did not attach much value to the machine-gun equipped armoured cars. In France they were nevertheless formed into 'Lambs' (Light Armoured Motor Batteries) and had the inoffensive animals painted on. The first setback was the use of armour-piercing ammunition by the Germans. The second was the trenches and the Flanders mud. Then the tyres created a problem. They were at first pneumatic with inner tubes, twinned at the back, at the enormous pressure of sixty-five pounds. They were easily shot out and a flat tyre put the car out of action. As an experiment the tubes were filled with a substance called 'Rubberine'. It only partly worked. Solid tyres were tried with transverse boring for flexibility. They were termed 'NAP' (natural air pressure). These were quite successful. Eventually static trench warfare brought the RRACs to a complete standstill. So they were sent to Gallipoli, South-West Africa, East Africa, and finally came into their own in the great land seas of the Lybian and Arabian deserts; and get honourable to enthusiastic mention from T.E. Lawrence (of Arabia) in the *Seven Pillars of Wisdom*, Sammy Rolls (no relation) in *Steel Chariots of the Desert* and Sir Miles Thomas in *Out on a Wing*. By this time they had become the outstanding fighting vehicle of the Great War, had given birth to the 'Tank', and contributed to the formation of the new (1921) states of Iraq and Kuwait, the explosive trouble spots of 1990. They had been in India since 1917 and were used against the French in Syria in World War Two. The famous 'One Hundred' (mentioned above) were the improved 1920 Pattern Mark I, the cars which arrived in Ireland to support the Auxiliary 'Terror' of that period.

*   *   *

Shortly after the death of Michael Collins the *Slievenamon* was spirited away from the backyard of Lee's Hotel, in Bandon,

9a. The W.S. Rogers' fantasy of Béalnabláth.

9b. The reality of Béalnabláth on Wednesday, 23 August 1922.

10a. The brass dashboard clock — in private hands — is all
that remains of the Leyland Eight. (*Photo: John Quaid*)

10b. The Monument (1924) . . . with the original plinth on right

1a. Free State recruitment in West Cork, with young Trevor
Roycroft merely posing front left.

11b. 'The Baby', companion to the 'Slievenamon',
with full complement.

12a. Commandant and Mrs. J.A. Smith, Oct., 1949.

12b. Jim Kearney showing where Sonny O'Neill stood to fire

13. The Spot where the 'Slievenamon' was found.
(*Photo: Fr. G. Casey*)

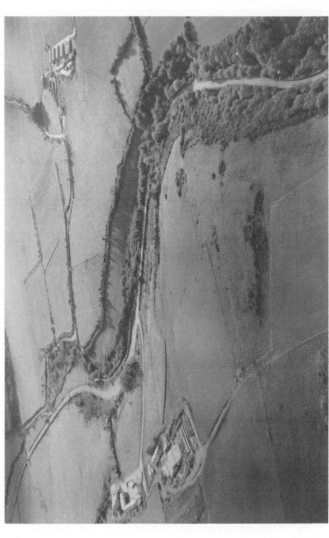

14. Aerial photograph of the Battle Scene. (*Photo: Daphne Pochin Mould*)

15. The Author presenting centenary rugs to Colm Connolly and Brendan O'Reilly of R.T.E.
(Photo: Eve Holmes)

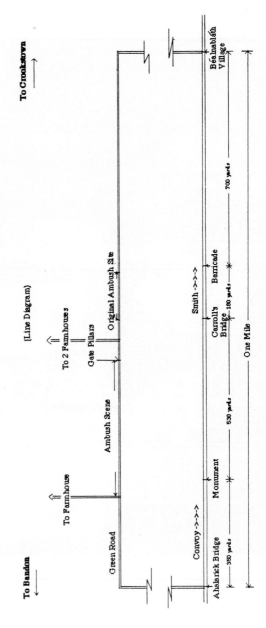

16. Computerized graphic of the Béalnabláth location.

(Katherine Walshe-O'Connor, B.E., Dip. Highway and Geotechnical Eng., M.I.E.I.)

and removed to West Cork into the custody of the Republicans (cf. next chapter, 'McPeak: the Mystery Man'). For a brief period it merited the attention of Ireland's most famous airman. Colonel James Fitzmaurice, as a young ex-R.A.F. officer, was commissoned in the Irish Army Air Service in 1922 and was appointed to command the air station in Fermoy. From there he did much reconnaissance flying during the Civil War. On one occasion, as he was returning from Kerry, his plane force-landed near Mallow and was burned by the Republicans. It was a Martinsyde 'Scout', from the same stables as *The Big Fella* (Martinsyde A Mark II biplane), the special plane bought by Emmet Dalton and two other Dublin ex-R.A.F. officers during the Truce negotiations in London and stored at Brooklands to ensure the safe getaway of Michael Collins in case the negotiations broke down . . . 'The next air patrol took him (Fitzmaurice) over West Cork in an endeavour to locate and bomb a Rolls-Royce armoured car which had been acquired by the Irregulars; he had to force-land once more, close to their headquarters in Cork City'. (Interesting but historically not very precise — from A.A. Quigley in *Green is my Sky*). Fitzmaurice had more luck in flying for old Ireland across the Atlantic, with a couple of Germans, in 1928, while Commandant of the Air Force at Baldonnel.

*　　*　　*

After the escape from Bandon the *Slievenamon* did not go directly to West Cork. John McPeak told the *Irish Independent* in 1971: 'We had one awkward moment. A soldier jumped on the back of the car and asked where we were going. I told him we were going out on a job and he got off. (In *The Day Michael Collins was Shot*, Billy Barry, the driver, is quoted as saying that the man was suspicious and hung on until McPeak threatened to shoot him). We were free. We then went out to a house in the country where they put us up for the night'. The house was Galvin's of Clodah, beside Crookstown village. They left early the following morning. It was well they did. Lieutenant

'Skeef' Murphy arrived with two lorry loads of troops and invaded the place. Nothing was found. The family had eradicated the tyre marks. The officer was very truculent but the valiant and widowed Mrs. Galvin gave him tit for tat, particularly upbraiding him for the fact that he had often been a welcome visitor to the house in 'the old days'. Nevertheless they were all carted off to Bandon but released after interrogation on the following day. The lieutenant left his binoculars on the fence of the yard and never returned for them. The glasses stayed in the Galvin family for many years until presented to a friend, Paddy Farrell, butcher, from Macroom, whose family still hold them in trust. (Mrs. Galvin — Mary Lordan from Newcestown — was the mother of big Ned Galvin, bishop to be, founder of the Maynooth Mission to China, the only man to my knowledge, from West Cork or anywhere, who could match big Mick Collins stride by stride, blow by blow, shove by shove, swear by swear, prayer by prayer and tear by tear — two conquerors of empires whose positions could conceivably have been interchangeable!). After a brief contribution to the Republican cause the *Slievenamon* ended up under a heap of 'lithar' forty yards from Cronin's front door in Derrinlunnig. That was where Commandant Peadar Conlon (next door neighbour of Seán McKeon in Ballinalee, Co. Longford, but 'hard man' in his own right) found it just on Christmas. He had been tipped off by a certain Denis Reardon ('Donncha a' Bhata') who lived in a cottage beside the road near Ballingeary and had the reputation of being light-fingered and a 'Tadhg a' dá Thaobh' — a turncoat. Conlon marched into Cronin's yard and set up a machine-gun right in the middle and facing the house. 'It was', Paddy Cronin, the present incumbent said, 'round on top' i.e. a Lewis-gun. The house was thatched and had a low attic Upstairs the old man of the house was sick in bed. He was Patrick Cronin — 'Paid Rua'. They questioned him but let him be. His two sons, Patey and Denny (the present Paddy's father) had taken to the mountain. The two girls, Mary and Ellie, were beyond in the stall milking the ten cows (this was eight o'clock in the morning!). A third young woman, Mrs. Denny Cronin (Abbey Creed from Oileán Eidhneach, across the river from Ballingeary, just married into the house) was in the kitchen. She was shocked and had to hold onto the stair rail for support. The two sisters and Mrs. Cronin were lined up against the wall of the little house and a firing-squad of riflemen was lined up in front of them. They thought they were going to be shot. Conlon barked: 'Where is the *Slievenamon*?' Mary answered. According to Paddy his aunt was 'a strong character, good to pray, great faith and wasn't the least bit afraid of them'. What she said was: 'Begor, Sir, I think you're gone astray. The last I heard it was a mountain above in County Tipperary!' His reply was a volley into the wall above their heads and mortar fell all over them. Just then Tom Daly and friends made their great discovery (cf. 'The Tom Daly Story'). The noble car was found under a heap of animal bedding between the stone wall and the cow-house. The 'comharsa bhéal dorais', the next-door neighbour, was Daniel McSweeney, known as 'Dan Mór' — Big Dan! (He was five feet tall and very bandy-legged from having been reared in a barrel as a child.) He knew nothing but was conscripted just the same and given a fork to remove the cover of 'lithar' in case the armoured car was booby-trapped. He went to work as if he had nothing to lose and when he spotted a nice hand-saw under the heap he said to himself — Here's something for me! He threw it over the wall when no one was looking. Unfortunately the handle hooked over a spar of bog oak supporting a gate, stuck on a splinter and was retrieved by the soldiers. (The spar still stands, a lasting tribute to the preservative powers of Irish bogs!).

Danny Leary, of the well-known family from Bawnaneel, was mechanically minded. He had dismantled some parts of the *Slievenamon* only the night before and was helped in camouflaging it by the brothers Jim and Miah Grey, from Cork City, Connie Cronin from the Gougane Hotel, the local Republican officer, and Jerh Shea from Ballingeary village (who had participated in the first ambush ever in Ireland, at Béal a'

Ghleanna, 'The Mouth of the Glen', 7 July 1918). Danny Leary removed the carburettor float, the dashboard instruments and the Vickers machine-gun. The smaller objects were stashed away in wall-niches of the old cowshed where Paddy Cronin found them eventually and played with them as a 'gossoon'. Later the wall was bulldozed and the instruments pushed into oblivion saving the onset of a new generation of archaeologists. The Vickers, however, has had an interesting career and is still 'to the good'. The first night it was hidden in a little rock cave above Cronin's farmhouse, 'the natest little place you ever saw', says Paddy Cronin, and, like the bog-oak spar, still extant. Two Free State sentries actually leaned against it while the search was on for the *Slievenamon*. Later the gun was moved to another Republican farm in the region, Sweeney's of Keimcurravoola, then to Glounthane, beyond Cork City, to the home of a noted rebel and public representative. That was in the Thirties. Following the trail of old and reliable 'call houses' the machine-gun arrived at Lisgoold, in East Cork, in the Forties. In the Fifties it was held by an American-Irish family in Glanworth, in North Cork, where Liam Lynch was accustomed to stay many years before, and from where it was moved to Dublin for the projected attack on Brookeborough Barracks, Co. Fermanagh. It seemed like the end of an odyssey visualized by Collins, and so many of his latter-day opponents, so long ago. The gun, however, failed to make the journey of destiny as ammunition belts could not be found for it. In the Seventies it surfaced once more when it was moved to the troubled Monaghan border for the purpose of shooting down British military helicopters. By now it had become known as 'the jamming gun'. True to its name, and Béalnabláth record, it jammed on the first attempt, was captured by the Garda Síochána and is now in military custody in Dublin, soon to be reunited with the *Slievenamon* in the Curragh Military Camp, Co. Kildare. The old bus has come to an honourable retirement in the workshop of Plunkett Barracks. The honour is somewhat tarnished in the book, *The Day Michael Collins was Shot*, which says: 'It has been alleged that the bullet marks on the turret . . . can substantiate a claim that a bullet fired from a particular position ricocheted off the armoured car and hit Collins. This can be discounted because the gun and turret . . . are not those which were on the armoured car on the day Michael Collins was shot . . . The Republicans removed the turret and gun section . . . it (i.e. the *Slievenamon*) remained beneath the furze for a number of years . . . until December, 1931 . . . the Staff of the Curragh Military Camp . . . took me on a trip (1988) in the *Slieve na mBan* armoured car . . .'. They did more. They unaccountably revealed information which the present writer gave to them in confidence in 1987 to the effect that I was on the trail of the illegally held Vickers machine-gun and would negotiate its reunion with its old comrade in arms. The bullet grooving on the topmost plate (8ft. 4in.) of the turret has been carefully triangulated to Mike Donoghue's position (cf.Chapter Four), and the turret is indeed the original having been found intact, not in December, 1931, as stated, but in December, 1922, just three weeks after it had gone missing. Truth is accuracy!

*   *   *

IL SABUESO

or

THE WHIPPET

(With apologies to John Milton, his
'Il Penseroso', and other breeds)

The War was raging; Rolls was dead!
But Royce dictated from his bed
To wartime draughtsmen, rule in hand,
At Derby, centre of the Saxon land.
Laid back in pillows, movement gone,
With motor-vision second to none,
He dreamed a dream of the 'Silver Ghost'
Spewing lethal metal coast to coast,
In Holy Land or Erin's Isle,
To dissipate Imperial bile.
A massive engine, tower of steel,
Sedulously inflated wheel,

A drab, incongruous hinder part,
Much as one finds a donkey-cart,
Completes the visual field-of-force,
So far removed from rabbit course.
Aristocratic frontal power
Propelled the ass-cart by the hour,
With eye of Cyclops spewing fire
To fuse the points of thorny wire.
Thus to the tribes of Orient,
And then to ultimate Occident,
A policy of do or die —
Theirs not to ask the reason why,
Those gallant hundreds, ten times more,
Would emulate the Lion's roar,
And show that Justice could not lie
In hewing the Treaty of Versailles.
Sufficient for the polity!
Let's scrutinize the harmony
Well synchronized by Henry Royce,
Which made his car the whole world's choice,
Without the presence of C.S. Rolls,
So long among departed souls.
In truth the year nineteen-o-six
Saw Rolls-Royce minions affix
A chassis to a side-valved block
And solve the curse of auto-knock.
For WAR the 'Ghost' would then avail —
Eschewing the mud of Passchendaele,
With Allenby to Egypt came
To share in his eternal fame.
And teach extrapolating Turks
How well the British drive-shaft works,
And hostile 'Wogs', upon the Nile,
The benefits of durance vile . . .
Then far away a cry was heard,
A cry that oftentimes had stirred
To ecstasy Westminster Chimes,
Appalled by all old Ireland's crimes:
The 'Ghost' then twitched his mantle blue,
And sought fresh woods and pastures new!

18

McPeak: the Mystery Man

Joe Curran wrote: 'I served in the Civil War under Michael Collins, and was a member of his firing squad to Glasnevin Cemetery. This firing squad consisted of fifty men drawn from 'A' Company, Second Battalion, Dublin Guards, of which I was a member. I myself am now (1986) going on eighty-four years of age, and my information of that time is that the gunner of the *Slievenamon* armoured car shot Collins. I would have to be talking to you to explain it all . . .'. Fine old Joe Curran, of No. 1, Oblate Drive, Inchicore, Dublin, was not alone in this strange opinion. Far from it. The whole Free State Army apparently believed it. It was the accepted view to the extent of being almost official. Some officers were so convinced of it that they tried to beat a confession out of Scotsman John McPeak and almost killed him. It happened like this . . .

A batch of Scotsmen came to Ireland early in 1922, during the recruitment drive, to join the Free State Army. They were stationed at Portobello (now Cathal Brugha) Barracks, South Circular Road, Dublin. Joe Curran held No. 3 Guard Post within the barracks perimeter. It was a dangerous position. From time to time fire was directed on them from the spire of the Rathmines church which could be seen above the wall. They dived for cover and fire was returned. On one of these exchanges the church itself caught fire. The *Slievenamon* came and went through the gates of Portobello Barracks and a man, whom Joe later surmised to be John McPeak, could plainly be seen in the vehicle as he travelled with the hatch open and his head protruding. The driver also was a Scotsman. Michael Collins had a house within the barracks (i.e. as Commander-in-Chief, though Kitty Kiernan makes no mention of it despite much correspondence with him on housing). After his death the house was occupied by General Richard Mulcahy. Joe frequently saw Collins in Portobello Barracks. He was the soul of propriety (said the old man) as Commander-in-Chief and as an Army man. There was never any evidence, as the story went, that he got drunk late at night and went roaring about the barrack-square. Joe always had to present arms as Collins passed by. However, he sometimes sat at his sentry post through weariness. On one occasion Collins caught him at it. As he jumped up to present arms Collins said, 'Soldier, you are asked to stand for only two hours! That's how Dundalk was lost!' 'We were beaten in Dundalk', Joe explained. Dundalk town had been under the control of General Frank Aiken and three hundred men of the Fourth Northern Division, who intended to remain neutral. The Free State Army captured the town while Frank, a northern Protestant, later to be a cabinet minister of high repute, was in Dublin negotiating with Richard Mulcahy as Minister for Defence. The town was re-taken by the Republicans on August 13. So Corporal (peacetime carpenter) Joseph Curran's 'run-in' with his Commander-in-Chief had to be on 14 August, the day before Arthur Griffith's funeral. Less than two weeks later Joe could have said something scathing (under his breath!) as he stood beside the renowned Commandant Vinnie Byrne and waited for Lieutenant (later Colonel) Harry Murphy to give the order to 'Present Arms' in Glasnevin Cemetery at the burial of Michael Collins.

'A few months after Collins was buried', Joe Curran said, he was stationed in Richmond Barracks, Dublin. At five o'clock one morning he and some other men 'were pulled out of bed'.

Joe saw a man in a grey trench coat and leggings standing there. The men had apparently been selected at random. The stranger, who was not in uniform, preceded them down the stairs and when they arrived in the yard he was standing beside a Crossley tender with a driver at the wheel. Without any identification, or insignia of rank, this man gave orders and they took them. There were three other men besides Joe himself. They all climbed aboard the Crossley, carrying their rifles, and proceeded to the B. & I. wharf at the North Wall. It was 5.30 a.m. when they arrived and 'a big ship from abroad' was berthed there. Two plainclothes men and a prisoner descended the slipway. He was put on board the Crossley and they all returned to barracks. The prisoner looked about twenty-four. On the return journey Joe got an opportunity of speaking to him and on hearing the accent asked him if he were a Scotsman and he said, Yes, he was. McPeak (for it was he) was 'kept a prisoner in the Depot' awaiting trial for the alleged killing of Michael Collins. The Army at the time had no legal procedures for major crimes committed by soldiers. They were tried by the civil court. McPeak was in Richmond Barracks awaiting trial for about a month. When the time came he denied the charge and was acquitted for lack of evidence. A short time after his arrival as a prisoner from abroad an attempt was made to force a confession out of him. Two high-ranking officers arrived in a motor car at the gate of Richmond Barracks at 2 a.m. Sergeant Moore (Joe could not remember his first name) was the duty officer at the guardroom. As the sergeant reported it later, one of the officers said — 'Where is he?', obviously meaning McPeak, and they ordered him to hand the prisoner over to them outside the guardroom. To the question — Did you know the officers, Moore answered, No! Would you recognize them? No, but one of them, the man who questioned him (i.e. Moore), could be a Colonel O'Connor. This was during a subsequent Army investigation as a result of which Sergeant Moore was demoted for having released the prisoner without proper documentation and for not having presented a release order for signature, or, as Joe Curran put it, 'a receipt for the body'. So, what happened? Joe heard the story from two soldiers who were talking in the square as he came on duty the following morning, They said — Did you hear what happened last night? But of course he did not. Two high-ranking officers, they told him, came to the barracks at 2 a.m. and took McPeak away in a car. Before leaving the vicinity of the gate they interrogated him with violence in the car about the death of Michael Collins. After some time they drove quickly up the road, opened a door and pushed the Scotsman out onto the roadway where he lay unconscious. They went on a little way, then drove back, picked him up in the car and delivered him once more to the sergeant, by which time he was a mass of contusions, or, as one of the soldiers said, 'he looked a bloody sight!'

As a matter of interest, Joe Curran joined the Army when recruiting began early in 1922. He signed on at Marlborough Hall recruiting station and after the split in the Army he favoured the Provisional Government. As he put it, he 'went with Michael Collins', and was transferred to Beggar's Bush military barracks. Eighteen months (others say fifteen) was the term required but for some reason he disremembers he served three months over and wound up in the North Dublin Union where Kevin Barry's sister, Sheila (as he said, but meant the indomitable Republican, Kathleen), happened to be a prisoner.

John McPeak went on to further endeavours. He tried bank robbery, Joe Curran thought, and was apprehended and spent a term in Portlaoise (then known as Maryborough) Gaol before being tried in Cork over the *Slievenamon* affair. Under the influence in a pub he claimed to have shot Michael Collins. And why not? Others did. With his undoubted though slight effect on the course of Irish History, the tough, sturdy Scotsman was entitled to his passing fancy of being 'Jock the Giant-Killer'.

Letter to *The Kerryman* newspaper from Jack Walsh, Moohane, Ballybunion:

With reference to what appeared in your paper about the shooting of Michael Collins (ref. *Cork Examiner*, 5 November 1985), I got a completely different story from the late Maurice Daly of East End, Ballybunion. Maurice, who originally came from Templeglantine, Co. Limerick, was a transport driver in the Free State Army, and was a personal friend and went to school with the famous Dave Neligan. He was based in Kilmainham and one night he was ordered to take a detail down town (Dublin) to arrest some Free State soldiers who were wrecking a pub. One of the wreckers was a Scotchman by the name of McPeak who was here with the British Army and stayed over and joined the new Free State Army. He was the rear gunner in the armour car with Michael Collins at Béal-na-Bláth. When the Civil War was over Maurice Daly got the option to either join the Civic Guards or the prison service. He joined the prison service and was stationed at Maryborough, as it was called, where he again met McPeak who was doing seven years for armed robbery with violence. McPeak's story was that Collins's death was accidental. The officer-in-charge wanted to pass through the ambush area but Collins insisted in stopping because it was his native countryside and, as McPeak said, he was so daring. When he came out at the left hand side (i.e. of the motor car) the fire was so intense that he had to run for cover. In so doing he was caught in the cross-fire from the rear gunner. Michael Collins was shot from behind. At the time I heard this story from Maurice Daly, I got his permission to contact your paper, which I did. One of your reporters was coming out on the following Thursday but Maurice Daly died on Tuesday . . .

*   *   *

McPeak was not really Scottish. His parents were from Tyrone. A member of that extensive clan (Fr. Patsy McPeake) was a fellow student of mine (author) in Maynooth during the war years (1939 onwards). Meda Ryan has got 'Jock' extensively covered in her book, *The Day Michael Collins was Shot*. It is interesting research for a somewhat unimportant subject. Connie Neenan tells a neat tale (to Uniseann MacEoin, in *Survivors*) of his own travels with McPeak after the delivery of the *Slievenamon*. The relevance of his defection to the I.R.A. is moot. He did not join the movement nor partake in its further activities. He simply moved the *Slievenamon* in their general direction westwards. His subsequent 'adventures' are of no matter. His 'price' for the armoured car never materialized, but a 'charitable' collection brought him a few pounds (the amount has varied much in the telling) which got him back to Scotland. His return to Ireland, however, involves some interesting features. He was interviewed for an Irish daily newspaper in 1971, having been living incognito in England all those years. Mrs. Ryan's information mainly comes from that source. The discrepancies are of some importance: 'The latest information available to me confirms that Jock McPeak spelled his name thus and not McPeake as many historians have believed . . .'. However the man may have signed his name, the variations in his surname appear as early as 1466 as 'M'Peake' and 'M'Pake' (Matheson's, *Varieties and Synonymes*). McLysaght's *Supplement* gives it as 'MacPeake' and 'Peake' from the census of 1659-60. Griffith's *Valuation* (1850) has 'M'Peak' and 'M'Peake'. What can I tell you? 'The trim six-foot tall McPeak' appears in Appendix 1, but cf. p.98 . . . 'lightly built and 5ft. 6in. in height'. Appendix 1 continues: 'On 2 July he was taken in for questioning by the Glasgow police . . . The Dublin Metropolitan Police arrived from Dublin and escorted him to Cork . . .'. Actually the Army escorted him to the guardhouse of Richmond Barracks where he was held for a fortnight and on 1 July, instead of being in Glasgow (as above), he was being remanded in Cork (according to the *Irish Independent*, 2 July 1923). 'Back in West Cork a rescue attempt was being planned . . . five men were ready to "jump him from custody" during his court appearance . . . because of the risk . . . Liam Deasy and Dan Holland decided it would be suicidal, so the plan was abandoned'. Strange! Deasy during this time was in custody himself in Mountjoy Gaol in Dublin (where he remained until 1924, originally under sentence of death), having been captured at Tincurry, Co. Tipperary, the previous January (cf. his *Brother Against Brother*), Liam Lynch had been killed on 10 April, and the remainder of the I.R.A. Executive (on Deasy's instructions from prison) had decreed a cease-fire on 30 April. Otherwise, armoured car driver Billy Barry's hyperbole adds colour but not credibility to the narrative, in detail fails to tally with McPeak's (thus!) reserved statements to Raymond Smith in the *Irish Independent,* 18, 19, 20, 21 May 1971. Likewise, the many names flip and flurry through the pages, dropping 'thick as Autumn leaves in Vallombrosa', names of men I knew and admired so much as a youth and as a man, old Republican fighters, humble, tolerant, religious (and sometimes irreligious for a reason), now like the leaves, dry, crowded, rotted, meaningless, faceless, unknown not only to this present generation but to the author herself — just names!

N.B.: John McPeak was twenty when he signed a pay-order receipt for a daily shilling in France with the Machine-Gun Corps in 1916. His signature, in upright copy-book style, indicates no further education after mid-Primary grades.

19

Five Local
People

They were all still with us in 1988. They were all knowledgeable about events of that historic day in 1922. They had all kept their minds to themselves over the arches of the years. They did so for disparate reasons. Into old age they had been afraid or proud or cautious or angry or indifferent — all of which are eminently understandable. Mostly they preferred to remain anonymous, but publicity was catching up with them. The information they offered was to my mind vital to future, precise thinking on the death of Michael Collins at Béalnabláth, which will be a vital issue forever and a day. Their politics — and in Ireland politics is still incredibly just for and against the Treaty or for and against Collins — were diverse. Sixty-six years previously these five local people were Kathleen Fahey (aged 15), Margaret Long (aged 22), Ellen Long (aged 19), Thomas Murray (aged 12) and Margaret Wall (aged 11).

The case of Margaret Wall was particularly interesting. She had to be one of the very few people in Ireland who could clearly remember being under continuous fire in the Civil War. Her home was on the hill facing the barricade site and about five hundred yards away. When the firing started at 7.30 p.m. her house was directly in the line of fire from the Vickers machine-gun in the armoured car. Slates flew off the house in splinters. The children of the family were made to lie down for safety inside the front wall of the farmhouse kitchen. The armoured car, the now historic pillars and the slated roof were in a straight line allowing for windage. One of the pillars has been demolished to make a dry stone wall where the five-bar gate of a field used to stand beside the roadway. They were the old stone-and-mortar capped 'piers' of long ago. The remaining one still has an iron ring or stay called a 'holding iron' or, in Irish, 'bacán' (still visible) which supported the gate. Oddly enough the 'bacán' points outwards into the roadway which clearly signifies that the gate when open closed off the 'boreen' to prevent the cattle going in the wrong direction. Young Maggie Wall cleverly counted five distinct bursts of gunfire over a period of 'about an hour'. She still counted them mentally. Wouldn't you! Then there was silence. The silence of the grave? There was a dead body being 'waked' in another house much nearer to the scene of battle. A little way up from the bridge, on the ambush by-road, there is an entrance to a farmyard where two families, O'Carroll (from whom Carroll's Bridge was named) and Holland, lived at the time. One or other household (according to Ellen Long) was waking the dead. They continued to do so undisturbed as they were slightly to the left of the line of machine-gun fire. It is, of course, futile but intriguing to try to distinguish the five bursts of firing. Tom Kelleher fired three warning shots 'in the air', he said. Jim Hurley engaged the Army in a burst of automatic fire, shattering the windscreen of the Leyland tourer and giving General Emmet Dalton the impression that there was a machine-gun in action against him. The soldiers on the roadway continued to fire even (according to guide John O'Connell from Mallow) when there was no one left to fire at. Michael Collins dashed up the main road to the back of the armoured car and presumably opened fire from a standing position on the retreating men. Mike Donoghue's unknown gunman fired one or possibly two rounds. Bobs Doherty may have fired a shot. Jimmy Ormond's group certainly did. And finally, Liam Deasy's men fired some rounds from the vicinity of the distant farmhouse to the back of the present monument as the convoy moved away. But Maggie Wall, seventy-seven years young, still heard five distinct bursts in her head!

Ellen Long, with her younger cousin, John Cronin, recently deceased, was sent to bring the cattle home. Home was at Béalnabláth crossroads. They stood at a gap in the old roadway across the brook, now no more than a cattle track (not the battle scene but the originally planned ambush site) and watched some men in the road directly below them dismantling a landmine near the barricade. (A clear line of fir trees at right-angles now marks the location). Suddenly there was a shout from beneath them and a man, invisible until now and obviously on guard, told them to get away from there or words to that effect. As they did so the first shot sounded from further up the valley. The two men who were actually handling the landmine were known to Ellen Long. They were from the locality. Their names she would not divulge because 'their people still lived in the place'. Reasonable!

Tom Murray was twelve sixty-six years ago. It made him quite a bit older than I was. Elderly? Yes, elderly! Seventy-eight now doesn't matter. But twelve in 1922! My God, I said to myself, what a story! I looked all around the old kitchen walls and into the old fireplace. If walls could speak! If an old hearth could murmur in its dreams! Cogadh cois teallaigh! The 'war beside the fireplace' — symptomatic of civil war! I looked at the spot on the floor where some parts of a landmine had lain ('in two separate sections in two cardboard boxes', the old man said) with its work undone, under the inside wall, the parlour wall. Suppose it had gone off! I looked at the parlour door, the same one still, and I could imagine I heard the tense murmur, the occasional shout, the ectoplasmic vibrations of an old I.R.A. conference long gone. I looked at the kitchen door into the 'back-kitchen' and into the backyard. I could really see Shawno Galvin come charging through that very door, an hour before midnight. I could hear him shout, wildly, almost hysterically: Mick is dead — and 'twas I shot him! The future bishop's

brother! Shot Michael Collins? Bishop Ned Galvin! The bishop
of the 'Far East' and the 'Chinese Missions' and the Columban
Fathers? His brother shot Collins? Impossible! I thought of the
monument to Michael Galvin, the other brother, killed on the
exact same date, two years previously, by the Tans down there
at Lissarda, on the main road to Cork, the finest monument to
one man, on the most spectacular spot for a monument in
Ireland where roadside and hillside monuments to the glorious
dead abound — Mick of the weak eyesight, they said, who
didn't notice for a moment that the battle was over and the boys
were pulling out, still sighting along the barrel of his rifle at the
outline of a foreign body, just as a lion sees his enemy or his
prey in outline. Others said that he stood up to call on the Tans
to surrender and was shot for his trouble. I looked across the
dinner table at the old man, crippled now, and thought of his
sprightly, rumbustious twelve years of age at Béalnabláth and
remembered another Civil War whose battlefields I traversed in
search of another book. All the great-sounding names anyway
you remember them . . . Chancellorsville, Chickamauga,
Chattanooga, Manassas (known for some reason as 'Bull Run'
and which the powers that be were just now endeavouring to
turn into a vast built-up area against the wishes of the people).
Then there was Mechanicsville — for what reason?; Antietam,
known as 'Sharpsburg' for an obvious reason; Fredericksburg,
that bloody battlefield where Irishmen on opposite sides and on
opposite banks of Rappahannock river sang together T.D. Sullivan's 'Song of the Backwoods', known as 'Ireland, Boys,
Hurra!'; and, of course, Gettysburg, where General Pickett
had charged hopelessly at his 'high-water mark' and General
Rommel had trained for another war with our own General
Costello. I remembered the Centenary in 1963 when nobody
turned up but myself — and a few school children who marched
in band formation among the rain puddles and blew sousa-
phones — 'Marching Through Georgia' up the miserable main
street of a small town in Pennsylvania, the 'woodland glade' of
that renowned Quaker who was possibly born, certainly reared,

in Macroom Castle. Small world! My father a prisoner in Macroom Castle and myself living then below the Mason-Dixon Line, in 'Dixie'. Michael Collins had his Mason-Dixon Line at Béalnabláth, a muddy fence of a country road, the mud still showing on his left coat sleeve, his rifle rest, in Dublin's museum, sixty-eight years later. They didn't like the term 'Civil War' over there in America, so they wanted a 'war between the States' or a 'war to save the Union', but they cheerfully accepted 'the first singing war':

> Break the news to mother,
> And say how much I love her;
> Kiss her dear sweet lips for me,
> For I'm not coming home . . .

Every war is a mother's war. The American Civil War involved boys of twelve to sixteen, hundreds of thousands of them. I looked at the old man across the table — twelve at Béalnabláth, not actively engaged but seeing all and understanding some. And the old mother over there serving apple-pie and cream! She had been under fire herself in the other farmhouse on the hill where they had to lie on the floor while Free State bullets were knocking chips off the slated roof — a young girl counting the separate bouts of firing. Which were they? Tom Kelleher's warnings shots, then Jim Hurley and his Mauser continuous with the Army, then silence, then Mike Donoghue's, then Jimmy Ormond's, and finally the latecomers from the pub below in the village? Five bursts in all over a period of an hour, she primly interposed . . .

The old man wanted to tell his story. He would prefer not to be named for it.

'That fella in the paper a while back had the rights of it', he said.

'What fellow was that?', his married son gently inquired from across the table.

'He had it right', he continued unperturbed, 'about that Kerryman and the group going home from Cork!'

His son smiled a slow pleasant countryman's smile and gestured to the head of the table. He turned slowly, his head stiff with arthritis. He took me in as if he were seeing me for the first time in context. He briefly eyed the clerical collar. Then his neck yielded to the pain and he turned slowly back to face his son across the table.

'This the man?', he asked, not quite disbelieving. He got a nod of assent and went on with his story as if it didn't matter. Which it didn't!

'They had a meeting at Sullivan's, Gurranereagh, in the morning and at our place, in this house, that night. The yard out there was full of motor cars. They came from all over. They were, of course, Republican motors. There was one even from Donegal with a man named Doherty. Dev's was easily the best one'.

'The biggest?', I asked.

'No, indeed, but the smallest. But you could see that it was better than the rest'. (It was a sports model Armstrong-Siddeley).

'A sports model?'

'I don't know — it was kind of low and shiny'.

'Did you see him leave?'

'I did'.

'Was he dressed — you know — like a priest?'

He took in the collar once more.

'I don't remember that — but he had his big black hat on'. (Eamon de Valera's black hat was famous from Co. Clare to London. There is a photograph).

'Mrs. Shorten said he was dressed like a priest!'

'She should know — she gave him the dinner, with my mother'.

'What about the barricade?'

'What about it?'

'Do you know where it was?'

'Why wouldn't I! I saw them setting it up. It wasn't much of a barricade. Only the dray from Bandon with the bottles.'

'Why Bandon?'

'That's where the brewery was. Stephen, the "Bottle-Man"
— I forget his right name — came from Bandon every Tuesday
to the pub down there and took away the empties. Beamish and
Crawford had a brewery in the town at that time. The lad
asked Stephen for the dray to make a barricade, so he emptied
his cases of bottles in the back of the public house and drove the
horse up the road. Then he un-tackled the horse and brought
him back down to the yard. (Ellen Long remembered him as a
beautiful chestnut horse with flowing mane and tail, big and
strong, but not a Clydesdale, the regular type of brewery dray
horse). They took the wheels off the dray and stood them
against it in front'.

'How did they know about Collins?'

'The motor bike scout told it!'

'Wasn't that man, "the Dane", on sentry-duty?'

'No, he wasn't! I was splitting blocks when the soldiers came
down the Kilmurry road. The scout was in front. He stopped in
the middle of the cross and took out a map. Longs owned the
pub then. Denny Long (he was no relation), "the Dane", was
standing at the door. The scout called him over. He went across
and leaned on the handlebars. I could hear them talking but
only later heard what was said. He asked for the road to Ban
don and Long pointed it out. Then he (the scout) put his hand
on the handlebars, in no hurry, and started talking in a friendly
way. I heard that he said — "We have the Big Fellow back there
in the car!" Then they drove away.'

(Note: For the record, Long's nickname should not be taken
by over familiarity, as pejorative or in any way denigratory.
Mr. Denis Long, later on in America and then at home, became
a very important and influential ally, an honoured friend, to
Mr. Eamon de Valera!).

'What did Long do?'

'I don't know. I suppose he told the story. There were men in
the pub. I heard it said that Dev was in a room upstairs and
guard with him with two revolvers ready.'

'What time was it?'
'About nine o'clock'.

*   *   *

In pre-Vatican Two theology Fear was defined as 'the shrinking of the mind from some impending or future evil'. It had its divisions and sub-divisions, and was declared to be slight or grave according to the frame of mind of the subject. A phenomenon apart is the reluctance of elderly people in Ireland to become involved in any publicity with regard to Civil War matters even at sixty-six years remove. It still amounts to grave fear. Living alone for an octogenarian is a frightening thing. It engenders sympathy even when one sees it as relatively unnecessary. To bring further distress on grey hairs, even when History must be served and reasons why are not forthcoming, strains to the limit the balance of one's conscience . . . Maggie Long was a young woman of twenty-two when summoned to a neighbour's house to assist in providing lunch for an important visitor. Strong-willed as always, she responded with a minimum of enthusiasm. She did not like the man, nor his politics. His name — Éamon de Valera. The place — Béalnabláth village. The time — two o'clock in the afternoon of 22 August 1922. She did merely as requested. He left at four. Others of her political persuasion would have him remain throughout the day while actively involved in encompassing the death of Michael Collins, his rival for the soul of Ireland. Not so this particular young woman. She was glad to see him go. She said so. It endeared him to her still less to see him dressed in clerical garb riding in a chauffeur-driven motor car. One would hope that much future service to the country, in difficult times, of this world-renowned statesman would have effected a change of heart. One hopes in vain. She saw the setting of the barricade at the S-bend and the laying of a landmine. The men who did so were well known to her, their names secure in the secret recesses of her mind from here to eternity. Her abstruse conviction of 'impending or future evil' is beyond the capacity of a younger mind to understand. Extrinsic causes, though long past and gone, are as palpable to her as the later ghostly 'ambulances', 'lights' and 'shots' which she claimed and in which she ardently believed. The shadow of reverential fear evoked no response to devious and desperate entreaty. Mulier fortis! A 'strong woman'! She could (like Hamlet and Florrie Donoghue):

> A tale unfold . . .
> But this eternal blazon must not be
> To ears of flesh and blood!

She will take with her, to where death shall be no more, a personal knowledge of startling and intriguing events, historical events, while we, the new-born, painstakingly piece together a jigsaw picture which at best can be only a 'seeing in a glass darkly'. She is not alone. She is, indeed, in the tradition of that conspiracy of silence, that even more startling phenomenon than fear, only come to light in recent times, among the very gunmen themselves!

*   *   *

There have been witnesses to the Béalnabláth ambush, with stories of greater or less degree, who preferred to remain anonymous. There is an old man in residential Alameda, San Francisco, named Andy Caverley, who could underwrite some technical problems on the matter being, as he is, the last remaining member of the Army convoy, but refuses to speak. Other old playboys of the far Western World, from Canada to Florida, ex-regular and ex-irregular soldiers, have elected to die of old age rather than reveal any complicity in Béalnabláth for fear of some imaginary reprisal at many years and many miles distant. There are speculators who would swear to stories so wildly contradictory as to be utterly ludicrous and counterproductive; and there have come book after book with versions and recensions somewhat or totally lacking in adequate research or literary criticism while shining brilliantly otherwise. But Kathleen Fahey is unique. She is an old lady who lives in 'Avondale' guest-house in Dublin who knew nothing of the ongoing controversy until she saw in a newspaper a letter from an old man in Australia. She resorted to the simple expedient of writing to Australia. In Australia is a garrulous nonagenarian with a sharp tongue capable of lashing out across continents and oceans. I happen to know. E.P. Timlin, of Collinswood (strange coincidence!), South Australia, is important historically, and he knows it. He was a member of the crew of the armoured car named *The Big Fellow* (which is now being restored in England), and on one occasion was escort to prisoner John McPeak. To E.P. the bould Kathleen, sensing some commercial advantage, wrote: 'Re the shooting of Michael Collins, this is a true story. I can swear an affidavit to it. I was born in 1907, and Michael Collins was killed in 1922 . . .' The gist of Kathleen's story is a certain amount of circumstantial evidence, small but valuble in that it bears out the Bobs Doherty story (as above), and lends some topographical assurance to my research to date with regard to the actual course of the battle at Béalnabláth. 'Our farm', she writes,

was about ten fields away from Béalnabláth (at Curraclough, Kilmurry). We had what was regarded as a 'safe house', in a 'boreen', with a view of the road (i.e. the Bantry Line), and the Tans in Crossley tenders passing at intervals . . . I was turning in the cows to be milked. Between seven and eight p.m. the shooting started (at Béalnabláth). Things quietened down after about half an hour . . . I saw five or six men — the 'Irregulars' we used to call them — all with Lee-Enfield rifles (I kid you not!) going through our land . . . About six a.m. next morning a knock came to our door for admittance. Two good-looking, fair haired boys walked in asking for food and beds. My mother always kept a 'Sacred Heart lamp' lighting before the picture of the 'Sacred Heart'. This happened the morning after the shooting. One of the boys pulled out a chair and knelt down in front of the picture and said the Rosary quietly to himself. We were preparing breakfast for them. The first words he said when finished — 'Poor Mick is dead!' The two men were supposed to come from Kerry . . . I well remember the evening. If you (i.e. E.P. Timlin) could forward the enclosed information to somebody who would be writing a book, it would be valuable to them, as I was there. This is a true account.

The six men referred to were rather obviously the Pete Kearney contingent heading for Newcestown or Kilmurry when the firing started. When Kathleen saw them he may have been already dead though Peter believed he himself shot Collins. (An alternative story about Comdt. Pete Kearney being on the hill at the back of the Free State contingent in the closing moments of the battle and firing a Thompson sub-machine gun at the behest of General Liam Deasy, either into the bushes as a distraction or towards the scene of the action, has like credibility though it is very moot if a tommy-gun firing regulation revolver bullets could reach so far. Cf. the Billy Powell account in *The Day Michael Collins was Shot*). About the pair who came to breakfast, a fifteen-year-old girl was quick to note, then as always, a couple of good-looking, fair haired young men, and with the addition of the strange Kerry accent they had an added attraction that has outlived the passing of time. Bobs Doherty and his clerical companion (cf. Chapter Six) must have remained in the vicinity overnight and picked up the awful news that broke in Murray's at eleven p.m. Bobs, always the hard man, stayed cool. The clerical student would undoubtedly have been the one to kneel and pray before making his fateful announcement.

20

The Tom Foley Story

Seán Buckley paced up and down the kitchen floor at Foley's of Bengour, nervously and intermittently looking at his pocket watch as if he thought that time might be controlled but finding it, naturally, uncontrollable. At the kitchen table sat his mate, Tadhg O'Sullivan, large and portly. Buckley's watch marked the stressful minutes of a battle taking place, from the audible sounds, a few hundred yards away. He was not a regular rifleman of the Third Brigade 'Flying Column', just the Intelligence Officer. Tadhg O'Sullivan was not the stuff either being now slow on his feet but with a highly creditable record in West Cork during the previous years of the War of Independence. As Brigade Quartermaster he succeeded Dick Barrett who had been captured in March of 1921 by the British and moved in his destined way to execution by the Free State. Tadhg's brother, Gearóid, friend and confidant of Michael Collins, was Adjutant-General in the new army of the Provisional Government. Now it was Civil War, so called, and the greatest West Cork man of them all was supposedly fighting for his life just down the road. Watching these two veterans (later to be public representatives and now wearing their Sunday clothes because they just came to a conference) was a young fellow of seventeen, a member of the Foley household, already mature in experience and size. Big, raw-boned, with somewhat of a crouch, young Tom Foley had power and drive written all over him. At eighty-four (Spring, 1989) he still carried an aura of those historic times, still had quite a sense of the power of his youth so long gone by. This is his story. It is an essential catalyst for the dark secret of Béalnabláth . . .

At eleven o'clock on the morning of the twenty-second of August, 1922, three men left Béalnabláth village in a 'Model-T' motor car. They had many models to select from but they chose the Model-T mainly because Denny Coveney, of Kilbrittain, was the appointed driver and he knew no other model. Beside the driver rested the large figure of Tadhg O'Sullivan and in the back, awkwardly arranging his long legs, was young Tom Foley. They were off to Newcestown, that pretty village two miles away from Mossgrove on the road to Enniskean. This was no joyride. They were in quest of two landmines which lay at the home of John Lordan just outside the village. The ambush had been decided on and this was necessary preparation. The mines were in two wooden crates, one of them three feet by two, the other much smaller. They were standard equipment for the job in hand. Without them there was no hope of dealing with the expected armoured car. Arriving back with their deadly load they found Liam Deasy, O/C of the First Southern Division, drawing the battle lines and establishing the field of fire. A gang of men set to work digging the road surface just below Carroll's (Glanarouge) bridge and on the Béalnabláth side of it. After much work the big box was set in place and the cables for firing were lodged in a shallow trench, covered and slung across the little river. The small mine was then similarly sunk in the surface of the by-road just across the bridge. The chosen ambush position stretched from there for one hundred and eighty yards to the S-bend further down where the barricade was to be erected. The purpose was to halt the convoy at the barricade while the big mine destroyed the armoured car or at least prevented its returning towards Bandon. In case of mishap the small mine was to be used to prevent the steel-cased

Rolls-Royce 'Whippet' from crossing the bridge onto the by-road and taking the ambush party on the right flank. A third mine from elsewhere was sunk in the roadway in front of the cart barricade, its cables visible to the motor-cycle scout. The attack, when it occurred, was to be a one-sided thing, the men being arranged all along the fence of a hidden track, the remains of an old road from Béalnabláth Cross which ran parallel to the present one and joined the now famous by-road, or 'boreen', at the first bend forty yards up from the bridge. Little more than a cow track, and now completely overgrown, it ran on the far side of the river and just a few feet higher than the road into Béalnabláth village. Strange to relate, no men were placed on the near or opposite side which climbed steeply to the high ground beyond. The visibility, which was good right then, is now completely obliterated with scrub, the old road's only place in history being as the eventual escape route for the men at the barricade. The 'Command Post', literally the high point of the attack, was 'The Rock' by Jake's Pool (also known locally as 'Poul Séc'), an elevation about fifty yards from the bridge and commanding the whole action. On this remarkable barbican the ubiquitous Foley found Liam Deasy setting up a Lewis-gun on its bipod. He lent a hand which was gratefully accepted. 'A bird', said old Tom, 'could not have escaped from the trap!' The gun was memorable to the young man's eye from its circular pan of ammunition on top of the mechanism. (Deasy has astutely omitted details of the arrangement, or even a mention, in his *Brother Against Brother*).

Nothing by way of obstruction could readily be found except the cart of the man of the bottles, and Foley remembered him traipsing disconsolately towards Bandon, the reins held in his two hands behind his back with his magnificent chestnut horse trailing behind, a picture which would have interested Jack Yeats, the great Irish poet's artist brother. Omnia parata! Deasy returned to Gurranereagh (according to his own account), leaving Tom Hales in charge. For political reasons the Divisional Commander had best not be present. The intention may have been to kill Michael Collins in the interest of an All-Ireland Republic, possibly to capture him, but some show of resistance in the circumstances was imperative. At the very least there was a concerted effort at the big gesture, and big it could have been. Nothing happened as planned. The day's battle happened in another position. Tom Foley went home to Bengour leaving the men to their work. A signal-man had been placed at 'the top of the height' near Bradfield's Cross on the way to Mossgrove. He had a white flag and was versed in the Morse code. 'We all learned it at school', said Tom Foley. (Séamus O'Connor, Republican school teacher, confirms this in *Tomorrow Was Another Day*). The signaller would be plainly visible from 'The Rock'. The first shots were heard in Bengour at 7.30 p.m. It was 'New Time' and 'still very bright', he remembers. The 'death in a fading light' idea (of Frank O'Connor's *The Big Fellow*) came a half-hour and ten minutes later by Séan Buckley's watch. At any rate no more shots were heard after that. At 7.30 p.m. the flag-man was seen frantically waving the letter U for warning — two dots and a dash. His signal read 'Coming!' Five men were making their way to their billets up the laneway off the by-road towards Long's farmhouse on the hill to the North-West. They were plainly in view from the Bengour kitchen window. Tom Foley could see them strolling in a group. Suddenly they turned about and ran back down to the little junction and then the first shot came. They took hasty positions along a fifty-yard stretch of fence facing where the monument now stands. Around the bend of their little roadway they could see nothing. What happened at the two-pillar position about two hundred yards away they were totally unaware of, ever afterwards for at least one of them. The cables from the two mines at the bridge had been rolled up as far as 'The Rock'. John O'Callaghan, battalion engineer from Newcestown, had them coiled and slung over his shoulder and had dumped the small mine on top of the fence. The big one remained covered and unnoticed in the roadway where the dust was soon to turn to mud. Beside it stood big Jim Hurley waiting for Tom

Kelleher to join him. Having got together they proceeded upwards on the by-road and took to the field at a stile which gave
on to an old school path forty yards short of the gate pillars.
When the shouts came from the five men ahead of them they
dashed back and took cover behind the pillars. On the high field
they were clearly in view. One of those pillars still stands, its
iron gudgeon (as Tom Foley called it) and heel-block (his word
also) still visible to this day. The other, to Foley's surprise, had
crumbled and the field level is now some feet higher completely
closing the gate entrance. He had constantly seen those pillars
on his way to school, he said, and their long lost iron gate frequently swung across cutting off the by-road to cattle. There
Hurley and Kelleher were joined by the men from the barricade
who had crossed the river and come on up to the old 'green
road'. There they made their way along to the turn of the by-
road, where the two ways joined, firing as they went at the
motor-cycle scout trying to rejoin his own group on the main
road. The firing from the pillars had been for the purpose of
warning them and drawing the fire of the Staters. They responded loyally by joining in the fray. They lined the fence from the
pillars onwards making a fairly complete line of attack with the
invisible five men around the bend, Dan Holland, First Battalion Q.M., being last in line and Joe Murphy, of Lissarda,
first in line at the next bend. Gradually they all slid away to
safety.

Tom Foley at seventeen was already a crack cyclist, champion of champions at competition level or 'flapper' meet. One,
three or five miles were all the one to him, he was proud to say.
He had been active on his bicycle as a scout for the I.R.A. After
the battle he did not go down to the scene. 'It was too dangerous
to go near the place!', he said. Sixty-six years later he still was
not aware that some Free State troops from Macroom had inspected the place that night — but they missed some vital clues.
Early the following morning, long before Press or sightseers,
he jumped on his bike and made a quick round of the battle
field, beginning at his own end of the cart track from Ahalarick

bridge to the by-road junction at Long's laneway. From there on a lot of shells were strewn about, some empty, some full. He continued on to the main road and the barricade position at the S-bend further down where he saw the horse cart tumbled into the ditch on the right-hand side. Back up the road to Bandon he saw where the armoured car had finally stood to fight (at the spot where the monument now stands). Just to the back of it, by the tail position, was a large splash of blood. He concluded that that was where Collins had died. He did not notice the Commander-in-Chief's military cap which was lying hidden in a deep water-dyke several yards further up beside the stream, nor was he aware of it until confronted by Jim Kearney, on the kitchen floor at Bengour, on the fourteenth of March, 1989. Nor did the two fine old gentlemen know of each other's existence until then. 'I thought you were in America!', said Jim. 'I went but came back after a few years', said Tom. (He had bought and worked the River Room public house in Macroom). Jim Kearney, an athlete himself, was well aware of the other's prowess in the old days and had often seen him ride. To me he said quietly — 'I thought he was dead!'. 'I'm very glad you were wrong!', I replied, and I meant it.

The blood on the roadway had to have been a further effusion from the great head as Michael Collins was being placed in the back of the armoured car by Major-General Emmet Dalton and his men. There was an object of equal, possibly greater, interest reposing that morning on the low earthen bank thirty or forty yards away — Dalton's revolver! It was the same gun he had drawn and brandished at the deep-sea pilot at Queenstown (Cobh) as he sailed up the Lee for the capture of Cork City. During the battle Dalton had used a rifle but he obviously had placed the revolver ready to hand. It was a long Webley .45, the British officer's regulation weapon, the vaunted 'service revolver' justly famous for its 'stopping power'. Tom Foley picked it up, examined it briefly, placed it in his pocket and headed for home. The wooden stock had carved on it the letters 'E.D.'. All six chambers of the revolving cylinder were loaded and unfired. The barrel was clean. Tom Foley knew about such things.

At seventeen young Foley was still in primary school, the 'National School' at Béalnabláth. Late attendance was common at the time even though 'we went only a day now and again', he said. Previously, under British administration, the Irish language was forbidden by law in schools. Under the new Free State government things were bound to change. Collins had guaranteed it. Patrick Fleming, the schoolmaster at Béalnabláth, was an enthusiast for the language. A Kerryman, as already noted, he attended Gaelic League classes in Ballyvourney during the Summer of 1922, and had his historic encounter there with De Valera on the evening of 22 August. One thing had not changed. The new school inspectors (like the new 'Civic Guards', the new C.I.D. men, and the new Army) were often quite as abominable as their predecessors. One of them had quite a serious altercation with Master Fleming soon after the school reopened in September. Tom Foley had Dalton's revolver with him hidden in the desk. As the voices rose higher he said to the lad beside him — 'Will I fire a shot?' It was a schoolboy jest — I think. Members of the Flying Column kept calling for the gun. 'They always came in twos', for some reason. Eventually he surrendered it to them and so far as anybody knows it may still be a treasured souvenir somewhere in West Cork, possibly even rotting in a barn loft.

Tom Foley in old age still rode a bicycle and made almost daily trips to Crookstown, to the consternation of his relatives. Only recently he had paid £200 for a new model. The 'pains' bothered him a mite — he thought I might have a 'cure' — but the dangerous traffic of this present age did not hinder him from occasionally reliving the days when he was King of the Roads. He was killed by a motor car at Ovens Bridge, on the Cork-Macroom road on 7 September 1989. He was walking at the time. Ironic!

21

The Tom Kelleher Story

It might be named: 'Fan Go Fóill Anois!' It was one of his favourite expressions. It means — 'Wait a while now!', or better, 'Hang on a minute until I think!' He thought rather slowly but extensively and when he did put his thinking into action he was one of the most courageous and determined of all Republican fighters, as attested to by his brigadier, Liam Deasy, in *Towards Ireland Free*. Commandant-General (Irregular) Thomas Kelleher, of Crowhill, joked with his captor, Lieutenant-General (Regular) Thomas Ennis, of Dublin, about how he (Kelleher) stopped a lorry-load of Free State Soldiers with a 'tommy-gun', standing alone at a crossroads. (Note: The variety of exalted military ranks, assumed by or bestowed on so many men on all sides in our little war for the Republic, has been a source of puzzlement to foreigners. It was a sort of military proportional representation, paralleled only in the civic and political honours list of so many others of later years, without evidence of much intellectual, academic, technical or linguistic ability, only an intensity of purpose). General Ennis said to General Kelleher, 'We're both Toms. Come and have a drink, Tom'. He might have said, 'We're both Irishmen. Come and have a drink, Paddy'. Tom Kelleher fired the warning shot at Béalnabláth but until his death, a few years ago, firmly

248

maintained that he did not fire at, only towards, the enemy of the moment. Others did. They had to — for survival. 'Tom Kelleher would not tell a lie!', said Denis Conroy, staunch friend of his declining years and presently (1990) Chairman of the Cork County Board of the Gaelic Athletic Association. Still, Kelleher was given to wild exaggeration and a pardonable bombast.

*   *   *

In 1980, towards the end of his life, Tom Kelleher, late O/C of the First (Bandon) Battalion of the Third (West Cork) Brigade of the 'Old' I.R.A., endured an extensive interview with the British Broadcasting Corporation (the B.B.C.) about 'being in an ambush', with specific reference to Kilmichael, Crossbarry and Béalnabláth, and made practically no sense at all. Most of the men of the old I.R.A. were the age of the century or less. Michael Collins was practically a patriarch at ten years older. Dev was a Methuselah. Tom Kelleher would have been quite an old man (eighty-five) when interviewed and heavy reading between the lines is required to put him in the picture (that expression which came into vogue only in World War Two). His version of Béalnabláth — like many versions of Béalnabláth — produces contradictions, miscalculations and some incomprehensible material 'by the new time', as he would say. But he was there! Still, another man who has recently and rather startlingly come to light as being still alive — Jim Kearney of Bandon — who was also there and in the firing line, says that Tom Kelleher was not there at all. Virtus in medio stat! The evidence points to a middle course. Ellen Long (Mrs. Allen who appeared in the documentary, 'The Shadow of Béalnabláth', shortly before her death) said that two men of the ambush party were billeted in the farmhouse above the ambush scene and at the far end of the winding ambush laneway. They were on their way 'home', as it were, when the trouble started. They were Jim Hurley and Tom Kelleher . . .

B.B.C. Interviewer: Tom, coming into the Civil War . . .

when the Civil War started, did you find that you got as much
support from the people in Cork as you did in the Tan War?

Tom Kelleher: Oh yes! We had support all the time!

B.B.C.I.:   You didn't have to worry about Free State
families?

T.K.:   No. Not exactly, but we were hoping that peace would
come.

B.B.C.I.:   Was that because the Free Staters started to execute
people?

T.K.:   Not really. We came to the conclusion that brother
fighting against brother was a bad job. Well now, look here
I'm in a very strong position to state that it was a British officer
shot Michael Collins.

B.B.C.I.:   I wanted to ask you about that, because you were at
the ambush . . .

T.K.:   I was.

B.B.C.I.:   You were in the rearguard after Liam Deasy and
the others had gone down the road?

T.K.:   That's right!

B.B.C.I.:   Now can you tell me about the ambush? Let me ask
you about Collins' death. You were going to talk about that as
well.

T.K.:   Oh, yes!

B.B.C.I.:   Can you tell me about setting up the ambush and
waiting for the whole day and then taking it apart?

T.K.:   I arrived there, I'm sure, about nine o'clock or
something like that. I think there was some meeting supposed
to be held, you see, but anyhow I was told that Collins passed
through and inquired the way to Bandon. (Fantasy Time: And
one chap — I forget the fellow's name — was talking to him and
told him the truth. 'When you get to Mossgrove', he said, 'keep
left for Bandon'. But Michael at the time, of course, wouldn't
believe what every man on the road would tell him. So, for that
reason, he stopped at Béalnabláth, in the pub, and he said to the
publican there — 'I'm looking for the road to Bandon'. And he
said to Michael — 'Well, keep left and you can't go wrong!'

Michael said to him — 'I was told that on the road but, of course, you can't believe what each and every fellow will tell you nowadays. I'm glad now that the fellow on the road told me the truth'. And he headed off). So then we all waited (i.e. at the ambush site). I didn't know too much about an objective in the ambush. I imagine they were anxious to capture him (Collins) for one reason or another (Fantasy Time: I believe before they left Dublin Michael Collins stated that Seán Hales was living in the same house as Tom, one against the other, and he said — 'There's something wrong somewhere. I have to go and do something about it when I get to Cork!'). But the remarkable thing was that he had four British officers guarding him. It is very hard to understand that from my point of view. Why should he have four (British) officers guarding him? And I believe one of the four said — 'We'll get him before we come back!' And they got him. One of the four shot him, I believe. The I.R.A. definitely did not shoot him!

B.B.C.I.: How do you know the I.R.A. did not shoot him?

T.K.: Sure I was there! They did not shoot him!

B.B.C.I.: Where were you?

T.K.: I was there with Jim Hurley and Tom Hales. Tom was at the barricade and I wasn't too far away from it and there was nobody else there when the shots went off. A couple of shots were fired nearer to Béalnabláth entirely different from where he was shot.

B.B.C.I.: As far as I know the story it is this, that the ambush party waited all day hoping they'd come . . .

T.K.: Not all day! I mean it wasn't so late at all when Deasy . . .

B.B.C.I.: Exactly, and as the evening came on they pulled out and Tom Hales was down on the road helping to clear the . . . who was the other one? Jim Hurley, did you say?

T.K.: Jim Hurley, yes!

B.B.C.I.: Were the rear guards . . .

T.K.: And Callaghan!

B.B.C.I.: And Callaghan?

T.K.:   Callaghan and Dan Holland and Sonny O'Neill.

B.B.C.I.:   And so there were six of you left behind as a rearguard as the main column pulled back to Béalnabláth.

T.K.:   We were left behind to disconnect the mine, to deal with the mine, you see. I don't think the mine was to be taken up but to be disconnected. And O'Callaghan, from Newcestown, disconnected the mine.

B.B.C.I.:   And then what happened?

T.K.:   There were a few shots fired on my side but . . .

B.B.C.I.:   I mean — when did you hear the convoy coming?

T.K.:   Tom Hales and I were talking at the barricade and Tom said to me — 'Come on down to Béalnabláth. We'll have a drink'. So I said — 'No, I'm not going down there at all'. Jim Hurley was further up. And all of a sudden he waved at us — he had big, long hands. So I went up and met him and on came the motor bike. And after the motor bike came down, a lorry of officers, I believe. I think they were nearly all officers in the lorry. After the lorry of officers came the private touring car and after the car came the armoured car. And I'm not sure now whether you had a lorry of privates after that, but it's immaterial anyway because they didn't come into operation at all. So there were a couple of shots fired. I said to Jim, 'We've got to fire very soon because the whole lot are walking down the road'. The barricade was a very temporary one. It was only an old back-to-back trap with a long stick thrown across the road. We cleared the road in a few seconds . . . I was talking to McPeak who was in charge of the armoured car. He joined up with us afterwards. They were all saying he shot Michael Collins. You may be sure he didn't shoot Michael Collins. But he came damn near to shooting myself. When talking to him I asked him why 'Oh', he said, 'if you saw them (the I.R.A.) you were under orders to open up on them — liquidate the lot'. But when they stopped, the men going down the road got away nicely. I was behind one pier, the first one (i.e. on the Bandon side) and Jim Hurley was behind the next one (i.e. nearer to the corner). I said to Jim Hurley, 'Go down to the corner!'. The corner (of th by-road) is about fifty yards up from the ambush site. When you come to the corner you can see the piers. And I said to Jim, 'Go down to the corner!' 'Fire away, Tom', said he, 'fire away!'. I said, 'If you're not going, I'm going!' So I'm aiming for the corner of the field and in the course of my going to the corner of the field a machine-gun tore a hole in the bottom of the fence in that part of the field, but I kept going and the gun stopped. I was under the impression that I had all the necessary cover. When I was talking to the gunner afterwards he said that he could have had I.R.A. casualties on that occasion. And I said, 'Now, Jock, what kind of nonsense are you going on with? How could you have I.R.A. casualties when you didn't see any I.R.A. men firing at you? Do you know where the two piers are?' He said, 'I know where the two piers are quite well and there was a man behind each of them. One of the two left the position and ran down for the corner. I was on top (i.e. in the revolving turret) of the armoured car and I had a great view. I fired in front of him. And another, I'd say, two seconds and he was dead — I had him cut in half. But my gun stopped'.

B.B.C.I.: Yes, but, Tom, tell me — When the convoy came with Collins, did you fire at it at all or did you fire in the air to warn the retreating column?

T.K.: No — I fired at the top of the car that Michael Collins was in. I said the man in charge of them (i.e. the troops) is inside in that car!

B.B.C.I.: Did you know it was Collins?

T.K.: Oh, no, I did not! I didn't know who was in the car. He was shot about a hundred and eighty yards up the road.

B.B.C.I.: But how did you know you didn't shoot him?

T.K.: Well, now, didn't I see the two of them jumping out of the car, and the whole lorry load took the necessary cover up along the fence. I escaped anyhow, and I got down to the corner where I meant to go. I'd be fairly well positioned at the corner, and I was right. I was there less than five minutes when all the legs started coming up. I saw the legs. Well, if the British were here I'd say I'd wait longer to see them coming into full view, but you see the fight was kind of . . . anyway, I opened up on the legs and all withdrew. And the next thing, right across the small field I saw a fellow coming up and I saw the Thompson gun, so I fired across at him to stop him from coming around us. (Note: This was Commandant Seán O'Connell). So he answered tat-a-tat-tat back at me and then he came up another bit. I withdrew up my own side and I fired at him again and he fired back. Anyway, there was more firing. It came from their side. I looked down from where I was and there was a bunch of them, so I fired down at them. They didn't answer me at all and I wondered if they'd taken cover. I went back down the road. I couldn't see them then and they didn't fire at me at all. And the next thing that happened was that John O'Callaghan, from Newcestown, came along and he had all the cables wrapped right round him. 'Great God', he said, 'I was disturbed for you! I was down near the road and I was able to battle my way up only for you holding this place.' So John came along with the cables. Then a young fellow came along. He had been set up on the road at the far side of the field (i.e. at the next bend on the by-road, about two hundred yards further on) that we were facing. (He was, in fact, Joe Murphy, of Lissarda, the only man Kelleher would not have known, as he belonged to a different Brigade. He was the man who brought the dread message to Lehane's of Ballytrasna, later that evening. cf. Chapter Eleven. Joe Donal Oge, as he was known, appears dramatically in the final tableau in the present work). It was a boggy field. This young fellow came along to us and he said Michael Collins was shot. I said, 'Who told you that?' He said, 'Seán Galvin'. I said, 'Where is Seán Galvin?' He said, 'He's right over there. He must have heard them talking about it!'

B.B.C.I.: So you didn't see Collins being shot?

T.K.: Oh, no, I didn't!

B.B.C.I.: Did you hear the bullet that shot him though? I mean — did you hear the sound of it?

T.K.: Oh, no, no, no! We heard shots in that direction, but I was concerned about my own side all the time. I heard no shot fired on my right side. At my right would be O'Callaghan. He couldn't fire shots because he was loaded with the mine equipment. Beyond him were Sonny O'Neill and Dan Holland. [Note: There is a fairly clear picture here of the final line-out along the ambush roadway, allowing for some inevitable switching of positions as the action progressed: Tom Kelleher (Crowhill), Jim Hurley (Clonakilty), John O'Callaghan (Newcestown), Dan Holland (Barryroe), Sonny O'Neill (Kilbrittain), Joe Murphy (Lissarda), Tim O'Sullivan (Kilpatrick), Jim Kearney (Kilpatrick), Ted O'Sullivan (Bantry), Shawno Galvin (Crookstown)]. Dan Holland was Commandant, First Battalion. He wasn't there all the time. I don't think he had any rifle. He'd have a small gun. Sonny O'Neill didn't fire first or he didn't fire last, because if he fired I'd have known it. I believe one of the four (British officers) shot him (Collins).

B.C.I.:   Were you on the side where the monument is now?

T.K.:   Oh, no!

B.C.I.:   You were on the other side?

T.K.:   Oh, sure! You know there's a small kind of boreen, a narrow road, and we had a good position where we were in the boreen.

B.C.I.:   On the other side from the monument?

T.K.:   We were on the left-hand side of the road going down into Béalnabláth (i.e. from Bandon). We were on the left-hand side, in a narrow boreen. We had a good position! (And I like Tom Kelleher's attitude of the knowledgeable and indulgent father explaining a vital matter of life and death to a clever but rather tiresome child).

*   *   *

Denis Conroy looked at me across the sitting-room fireplace, and I looked at him. We were occupied a moment with our thoughts, and we looked at each other wonderingly . . . 'They wouldn't do it now!', said he at last. 'They would, Denny', I said, 'if the occasion arose!' And we looked into the fire figuring what the occasion might be, and if they would.

*   *   *

Michael J. O'Hea was a bank manager in Tallow, Co. Waterford. Before his retirement, twenty-odd years ago, he told a strange story to a friendly client, Jack Hegarty, of Ballynoe. As a young bank clerk in 1922 he was appointed to a post in Monaghan town. A native of Barryroe, he was on his way through Clonakilty to take up the appointment, knowing that he would have to travel by boat from Cork to Dublin. It was 22 August and the Collins convoy was in town. He went into a shop and met Collins on the way out with the *Cork Examiner* in his hand. Shortly afterwards O'Hea was in a pub where he heard some soldiers from the convoy talking about Collins. They had English accents. One of them suddenly ejaculated — 'We'll get the bastard yet before the night is out!' Well, maybe Tom Kelleher had a point after all!

22

The Parallax Dilemma

And the dark secret of Béalnabláth slides, as it were, into the labyrinth of Cretan mythology, gloomy, sinister and incomprehensible. A spanner in the works or a cat among the pigeons are mild metaphors compared to what Mr. James Joseph (J.J.) Kearney of Bandon, late of Kilpatrick, has done to the accepted notions and the reports to date on the battle of Béalnabláth. In fact, 'OUT OF the valley of death charged the six hundred!' It was fought, he says, in quite a different location from the accepted one, a quarter of a mile up the road towards Bandon, around Ahalarick bridge. On the side of the Irregulars were three young men (and three only!) armed with pistols. They were John O'Callaghan (of Newcestown), Tim O'Sullivan and Jim Kearney himself (of Kilpatrick), and their weapons, reading from left to right from where I sit, were a Mauser, a Luger and a Colt, 'If you know what that is!', he said to me a few short hours ago on this Thursday, 22 September 1988. I knew what a Colt was quite well, having used one in foreign parts. I also was familiar with a Luger 'Parabellum', said to be the best automatic ever made, and I had test-fired a Mauser 'Peter the Painter' many years ago in Ballyvourney. He also asked me please to believe that three young men of twenty or thereabouts took cover behind a slightly raised bank of clay, grass and rubble and replied as best they could to an armoured convoy of Free State soldiers ranging up and down the main road, across the brook, thirty yards or so distant from their 'green lane', firing at them incessantly with a Vickers machine-gun, two Lewis-guns, some Thompson sub-machine guns, assorted rifles and pistols, but left 'after fifty-five minutes to our great relief' just as John O'Callaghan whispered to him to ask if he happened to have a white handkerchief 'because we might think of surrendering'! Jim is a mild and gentle old man who wants the 'truth' finally to be told because he has torn out practically all of his hair at the enormity of the lies and blatant inaccuracies that have been printed to date about the death of Michael Collins. J.J. Kearney certainly corroborates the principle he knows to have passed between two writers of history of his acquaintance — 'Feehan said to Meda: "Stick to the sensational! Nothing else will sell!" '

The whole action of the day, Jim Kearney says, centred around Ahalarick bridge (i.e. 350 yards from the present monument and a further two-hundred from the original centre of the battle as it is generally understood); and in his own good time Michael Collins walked 'down the road' (i.e. towards the monument location) in full view, carrying a rifle at the slope, and fell two hundred yards from where he was believed to have fallen, having been hit by a rifle bullet fired from the hill above by Sonny O'Neill using regular dum-dum bullets captured from the Black-and-Tans. 'I dropped him', said Sonny O'Neill to Jim on the following morning, 'with one of these', showing him the flat-nosed slugs, 'and I dropped Smith (i.e. the lieutenant) with another!' At the time, Jim said, he had heard the shots being fired from that particular direction, not knowing who fired them. He thought it might have been 'a well-known Republican officer who was in the farmhouse above (Long's) during the battle and didn't bother to come down'. Caveat! Let one beware! Snap judgements and hasty rejoiners are not of the order of this day. At eighty-six James Joseph Kearney was still a Peace Commissioner. He was a non-smoker and a golden jubilarian of the P.T.A.A. He has, in his day, been an accomplished athlete, a regular soldier, and is still (1990) in almost perfect health. Other credits are: Cork County Chairman of the N.A.C.A. and national vice-president, and a life member of the National Historical Association under whose auspices he has frequently lectured — and he is a poet of gentle and saintly feeling. How is that for credibility! And he firmly believes that his old friend, Tom Kelleher, was mad. Against Jim Kearney is the weight of evidence to date. His still, small, gentlemanly voice, pleading sadly for a belated truth, may be highlighting an even darker secret of Béalnabláth — but probably not!

*   *   *

I handed a plastic 'Peter the Painter' (Honk Kong issue), perfect in almost every detail, to old Jim Kearney. He took it gingerly in his hand and said — 'For a moment I thought it was the real thing!'

*   *   *

Mrs. Meda Ryan, author of *The Day Michael Collins was Shot*, took Jim Kearney's story as Gospel truth, and drew a map to illustrate. She also had Jim Wolfe, the driver of the armoured car on the day, inspect the ground. He explained how he drove the *Slievenamon* up and down beyond the Ahalarick bridge entrance to Foley's, of Bengour, during the course of the battle. The sketch-map (supra) was adroitly montaged to suit the narrative, and incorporated the rather tricky skirmish taking place around the gate pillars half a mile away. Sonny O'Neill is accommodatingly shown as appearing in Foley's avenue (Bengour) to fire his fatal shot, whereas Jim Kearney showed the present writer the spot where he said O'Neill had stood, at Long's junction three hundred yards away, to fire the brace of shots. At this point the analysis becomes a dilemma — the parallax dilemma!

I stood on the road beside Ahalarick bridge with Jim Kearney and pointed to his stated position across the brook some thirty or forty yards away and on the level. 'They could have reached you with stones, Jim', I said, 'not to mention grenades, machine-guns and rifles!' The old man looked puzzled and then confused. 'Have it your own way', he said, not truculently but patiently. How to explain the mistaken position! It is understandable that battle conditions produce related fatigue and trauma, which in turn produce illusion . . .

In all kinds of combat the whole body is battered by emotion. The ductless glands pour their fluids into the system to make it stand up to the great demand on it. Fear and ferocity are products of the same fluid. Fatigue toxins poison the system . . . In the dullness all kinds of emphases change . . . The whole world becomes unreal . . . The outlines in your memory are vague . . . Men in prolonged battle are not normal men. And when afterwards they seem to be reticent — perhaps they don't remember very well. (John Steinbeck, *Once There Was A War*).

Now, the parallax dilemma is simply this, that an object appears to change shape, position and distance when looked at from different points of view. The confusing of J.J. Kearney, whether subjectively or objectively, created a new problem for this present investigation, as well as for the study for Irish Television (R.T.E.) done recently, in the form of a large-scale documentary named 'The Shadow of Béalnabláth', by journalist Colm Connolly of Dublin. Undoubtedly Mr. Kearney misplaced his battle. At least all the evidence pointed that way. In extenuation, there are five similar L-shaped positions to choose from, two of them almost identical, the latter being the laneway from Bengour onto the 'green road' by the river bank at Ahalarick bridge, and the laneway from Long's farm onto the accepted ambush by-road. Next, Holland's laneway is parallel to Long's, and finally the two by-roads themselves come onto the main road at ninety degrees at both bridges. Perhaps old Jim Kearney did not remember very well. Perhaps the others did not. He at least had the wit to enjoy the spectacle of R.T.E.'s man at Béalnabláth attacking a clump of bushes and briars, in pouring rain, with a nail scissors in search of an historic heap of stones!

The problem of Michael Collins' military cap is a persistent aggravation. Is it the one in the glass case in the National Museum in Dublin? It is, everybody says. It is not, everybody else says. Does anybody know? Yes! Jim Kearney knows. He found it himself early the following morning after the ambush. It was lying in a deep trench, a one-and-a-half foot surface-water dyke, beside the road at the point where the little river touched. There was no river bank at that point. He lifted the cap out and found it full of blood and, as he said, brains. The stream was so close to the road that he was not able to reach down to wash the cap in the flowing water. So he simply emptied the contents in the drain. In the cap itself he found a large hole, not a tear, in the back and just at the right of the vertical seam, into which he could place the tips of his five fingers in a bunch. From where Collins fell the cap had been blown right across the road, showing that he had been hit from the back. No other tear showed, so the fragmented or flattened bullet may still have been in the cap when he emptied the contents. A gruesome but historic souvenir is still probably reposing a few inches below ground as that particular spot has not been changed in the meantime. Which spot? Ah, yes! There are two spots where the stream touches the road. One is the location of his death as pictured in the *Pathé Gazette* a couple of days later. The other is almost two hundred yards further up the road where Jim said he saw Michael Collins fall. Tom Hales had been billeted in Long's farmhouse on the hill. Jim found him still in residence. Hales removed the military badge to keep as a souvenir. Jim went over by the 'Green Hill' to Murray's house (not to be confused with Murray's above Béalnabláth village). Finding a shovel in an outhouse he buried the cap between two large sycamores of a row just below the garden gate. On the following morning the man of the house thought it improper to leave the cap so. He dug it up, washed it in a bucket of water, brought it into the house and placed it in an alcove under the stairs. Three weeks later Fr. Coffey, the curate in Newcestown, came to say the 'Station' Mass. Mr. Murray removed the cap, as a bad omen, before the Mass began and then gave it to Fr. Coffey who took it to the Military H.Q. in Bandon.

The cap as worn by Michael Collins had a circular spring in the crown, according to Jim Kearney, to keep the shape. The cap, said to be his, in the Dublin museum is without the spring, has no tear in the back (only a rent in the seam) and looks (from extant pictures) very like the one worn by Emmet Dalton. Some say the original was removed and replaced by the present one. Likewise, many years ago, a military uniform was on display in the museum where now there is just the overcoat. That uniform had a button missing, and there was a note which said that it was the uniform of Michael Collins and that no none knew the whereabouts of the button. (The present writer received it from San Francisco some few years back, with 'Commander-in-Chief: Michael Collins' engraved on it). No one now knows the whereabouts of the uniform itself.

We called to a house, Jim Kearney and yours truly. We were looking for a house. We were told that there was no household of the name of Murray around here. But there might have been one time. Better ask the old man. We did. I saw recognition dawn, mingled with disbelief, as the two senior citizens confronted each other on the kitchen floor. Tom Foley not only remembered Jim Kearney but he remembered the story of the cap. The relief of J.J. was enormous. We had failed to find a road where he expected a road and he had begun to doubt his own memory. 'You are right about the house!', said Tom Foley. 'Congratulations!', I said. We were home. Tanner's was the house we sought. The present occupant's father had married old Patrick Murray's daughter many years ago. We all went up to Tanner's. The house was unoccupied. Jim recognized it right away. 'But where is the laneway to the house?', he asked. 'Not from here!', said Tom Foley. 'You go under the "Green Hill" beyond Long's and COME DOWN the laneway!'. 'Right you are!', said old Jim. We found it exactly as they said and a few minutes later I stood reverently on the spot where Michael Collins' military cap, which he wore at such a proud and defiant angle, had lain buried for awhile after the battle of Béalnabláth.

23

The Gemini Syndrome

There were two men of the name of 'Lieutenant Smith' attached to the Army in Cork at the time of, and subsequent to, the death of Michael Collins. One of them was the motor-cycle scout at Béalnabláth. The other was in charge of the lying-in-state of Collins' body at Shanakiel hospital on the following day. They both left the Army after the Civil War. One of them disappeared without trace. The other reappeared two years later, rejoined the Army and got married in Collins' Barracks in 1925. Twenty years later, during the Emergency, he claimed to have been the scout for the Collins convoy. In the Army he became a famous horseman. After the Emergency he was for a short while equerry to the British Royal Family, went to Canada to take over a riding school, died there and was buried with full military honours in St. Finbarr's Cemetery, in Cork, in 1956. Lieutenant A was said to be a native of Wexford. Lieutenant B was born in Westmeath but left at an early age. Lieutenant A rode out of Portobello Barracks, Dublin, at the head of the Collins entourage on Sunday morning, 20 August 1922. Lieutenant B was sent from Cork to Limerick to meet the convoy on the same day. Two motor-cycle scouts left Limerick with the convoy. One of them led Michael Collins into Cork on his fateful last journey. Who was he? Or were they both the same man? 'You can't prove it!', said Colm Connolly. 'No, but I can write it!', I replied.

*   *   *

Maurice Donegan, 'Mossie' to his friends and acquaintances, was O/C of the Fifth (Bantry) Battalion, Third (West Cork) Brigade, and an active member of Tom Barry's 'Flying Column', when he was captured by the British on the twenty-first of November, 1920. Thus he missed some major engagements of the Black-and-Tan War, but emerged again in good time for the Civil War. His calibre as a leader and fighter was (according to Liam Deasy in *Towards Ireland Free*) on a par with Barry's own. His calibre as a joker and opportunist was on a par with any other Irishman. Thus he accosted a Free State Army officer, a lieutenant, in a pub in Clonakilty when he needed to get back home to Bantry. He was a 'wanted' man. He acted the worse for drink. The officer was a kindred spirit and, suspecting no Republican affiliations or likely not caring much, provided him with transport. The Civil War was as good as over anyhow. They met once again, Mossie Donegan and his benefactor, when many old Republicans answered the call of their country during the 'Emergency' (1939-1945) and returned to the Colours bringing with them their long concealed weapons. The Free State Army was now Dev's Army. The lieutenant was now a captain. The order in which one hears the lieutenant's name and the captain's name is immaterial. The chronological is convenient. The lieutenant was John Joseph Smith. The captain was James Austin Smith. Believe it or not! Positively not, said Lieutenant-General (retd.) Seán Collins-Powell. Can't say for sure, said Lieutenant-Colonel (retd.) Seán Clancy of Dublin, but the thing was frequently mooted, he added. Absolutely yes, said Lieutenant-Colonel (retd.) George McEnery of Tralee — 'I was present at the reunion' i.e. of Mossie Donegan and his lieutenant. One would have thought that Béalnabláth had no further mystery to offer.

*   *   *

Lieutenant J.J. Smith certainly could a tale unfold. All others who have essayed to do so, on his behalf, have invariably referred to him simply as 'Lieutenant Smith' except, that is, Calton Younger who called him Lieutenant plain Jack Smith as if it seemed necessary to him to hang a label somewhere. Reading between the lines of his ebullient account (*Cork Examiner*, 24 August 1922) of the Béalnabláth ambush, or 'engagement', as he would have it, makes a lot of sense. His terms of reference are worthy of careful scrutiny, allowing for exaggeration. In one literary effort running comments in italics, on his disclosures, are mainly arbitrary and totally trivial, while being seen to be erroneous in the light of later evidence. 'Lieutenant Smith', cut down to size, may be seen to be right as far as he goes. His 'profuse strains of unpremeditated art' may turn out to be the authentic notes of Shelley's skylark whose blithe spirit soared over all while blithe newcomers of his time and ours may conceivably appear as emulators of Wordsworth's cuckoo. Which is not to say that books on Collins ever dare to aspire to the 'raison d'être' of Delaney and Feehan's *Comic History of Ireland* (following *1066 and All That* of the early thirties); but the political bias of Piaras Béaslaí, on the one hand, on the other, of Dorothy Macardle, the wild imaginings of Desmond Ryan, the elaborate flounderings of Margery Forester, to each his — and her — own right through the vast Collins biography, including the emotional 'volte-face' of Frank O'Connor, all in one way or another catch at water-logged straws in an effort to exorcise themselves of a ghostly chimera in place of a simple and complex, rough and gentle, sweet and sour, lovable and hateful, hard and soft, brave and craven, heroic and abominable, vulgar and courteous, devout and irreverent, civic and anarchic, capitalistic and communistic, radical and monarchic, fairly typical Irishman named Michael Collins who happened to be born great, to have achieved greatness and, sadly, to have greatness thrust upon him. It is the story of the Celtic nation since before even recorded Classical times. And already a well known Irish journalist has perpetrated a massive volum to end all volumes for the Collins Centenary of 1990.

At home in 'The Hollow', Irish Street, Enniscorthy, Co. Wexford, Lieutenant J.J. Smith had been known in his youth as 'John-Joe'. What else! Oh, yes! — 'Jeersy', for no known reason. He joined the freedom-fighters during the 'Trouble' times, became a member of the First Battalion, Wexford Brigade, I.R.A., and in the fullness of time joined the Free State Army. His designation was 'Scout Officer' and by curious coincidence, when Emmet Dalton led a large armoured column from Dublin down through Wicklow and Wexford, in the previous July, 1922, Smith proudly led them into his native Enniscorthy from which the Republicans had just been ousted. When Dalton had been established in Cork City, on 10 August, Lieutenant Smith was transferred there in the same capacity as scout officer. He was sent to Limerick to meet the Collins convoy, replaced a Lieutenant Corbett, another scout officer, and proudly led Collins home to die.

Lieutenant J.A. Smith was a blithe spirit. His personality was such that he was known throughout the Irish Army, into the 'Emergency' years of World War Two, simply as 'James Austin', and at a time when 'parameter' still merely expressed an independent variable in a Higher Mathematics formula. James Austin's parameters were fluid and far-flung. He was a fun-seeker, an entertainer and a ladies' man (according to some who knew him). His rank and superb horsemanship he obtained somehow. Obviously the expression, 'to make a horse laugh', comes to mind as does the superb horsey character of Ivor Claire in Waugh's *Officers and Gentlemen*. James Austin was wounded, though only slightly, at Béalnabláth i.e. assuming that he may have been the 'Jeersy' Smith who is still accredited in his native place with having identical characteristics with the above. His account of the battle to the Press was naturally hilarious. Even the imaginative painting of the battle by W.S. Rogers, rather obviously based on his account with no regard for locale or other necessary particulars, had him sitting on the ground wounded even before Michael Collins himself was hit. George McEnery, one-time personnel officer at the Curragh Military Camp, has suggested that Smith was in command at Kinsale during the remainder of the Civil War. Undoubtedly he gave safe passage and transport to the discomfitted and 'legless' Republican from Bantry. Major Mossie Donegan, now his superior officer, and himself 'laughed heartily' at the memory when they met once again and all were friends in a different cause. Did the lieutenant change his identity? If so, why? Die-hard republicanism was rife for many years to come and reprisals were not unknown. 'We picked off a couple of them', he said in public, 'and could see them fall'. Also, from the Free State point of view, he had betrayed the presence of the Big Fellow to the watcher at Béalnabláth Cross. In the disturbed times that were, the blow might come from either side to an unarmed civilian as he later was. At any rate the scene had changed radically when Captain James Austin Smith met Major Maurice Donegan, two decades later, at the Curragh of Kildare.

Willie 'Whack' Gleeson, late of the *Limerick Leader* and the Free State Army (cf. Chapter Eleven) came to know ex-Lieutenant Smith in Limerick just after the Civil War. He had been the scout at Béalnabláth, freely talked about it and showed the wound in his neck as corroboration. He stayed at the home of Gleeson's Uncle Mick in the Assembly Mall (also known as Charlotte Quay), who was owner of the *Record Printing Works*. He was known to them as 'Jimmy'. I showed Willie Gleeson a picture of James Austin, in dress-uniform, dancing with his wife. 'That's the man', said Willie without hesitation. 'Looks a bit older, but that's Jimmy Smith all right!' All right

24

History as a Moving Target

> And all our yesterdays have lighted fools
> The way to dusty death.　　　(*Macbeth*)

A young American journalist from a Florida newspaper, who had somehow got wind of the Bobs Doherty story, arrived at my front door and asked, 'Have you yet got the name of the man who shot Michael Collins?' I said, 'Not quite, but let me explain to you the various groupings and the near impossibility of ever knowing who fired the actual shot which killed him, or indeed the kind of missile, without an exhumation of the body'. 'Why should it matter', he asked, 'if it is just between one Republican group and another, known or unknown, all of whom happened to be on the spot?' And do you know, I hadn't thought of that! Self-consciously I replied, 'There is still the political situation which affects the peace of mind of this country, and you would need to be Irish to understand that — if at all!'. 'I am Irish', was what he said.

* * *

Then some film makers came from Hollywood 'to do a movie' on the life and times of Michael Collins. They wanted a Pancho Villa. They needed a Pancho Villa — murderous, treacherous, wenching and stenching, a-sexual, b-sexual, c-sexual, x-y-zee-sexual, drunked, flunked, and debunked, valued and devalued, signed, sealed and delivered! They said so. We said No! So, Mr. Director went home and got fired! End of film!

*   *   *

Who, then, was this man, Collins? Did anybody really know? Was the 'Finis Poloniae' of the Polish republican hero, Kosciusko, in any sense a 'Finis Hiberniae' when Mick fell at Béalnabláth? Was he a Sarsfield at Landen wishing his ebbing life-blood was for Ireland? Was he a Leonidas at Thermopylae? Was he a Brian Boru at Clontarf? A Roland at Roncesvalles? To be any of these historically he should have died in Dublin in an alternative endeavour, a different cause. Perhaps he meant to. The village at my door was the Pass of Thermopylae, alternatively a rallying place for Republicans and a salient of the Free State Army. The cliffs of Mount Oeta and the Gulf of Lamia were the Ballyhoura Mountains and the Blackwater River, and Collins was Xerxes. The defenders were few — Commandant Jim Brislane of the Charleville Battalion, Brigade-Staff Commandant Paddy O'Brien, both from my next village, Liscarroll, and some others from the locality, with the great General Seán Moylan brooding over all like a classical god of war. One of the defenders, Peter O'Farrell, published his memoirs in New York City and with a pardonable hyperbole of age, time and distance, has this to say:

We then retreated along the Kilmallock road to Garrienderk Bridge. I was placed on the railroad at Charlie Culhane's with three others, as the Staters had taken Knocksouna Hill and we expected an attack along the railway. Ned McCarthy had a section in Ballinagoul, at the Maigue Bridge, and kept Knocksouna busy. John Pender supplied the boys with plenty of milk as we retreated past the pub. Seán Moylan came and inspected the defence positions and marked the road every hundred yards for rifle range as far as Buck Moloney's. The retreat from Ashill Towers was under deadly fire. They had the range from the hill below the Church. They knew that as our only line of retreat and they put everything into it — Lewis guns, Thompsons and Vickers. It was a veritable rain of lead. We had to crawl through it as far as Emmet's Bridge, and luckily there was not a casualty. We held these positions for approximately a week, and then received orders to break the lines and to return to our local units 'on the run' to form local columns. . . . About two hours later (i.e. after Collins had driven by on 20 August) two scouts (Pa Motherway and Seán Riordan, Charleville) arrived at the house and ordered us (J. Tarrant, Ned Treacy and myself) to report to Cooline (i.e. in Ballyhea) to form a column. When we arrived in Cooline a group of about twelve were picked to act as a retreat unit and proceeded to Fortlands House (near Charleville). Eight hundred Free State soldiers had just arrived in Charleville. They were lying down on the street due to the heat of the day, dog-tired, coming from Limerick and Tipperary on the way to Cork. The unit, as best I can remember, was Mick Denny Sullivan, Column Commander, Con McCarthy, Mick Ryan, Tom Culhane, Kid Donoghue and myself. Our assignment was to go to Ballysally graveyard and railway road, and rake the main street with Thompson and rifle fire. The Commanding Officer, who was facing a large bay window overlooking the back of the town, saw about two hundred Free State soldiers in open formation approaching the house. We got out and fought a retreating action all the way back through Spring Fort to Cooline . . . In the meantime, at the Cross of the Frolic, Commandant (Paddy) O'Brien had arrived by car. (Note: With him was his adjutant, Captain Mick Geary of Charleville, still to the good in 1990, and Mossie O'Brien, the Free State officer wounded at Spur Brien's, who had now joined his old comrades). There were two or three other cars being shifted and there were also some stragglers showing up to join the Column. At the same time a column of Free Staters went as far as the brickyard in an encircling movement to cut off our retreat from Fortlands. The Frolic (a crossroads position a mile from Charleville) was bombarded with rifle fire, grenades and Thompson fire, but all (of us) got away without any casualties . . .'.

The compelling nature of the advance into County Cork was much as to preclude any significant resistance. From here on the fields of home were literally crawling with soldiers, frequently on their bellies or advancing in open formation across the boglands, streaming over the Awbeg river and along by the banks of Spenser's beloved Mulla where he had wandered and dreamed of his far distant and elusive *Faerie Queene*. For all it matters now the 'Staters' might have come in 'Plus-Fours' and sports cars, with placards announcing, 'We are the new Civil Service', and would have been received with amusement and disbelief. (For an insight into the nature of Collins' new Civil Service, Mervyn Wall's stories, in *A Flutter of Wings*, are incisive, somewhat surrealistic and extremely funny). Collins had been restive all day, Sunday, with moods changing by the hour. In Limerick he went on inspection of guard posts about the city and environs. He kicked in the gates of the post at Bruree, startling little Willie Gleeson who was on guard duty but on the safe side and had, therefore, nothing to fear. At Kilmallock the Commander-in-Chief was confident. Limerick was under his control, and he was about to enter County Cork. At Garrienderk bridge, broken and dilapidated, he was once again restive and hostile, at Charleville impatient to be on, at Mallow sullen and non-communicative at having to stop and consult. Entering Cork he was exuberantly looking forward to returning to his native heath. Poised for the kill, he died simply and easily by a lonely roadside . . .

> Hope, for a season, bade the world farewell,
> And Freedom shrieked — as Kosciusko fell!

Take it anyway you please, but only this: an enigma General Michael Collins may have been — a mystery he need not remain!

Did Florrie Donoghue inadvertently blow Michael Collins' cover? After that vital meeting Florrie moved about the town of Macroom, acknowledging, and acknowledged by, both sides to the controversy. On the Republican side he talked to Commandant Dan Corkery, the Browne brothers, Charlie and Dick, and some others, and headed for Ballyvourney where Dev's last stand was being considered, and to where the man himself was frequently commuting from Gortafludig. So the Macroom men already knew that Collins was coming back to receive

Florrie's report, and the town was linked company by company with Crookstown. Florrie was neutral and conscientious, but also disillusioned and bitter. In his *No Other Law*, a good thirty years later, quoting a reply dated 4 August 1922, which Collins sent to Cork negotiators Mr. T.P. Dowdall and Fr. Tom Duggan, referring to 'the duties of Government, and to the fact that the time for face-saving had passed, the letter ended on a challenging and provocative note'. Florrie never saw Collins again. It is doubtful if he wanted to.

* * *

A few short years ago an enormous brush fire on the battle site of the Little Big Horn river, in Montana, U.S.A., where Custer made his last stand in 1876 fighting the Sioux Indians, disclosed such an amount of battle relics, including fired and unfired bullets, that the course of the battle was finally and completely clarified. Stranger still, the body of a young cavalry man from the U.S. Seventh Regiment, was found where he fell, just as the body of another young soldier was discovered more recently on a remote island of the American north-west where he had been sent, and somehow overlooked, during the course of World War Two. Michael Collins had a famous name and holds an unique place in History, but we still have not adequately examined the undergrowth (which is progressively obliterating the site) for clues of how he died, nor do we have military reports, and there must have been some, with regard to what was found on the immediate examination of the terrain following his death. So for the moment we may merely choose our words and construe our phrases on the perpetual subject of extraordinary men we call soldiers, known or unknown, who faced imminent annihilation in the fullness of life and 'died with their boots on' — or managed to survive. Collins deserves better than we have given so far.

* * *

The historic mile at Béalnabláth divides broadly into four relevant sections, the five salient features being: 1) Ahalarick

Bridge; 2) Collins Monument; 3) By-Road Bridge; 4) Barricade; 5) Béalnabláth Cross. From one end of Glanarouge to the other it savours of ancient warfare, this 'Valley of the Rout', from Ahalarick, the 'Ford of the Slaughter', to Pullerick, the 'Pool of the Slaughter'. The direction is precisely North and South, the elevation from 300-450 ft. Ahalarick Bridge is off the main road on a by-road crossing the stream and going off westwards to nowhere in particular but it marks the 'Top of the Height' from where things began to happen, that harvest evening in 1922. Michael Collins died forty yards distant from the present monument, on the road upwards towards Bandon. Though often referred to as such, it is not a hill, the gradient being only one in sixty. The monument, erected in 1924, was placed in its present position for convenience (whose, I have no idea!), against the rising ground on the right, or eastern, side of the road facing Béalnabláth. Shortly after his death a rough wooden cross was erected at the southern (Bandon) end of the 'quay-wall', a makeshift structure of stone and clay built where the stream touched the roadside. This cross was later removed (there is a story that it was smashed and replaced twice), and was unearthed some years ago in the sacristy of the chapel at Collins Barracks, Cork City, and erected in the military museum. In its place was set up a small, round-topped cone of cement, white-painted, and upon the face of which a black-painted cross was incised — 'Cloghafaermore', a new landmark in Irish History as it was in ancient legend in County Louth where Cuchulainn stood and fell mortally wounded having tied himself to the stone. Collins managed in life to give the impression of standing alone against the might of empire having tied himself to the 'Lia Fáil', the Stone of Destiny. The tiny pillar was moved when the stream and road were moved and is now across the road standing demurely beside the great monument, the authentic 'Cloghafaermore', the Stone of the Big Fellow. This is not going to be about ballistics 'per se'. It has to be about that great Irishman, Michael Collins, getting hit unexpectedly in the back of the head by some flying object, resulting in his premature death. Many people have studied, talked and written about the matter. Their efforts were various, their success 'comme il faut'. Philosophically ballistics is a sad business — it has to do with killing things. If the objective is animal life, it may touch the heart-strings, if human, it may bear the curse of Cain. And it goes on all the time. One of those countless times is vital, in fact central, to the history of our country resulting, as it did, in the death of Michael Collins. Who did it to him. Why? Where? How? When? . . . Who? is Politics. Why? is History. Where? is Graphics. How? is Ballistics. When? is immaterial.

*   *   *

The old Rolls-Royce 'Whippet' armoured car, designated 'A.R.R. 2' and more familiarly known as the *Slievenamon*, is eight feet four inches to the top of its revolving turret. The first time I made its acquaintance I climbed precipitately (quite a feat for an ageing cleric) to the top of the turret. I was looking for something. I found it. To me it was something more valuable than the controversial Derrynaflan Chalice of the same time. My calculations had told me that there could be a distinctive bullet scar on top. There were two, ten inches apart and four inches long. The Army said: No! No! Impossible! An expert suggested infra-red photography. The Army said: What about all the cleaning and polishing and painting over the years? What about soft lead and hard steel? What about the relative scale of hardness? I said, What about that? The photographer took a regulation picture and there they were. Nobody, it seems, had gone up there before. The small square plate set in the centre of the hatch cover carried the two scars. They are parallel to each other and lie at an angle of eighty degrees to the direct line of fire of the Vickers gun. Extended they would lie just on the brow of the hill where the Kerrymen lay that evening and from where Dalton heard some firing. They are, as I have said, eight feet or so above ground. A tall man stands six feet. His gun, if he used one, would be at most five feet up on the horizontal plane when in a firing stance. The only times I knew of the *Slievenamon* being in action was at Béalnabláth, at Ballyvourney, and the time when Mick O'Sullivan ditched it with a 'Lancia' near Kilmallock. The old bus has two or three head-on bumps on her outer crust, dimples as it were. The ambush thing was an open country attack from behind rocks and walls and so forth, usually not to any great height above the ground. The 'Whippets' made fast, transverse runs firing as they went, and to the extent that anyone would bother aiming a rifle at a steel tower, it had to be the driver's or gunner's peep-hole or slit. Even in a town or city attack, it would still be true that it would be wasteful or futile to aim at the turret, more especially the turret top. McPeak had the hatch open coming into Glanarouge. One of the first bullets sheered off the hasp before he could get it closed. The elevation at Béalnabláth is, of course, the relevant point. The two gunmen by the pillars on the by-road, Jim and Tom, were on a higher level than the *Slievenamon* (about thirty feet) but the distance was too great against such an acute angle to cause the short, deep scars, or any scars at all. But Mike Donoghue and Bobs Doherty were eighty feet up in the air, and a bullet travelling at such a depressed angle was so much the more affected by the pull of gravity and air resistance, vital factors in ballistics, bringing the point of the bullet further down . . .

But if he was not shot by a .303 rifle, what kind of gun would inflict the type of wounds seen by the witnesses? The most likely answer to that question would seem to be: the Mauser pistol. The barrel and the body of the Mauser pistol are in one piece and it is normally supplied with a wooden holster which can be attached to the grip of the pistol and so turn it into a mini-rifle which can be fired from the shoulder. It usually fires a 7.45 mm or a 9 mm bullet which, when it strikes and enters the object, expands and tumbles and can tear the flesh to pieces inside. If the bullet emerged it usually leaves a large open wound at the point of exit. It is now considered a savage, uncivilised weapon which the Geneva Convention on War should have banned long ago! (From John M. Feehan, *The Shooting of Michael Collins*).

When I first read this paragraph I could hardly believe the 'site o' me eye'. I rang up a knowledgeable gunman. 'Listen to this!', I said, and I read the piece for him over the phone. 'That's all bullshit!', was what he said. Experts sometimes let the hair down and talk in simple language that can be understood by ordinary people. The 'tumbling' bullet interested me because that is the characteristic of the rather new and politically explosive 'Armalite' rifle, and more than makes up for the small calibre which is little more than a point-two-two 'Rook' or sporting rifle. The 'Armalite' bullet is boat-shaped for the purpose, which means that it tapers at both ends. Reading on from the above paragraph I find:

To aim at and hit a small target, such as a man's head, at 130 yards with a Mauser pistol, even with the stock on, would be little short of miraculous. Theoretically the Mauser can fire up to 500 yards but there is a vast difference between the distance a bullet can carry and the distance one can get an aimed shot on target. It is also unlikely, if they were really out to get Collins, that they would have waited till dusk and the uncertainty of a Mauser bullet.

In the interest of truth, the 'Peter the Painter' (Mauser) carries fixed sights set at 1,000 metres. The propellant is a high-powered powder which gives enormous velocity and the bullet itself is relatively small and, therefore, very little affected by gravity and drift. We have, then, a powerful, handy gun, extremely accurate at long range. With regard to the 'miraculous' nature of hitting a small target, such as a man's head, at 130 yards with a Mauser automatic, there is this from a training schedule of the British Army during World War Two: 'At two hundred yards all parts of the body are distinctly seen. At three hundred yards the outline of the face is blurred. At four hundred yards — no face. At six hundred yards the head is a dot and the body tapers.' With the sights pre-set at almost eleven hundred yards, the Mauser was tested, designed and meant for serious business at long range and was far handier than a rifle. Its 'bark' was very distinctive. On the occasion of the series of tests mentioned already, an old Republican wandered onto the range and said: 'Was that a "Pether" I heard?' Finally, there is a nice piece on it in the *Encyclopaedia Britannica* (1950 edition):

For although the latter (i.e. the Mauser as against the bigger bored revolver) may exhibit more 'calculated' energy on paper, its metal case causes it to penetrate cleanly and its limited diameter results in an almost tiny perforation through the tissues, with little bleeding; and by reason of its high velocity it usually passes on through the target to expend most of its energy upon the scenery beyond.

I have seen in my time just one clip of 'dum-dum' Mauser pistol ammunition. I believe this kind of ammunition was rare, but it did exist. The copper casing, I remember, was so neatly stripped back, though slightly, from the lead point that it was obviously manufactured in that condition i.e. not done deliberately by the operator. Now that would be damaging, but far less so than a rifle bullet.

What has all of this to do with the death of Michael Collins? Everything, in fact. 'One of these two (i.e. the watchers at the pillars) was firing a Mauser pistol and was quite an experienced soldier'. (Feehan). Reading between the lines, this had to be Jim Hurley, twenty-one-year-old Commandant of the Second (Clonakilty) Battalion, big, powerful man, hurler, footballer, soldier, academician — the embodiment of an Irish rebel. (Jim Hurley never spoke of his Civil War activities, and Tom Barry's account, as a codicil to *Guerilla Days*, was so garbled that he must not have spoken to Barry either, though Jim was one of his top men. Neither did he divulge anything to his relations or close friends, of whom my father was one. Tom Kelleher spoke openly to anyone and everyone, loved automatic weapons — latterly he used an umbrella to demonstrate the use of a 'tommy-gun' — was justly proud of his achievements but he fired only a rifle at Béalnabláth). Jim Hurley's rapid Mauser fire was one of the outstanding features at Béalnabláth. It was that which shattered the windscreen of the Leyland Eight, stopped the clock and gave Emmet Dalton the impression of being under machine-gun fire. But Jim Hurley did not shoot Collins. He was gone when the 'Big Man' fell. The renewed burst of firing which Dalton mentioned, as they were removing the body of the Chief, had to come from Jimmy Ormond's group, if not from himself. It was then Smith got wounded in the neck, and the nature of the wound was such that it did not prevent the lieutenant from carrying on. Only a Mauser flesh wound would have left him in that condition.

*   *   *

'Speculation apart, the shot which killed Michael Collins came at a time when the fire of ambushers and ambushed was silent — in itself a point which favours further investigation' (Rex Taylor).

*   *   *

The enormity of the wound at the back of Collins' head has been laboured to the point of wonderment. For sure, Ireland's greatest revolutionary will never, to the end of time, be let die from a mere shot to the head. It is important to analyse the nature and extent of the damage. A Lee-Enfield rifle bullet (.303 in.) is sharp-pointed, made of lead and either nickel coated or antimony hardened. Off the perfect trajectory it is capable of two curious tricks known as 'key-holing' and 'yawing'. The former means that it stands on its nose or tail as it flies, the latter, that it spits weakly out of the gun muzzle. Either way it indicates faulty loading of powder grains in the shell case, but it still moves at high speed and tends to cause a tearing of flesh rather than a clean puncture. It is just possible, but difficult to believe, that one such bullet caused such extensive damage to Collins' head. The area of detrition, by all accounts, was vast. What if a .303 bullet bounced off the top or side of the *Slievenamon* — what is called a 'ricochet'? In this case it gets flattened to some extent, and may also be set spinning, resulting in extensive, but superficial trauma. Even still it scarcely meets the facts of the case. German Mauser sporting rifles were reasonably common during the 'Troubles'. They were meant for heavy game (the image of the fat, belted, booted, stockinged, feather-hatted and smooth-faced German, stalking wild boar through the forests, is familiar to all), and had a larger bore (8mm or .315 in. An earlier Mauser repeating rifle had a massive 11mm or .433 in. bore). The bullets were longer than those of the Lee-Enfield, had round tips, were encased merely in soft copper and were meant to flatten, 'mushroom' or even disintegrate on impact. A ricochet of this kind would flatten to an inch in diameter (or three inches in circumference) with serrated edge, and do vast damage. Moreover the Mauser rifle bolt was quicker to work than that of the Lee-Enfield and two shots could be got off in as many seconds (I have seen it demonstrated!). Bobs Doherty heard someone say: 'I put two into him!', before he 'saw the Big Man fall'! The glancing blow with no exit wound (as described by Dalton) could easily have been a Mauser rifle bullet bouncing off the armoured car. At close range a Webley (or other) revolver bullet (bare lead .455) bouncing off the back of his skull, might have created the type of wound suffered by Michael Collins, but there was nobody near enough to fire the shot. For the record, Mick O'Sullivan (*Where Mountainy Men Have Sown*) was shot literally in the teeth with such a revolver bullet in an attack on Free State troops stationed in the Carnegie Library, Millstreet. As he rushed the door the bullet hit him in the mouth, blew in his teeth and disintegrated into six pieces which lodged against and around his spine remaining there, of necessity, until his death in 1986.

*   *   *

At last I get the whisper of a name. It came with St. Swithin and in a strange manner. A Limerick family wanted to visit Béalnabláth, a sentimental journey. Their granduncle had been there for that Tuesday conference of the First Southern Division. It had taken him four days to make the journey. Because of the death of Michael Collins he returned home and opted for neutrality, washed his hands of the business, as they say. But in some strange manner, unspecified, he got to know, and passed on the knowledge to his family before he died, that Michael Collins was shot by a man from Glenflesk, named O'Connor. Now, Glenflesk, Co. Kerry, is intrigued rather than disgruntled by the claim to fame that a local man was responsible. It seems to be generally accepted there (qualified by a well known man of the place) that, 'Those who knew something wouldn't talk and those who knew nothing talked too much!' For many years Bobs Doherty had been the front runner, as it were, but the Glenflesk angle seems to indicate secret lines of communication between the higher echelons. This family, at any rate, knew enough to pick the 'right man' in Macroom to act as guide to Béalnabláth and in return passed on the long kept secret. I hastened to check my roster of Glenflesk men hoping desperately for an O'Connor. There were three. There was Pat at Loo Bridge. He was quite a young man. His father was known as 'Patsy Charlie' who worked as a forester for Lord Kenmare. He lived near Mike Donoghue. Could young Pat O'Connor be my man? No, said Pat Riordan — he got sick (as so many did) fighting the Black and Tans and died even before the Civil War began. Of the two brothers, Dan and Tom O'Connor from Cloghane, four miles away on the far, or Killarney side, of Glenflesk chapel, Tom was the younger and was the perpetual dispatch rider. So said his brother, Neily, the only survivor from a family of eleven. Tom was born to the bicycle and covered all that territory — with a sweep of the old man's hand — from Sliabh Luachra to the County Bounds. He never had a gun until a vast quantity of Free State stuff was captured at Kenmare in September of 1922. A truck load was transported to the home of Mike Quill (later the well-known American trades-unionist) in Kilgarvan, and of these, six rifles were deposited in Mike Donoghue's. Tom finally got his, but too late for Béalnabláth. This leaves Dan. Now, Dan was a man of mystery to the young brother, Neily, at eleven years of age, and an inveterate soldier. Many's the time young Neily saw his big brother, Dan, sling his trench coat over his shoulder and stroll off down the line to anywhere. The railway ran beside the house as it still does. Sometimes the train stopped to pick him up. This was pre-arranged through the oldest sister who worked at Tangney's Bar facing the entrance to Glanmire (now Kent Station in Cork City, where all the railway men went to drink. The oldest brother worked in Ford's of Cork, a hotbed of intrigue in those dangerous times. On one occasion the train driver only slowed down beside the railway bridge at Cloghane sufficiently to let Dan swing aboard where he found a train load of British soldiers, but the driver gave him a boiler suit and put him to work as a stoker. He was a 'great gunman', Pat Riordan said. In the Glenflesk company there were only three rifles. One was a Lee-Enfield rifle. This was in the possession of Pat Cronin who had been seconded to the Brigade 'Flying Column', the only Glenflesk man in it. He naturally took with him the Lee-Enfield rifle. Then there was the police carbine, a light short .303, for cycle or horseback use, captured in an attack of some patrol or station. Finally, there was the Martini Henry, standard for the British Army at the end of the previous century, the magnificent, long-barreled single-shot, the perfect sniper's weapon, the gun that vanquished the Zulus. Two shells in a man's fist could be slipped into the peculiar slide-block before the breech and fired twice as fast as the rough-and-tumble of the Lee-Enfield bolt could do so. It had a massive .45 inch (11.4mm) lead bullet. It was Dan's gun . . . The Glenflesk men went to Limerick to help oppose the advance of the Free State Army. When that failed they returned home, arriving by lorry about two weeks before Béalnabláth. 'Where did Dan go after that?'. 'I have no idea', said Neily O'Connor, 'But he was away somewhere!'. 'Did he go with Mike Donoghue's group to Cork Harbour?'. 'I don't know', said the old man pensively and then he laughed, 'But if he did, they arrived too late!'. Dan O'Connor, of Cloghane, Glenflesk, managed to avoid capture when things went completely wrong, and went to the States in 1925. Returning home some years ago, he bought a place near Rathmore, where he died leaving one daughter who now lives in the U.S.A. Was he the sharpshooter whose destiny it was to kill Michael Collins at Béalnabláth, and whose Martini-Henry rifle Mike Donoghue hit down after he had 'put two into him'? . . .

And now for the Co. Limerick family who went on a sentimental journey to Béalnabláth in 1974! The name was McNamara, from Cappamore at the foot of the Slieve Felim mountains. The granduncle was Maurice McNamara who had been a captain in the East Limerick Brigade, became a priest in the Cistercian Abbey at Mount Melleray and died in 1973 at the age of ninety. As an I.R.A. officer during the Tan War he was a judge of the Sinn Féin 'Arbitration Court' in the locality when British administration had broken down. He conducted two 'law cases' in his time, both at Walsh's of Bilboa (between Cappamore and Doon). The first was of a man accused of stealing apples (in the Black and Tan era), the second, a courtmartial-type trial of a man accused of shooting Michael Collins — the sublime and the ridiculous! All that is known is that this man was 'O'Connor from Glenflesk in Kerry'. The story was that he went on the run after Béalnabláth. Wearing a boiler-suit, he came from Kerry to Mallow on a train full of Free State soldiers, skipped the train in Mallow and made his way northwards to Cappamore. The result of the trial was merely that he was dismissed from the Republican Army. Disgruntled, he went to Cork where he worked until he went to America in 1925. Was he Dan O'Connor? Or was this some fantastic coincidence? There is yet another! Denis 'Sonny' O'Neill also went on the run after Béalnabláth. He also headed for Cappamore where he had a cousin named Bobby O'Neill (whose son, a vet, still lives in the place). This Bobby O'Neill was an officer in the Free State Army, met Collins in Limerick on his way through, and 'had a row' with the Big Fellow. Sonny O'Neill stayed for quite some time at Paddy Ryan's 'safe house' at Kilcommon Cross, seven miles away, and became well known in the region. He is still remembered as 'middle-sized, stocky, fair-haired and round-faced'. He later married a nurse in Nenagh where he lived until he died in 1950. He became an election agent for Eamon de

Valera in the 1932 campaign which got the Long Fellow finally into power. At one of those election gatherings he met Miss Kitty Teehan of Shipton, Co. Kilkenny (cf. Chapter Ten: 'The De Valera Story'), to whom he revealed the dread secret that it was he who had shot Collins at Béalnabláth. He did likewise on two other recorded occasions. He made a statement to the effect to Máire Comerford who typed out the statement and sent it to Seán Dowling, Director of Intelligence for the I.R.A. The note is now in private hands (See 'The Shadow of Béalnabláth' documentary). Finally, Sonny O'Neill told Jim Kearney, on the morning after the ambush, that it was he who had shot Collins. As he did so (according to Jim Kearney) he took a couple of bullets from his pocket to show the type he used. 'Dum-Dums' is what old Jim told the present writer they were, but on questioning it transpired that they were just a couple of antique round-headed Lee-Enfield bullets. So much for expertise!

*   *   *

The evidence, such as it is or ever will be, is now in for the seven soldiers of the Republic one of whom has to be the still unknown gunman who laid the great Michael Collins low. Which was he? It is fashionable now to ask — Does anybody care? 'Revisionist' History may be the style of the trendy times that are but, as in the 'revisionist' or avant-garde in Art, Music, Poetry, Religion, the question may likewise be asked — Does it help? Does the revisionist notion contribute to the good of the people, the nation and the world? Or should we stay with the wise and ancient dictum, 'nihil innovetur nisi quod traditum est? . . . A bright and erudite correspondent of the *Cork Examiner* (name of Seán Dunne) had a feature published in August, 1989, entitled: 'A PLAGUE ON BOTH YOUR HOUSES'. The final paragraph ran:

And as for the Civil War, which soiled our country and tore it apart, all I can say is this: A plague on (sic) both your houses! It is like a dusty old curtain over the window of a disused room. I think it would be best to rip it away, open the window and throw out the books and the video and the programmes and the blood-drenched songs. That way, the light might at last break through on a land fit for young and old to live in!

But what light is coming through in the Ireland of today? I am in the process of trying to let some light into the dusty room, but the view from that room, nowadays, is a physical, moral and social turpitude compared to which the Civil War was a noble episode in the country's history, and the death of Michael Collins was a noble sacrifice liturgically presented on the altar of a Celtic druid. You may keep your illicit sex, bubbling booze, cash flow and international acclaim! I'll continue to sit and think in my dusty room among the noble ghosts!

*   *   *

Henry Good was a Ballyvourney man, albeit a Protestant, who lived and worked in the safe custody of St. Gobnait's Shrine. A Tipperary man originally, his home accent, with latter-day Ascendancy overtones and strange diction peculiar to himself, was much mimicked and gave enjoyment in times when such was in short supply in a place where mutual mimickry was a way of life. A good Christian man was Henry who worked late and early, minded his own business and was well in with the neighbours. I knew him personally and have one regret that I was precluded from attending his obsequies, thirty odd years ago, by Church Law. He also kept a 'safe house' for the 'boys' in Trouble times, but retired into his shell, as it were, when Civil War loomed. In September, 1922, Ballymakeera village was occupied by Free State troops from Macroom, under Captain Dan Dineen (a cousin of mine from Peake, near Coachford). Henry was harvesting up near St. Gobnait's, high above the village. His workman kept a rifle handy by the ditch of the field and every so often ran down to fire a nuisance shot at the village far below and send the 'Staters' scurrying for cover, then ran back again to his binding of 'shaves'. Henry bore this with Christian fortitude until it finally got to him. 'Wot runnin' hafs you?', he yelled, 'Runnin' an' firin' an' firin' an' runnin'!

When they lafts you alone why don' you laf thum alone?' Or so my father said. What I am saying is that the much vaunted battle of Béalnabláth was a mere 'runnin' an' firin' an' firin' an' runnin' 'to the eye of a foolhardy bird, while the 'inadequate' convoy proved more than adequate — but Achilles died nonetheless.

*   *   *

'That's the type of mercenary that is doing the Irishmen's killings for them. He isn't a heroic or even a dramatic figure. He just sits hunched over his whiskey glass, worries about how to invest his money, lets his weasel mind run on and wishes the boys luck. The boys seem to be having it'. Ernest Hemingway wrote that as a 'point d'appui' and it was published in the *Toronto Star Weekly* on 11 December 1920. In December, 1920, any luck the 'boys' were having was considerably helped by one man. That man was Michael Collins. Hemingway was a young reporter who had run away from home to escape his mother. The suicidal tendency was already in embryo. In the Great War he had helped an impecunious Italy against a domineering Austria. Evidently he did not like the Hapsburgs. In the Spanish Civil War he assisted the Popular Front against Franco. He did not like the idea of monarchy . . . 'The world is a fine place!' he wrote in context. 'It is worth fighting for!' (From *For Whom the Bell Tolls*). A West-Cork man fleeing before the British forces in 1921, across the border mountain and boglands, exclaimed, 'Look what we're fighting for! It isn't worth wan clout of a fisht!' Ernest Hemingway led an irregular killer-group (or so he said!) against a retreating enemy in the Normandy campaign in World War Two. He disliked the Germans. He insinuated his men into Paris even before General Giraud. Perhaps he despised the French. 'War is hell!', said Sherman; 'War is fun!', said Hemingway. He relentlessly gloried in the destruction of big game animals, big bulls, big fish, big fighting men. The curse of the Gadarene swine eventually caught up with him. He lived to hate himself most of all, his disturbed genius wasting four good women while he still 'loved' the first and wished he were a better Catholic. 'Gunmen from the United States', he wrote, 'are being imported to do killings in Ireland'. Proof? 'That is an established fact from Associated Press dispatches'. Hard evidence?

In the Red Island they do their job of killing, collect their contract price and slip back to England. It is said that the price for a simple killing, such as a marked policeman or a member of the Black and Tans, is $400. It may seem exorbitant when you remember that the old pre-war price in New York was $100, but the gunman is a specialist and his prices, like those demanded by prize-fighters, have advanced.

. . . In Dublin, a couple of years ago, a little old man watched me as I chaired a meeting of the 'Friends of Michael Collins', called to prevent his memory being vulgarized by American film makers. The fading old eyes were still guardedly watchful and intense. They had once looked into the eyes of the only American known to have functioned in this country in a killer capacity — name of Lieutenant Ashley Aimes of Titusville, Pennsylvania, late U.S. Marines, leader of the 'Cairo Gang' working for the British. The Dubliner told the Yank to 'say an Act of Contrition' before putting a gun to his head. I looked in the old hooded eyes and wondered what else they had seen in the employ of Michael Collins as a member of his 'Twelve Apostles'. I was drawn to the old man, not repelled. I offered him transport to his home. 'No', he said shortly, 'I can manage!', and straightening his stooped shoulders with an effort proudly added, 'This is my town!' Commandant Vinnie Byrne walked home alone. But Hemingway wrote:

According to underworld gossip in New York and Chicago, every ship that leaves for England carries its one or two of these weasels of death bound for where the hunting is good. The underworld says that the gunmen are first shipped to England where they lose themselves in the waterfronts of cities like Liverpool and then slip over to Ireland.

One wonders what those places were that he fancied about, this England and this Ireland. Which was which? One, a large island, a mighty nation and empire with tentacles spreading far East, far West, far South, whose armed and motorized forces, for no certain reason, traversed the highways and byways, the lanes and back-alleys of the other which was a small island of no resources but a few thousand working men and women, constantly in danger of slipping off the Continental Shelf into the depths of the Porcupine Basin. One wonders which island was which to Hemingway, or whether he disliked working people and, in good old American style, loved decadent Royalty!

'For killing a well-guarded magistrate or other official as much as $1,000 is demanded . . . In the course of an afternoon I learned a number of things about the trade'. Hemingway is dead. He killed himself. De mortuis nil nisi bunkum! His motto as a writer was 'Integrity'. Displaying a degree of greatness, a brand of genius, he received the Nobel Prize for Literature, his citation reading that he was one of those who, honestly and undauntedly, reproduced the genuine features of the hard countenance of the age. Why, then, in a selection of his early and immature newspaper work, should appear (1976) long after his death, an atrocious piece of misinformed writing of which he was heartily ashamed, called 'Plain and Fancy Killings, $400 Up'? The citation this time was an editing by William White with commentary by Philip Young for *Penguin Books of Canada*. Men die but old hatreds live on and turn up in the most unexpected places, and for no certain reason. Papa Hemingway's 'volte-face' is a small concession to his memory . . . 'We walked up on him like a posse, or a gang of Black and Tans, guns ready and cocked . . .' (From *Green Hills of Africa*, 1935). The idea of a hired killer surfaced at Béalnabláth, ironically against the man who should, if he would, have paid Hemingway's 'weasels of death' in the first place. The idea has been taken up for serious consideration and publication. In Literature integrity and naïvete are strange bed-fellows.

*   *   *

So the Dark Secret of Béalnabláth will go on into Eternity and the identity of the man who killed Michael Collins shall never become known. Meanwhile the 'Utinam Factor', the 'What if he had lived!' idea, is sure to fill the long Winter evenings of those who like to speculate on what might have been. The circumstances of his death and the absence of an autopsy have exercised historians, agitated politicians and bemused the general public ever since. He was born just a hundred years ago. He 'should have died hereafter'! In the context of the Centenary Celebrations at Woodfield, the other day, his nephew Liam Collins, Johnny's son, said that his uncle Mick simply 'died in a battle in Ireland's Civil War, and there the matter should rest'. Another nephew had already said, in answer to the suggestion of exhuming the body, 'Let the poor man rest!' Rest for the 'Big Fellow', even in his grave, seems like an anomaly. Just one more grave among the hills he personally provided for so many young men of his time but would not have wanted for himself. Leaders of humanity, for good or ill, make that choice deliberately. The world accepts it. Consequently they cannot be let die or the world will die — and the nature of their passing is a sacred trust. Michael Collins was killed by a transverse shot fired by Jimmy Ormond of Lismore, Co. Waterford. Who is Jimmy Ormond? No one you know! Who is Broder the Dane? No one you know, but he became world famous for killing Brian Boru at the battle of Clontarf, as did Lee Oswald for the slaying of John F. Kennedy. Richard the 'Lion-Heart' was killed by a crossbow bolt while besieging a castle in Limoges, France, and a lowly and unnamed bowman was put to death by his own people for firing the shot. Life is sweet and when the bullets fly and the bombs burst it is every man for himself. In the case of Michael Collins the bullet entered behind the left ear and exited in a massive contusion behind the right ear. The case might rest there but for the fact that there are other contenders besides Jimmy Ormond — six, in fact, possibly seven, maybe even more. Imagine a clock face, and the figures in proper order from one to twelve! Mick Collins is the pivot and Time is the Historic Present. At 'Twelve-o'clock High' stands Denis 'Sonny' O'Neill. Through the bushes and impending dusk he sees the figure of a man and fires. The man falls. Down the line is Joe Murphy, of Lissarda, crouching at the Figure One. He fires slantways at the armoured car. A man falls. Joe moves elsewhere that evening and tells the tale. At the Figure Three fluctuates Tom Kelleher between a pillar and a bend. He is still firing in the general direction, but at an oblique angle, at the moment the man falls. Over beyond, under the Figure Four, lies Bobs Doherty on the newly wet grass. He hears a gun go off. Perhaps it is his own. Simultaneously a big man in his line of vision falls forward on the visible roadway, and one figure away, on Five, Dan O'Connor's 'Martini-Henry' is being hit down by his commanding officer. Liam Deasy has taken his stand where the Figure Six should rest, having ordered Pete Kearney, for whom the evidence to hand provides a condition of bilocation, to open fire with a 'Tommy-gun'. At the Figure Eight Jimmy Ormond peeps breathlessly over a dividing fence, levels his 'Lee-Enfield' and lets fly at the only man in sight, a big, uniformed man who crumbles at the touch of his finger, while at the Ten position, if Tom Kelleher is to be believed, Pete Kearney returns on his tracks from somewhere to fire a single shot and mourn forever in this macabre Dance of the Hours!

APPENDIX A

Synoptics and Antithetics

1. Official Notice: 'General Michael Collins, Commander-in-chief of the Army, was killed in an ambush by Irregulars at Béal-na-Bláth, between Macroom and Bandon, on last night. Towards the close of the engagement, which lasted about an hour, the Commander-in-Chief was wounded in the head.' (As quoted by Dorothy Macardle in *The Irish Republic*) . . . 'Ambush', however, was a misnomer. The ambush as planned did not take place. What did take place was a sudden and unpremeditated skirmish due to a warning shot fired some two hundred yards from the chosen spot.

2. Impressions of Ireland: (Peter Golden, 1923).

'I am in Macroom when the news comes of Michael Collins' death. It is not credited at first, but is dismissed as one of the many wild rumors constantly afloat. Michael Collins dead? No. That's unbelievable. That can't be. Anyone may be dead. Anyone else. But Michael Collins? No. Not Michael Collins. In a little while, however, word comes officially through the post office . . . The facts of the case in Collins' death seem to be that those who prepared the ambush — a few men — had no knowledge whatever that Collins was in the party they were ambushing, and were perhaps the most surprised people in Ireland when they learned he was . . . As the body of Michael Collins is taken from Cork to Dublin huge streamers adorn the lorries that convey the body to the boat. On the streamers there is printed in letters large and flaunting, ''REVENGE FOR MICHAEL COLLINS'' ' . . . Macroom-born American journalist Golden's on-the-spot and on-the-dot impressions of the Béalnabláth situation indicate the original confusion which still reigns supreme.

3. Michael Collins and the Making of a New Ireland: (Piaras Béaslaí, 1926).

'It was later ascertained that, after Collins and his escort had passed through Bandon in the morning, three girls left the town on bicycles, and got to the Irregular ''flying column'' with the news. It is a remarkable coincidence that Mr. de Valera, on the same day, is known to have been on the road taken by Collins's party, and not far from the scene of the fatal ambush . . . There were circumstances in connection with the death of Michael Collins which have never been fully cleared up' . . . A labour of love, which should probably have remained the definitive 'LIFE', two great volumes is indeed an excessive monument when the dear departed was a soldier and one is just a daring academician and littérateur calling oneself a general. 'Ah, let the baby have his stripes!', said Collins to a protesting Mulcahy. Béaslaí more than repaid the grudging compliment. A short-term general, he liked to pose in army uniform. Daring and persistent he was in the cause of freedom, and a good, working writer. The present effort, while comprehensive and informative, is marred by a pungent bias and has absolute truth only in the title. Nineteen-twenty-three: twenty-five was perhaps too near the life, death and resurrection, the sound and fury, to relish alternative elements in the making of a new Ireland.

4. *The Invisible Army:*   (Desmond Ryan, 1932).

'As the lorries tore along the road to the rescue, winding and speeding in the darkness, Harding felt a foreboding which deepened to certainty . . . The attackers faded away. A solitary shot echoed down the slopes, where Michael Collins was fighting for his life — two miles from his mother's blackened ruin of a house. Macken hastened forward . . . He had died, a melancholy group of officers told Macken, firing to the last, while bombs and bullets hurtled round him' . . . For real historical trouble an historical novel is all one needs. Desmond Ryan's motivating cause, his 'primum mobile', totally eludes me. The resulting 'confusion worse confounded' is nothing short of disastrous, almost criminal in the circumstances. The need for such a novel, even a good one which this definitely is not, seems quite remote but for the fact that his veneration for both Pearse and Collins reached extravagant heights. Collins, at any rate, needed such schoolboy exuberance and diction like the proverbial hole in the head. And the novel is still in print!

5. *Legion of the Rearguard:*   (Francis Carty, 1934).

'One morning, about a week later, a small party of republicans occupied an ambush position overlooking a road in the county Cork . . . The republican sentry opened fire and the party stopped. A tall officer jumped recklessly out of the touring car. He stood defiantly on the road, a rifle in his hand, the men on the hillside watching him through the trees. He saw them and levelled his rifle. One of the republicans fired first. The tall officer dropped . . . Next day they heard it was Michael Collins' . . . One morning, about two years later, Francis Carty did the same thing — he produced a novel on the theme of the life and death of Michael Collins. It lacked the contrived flamboyance of Desmond Ryan (to whom it was rather obviously a political response) to the extent of being almost cryptic, and approached so close to a simple statement of the actual happenings at Béalnabláth as to produce a kind of verisimilitude, thereby making the statement of fact even more misleading. The image of a duel, when 'he saw them and levelled his rifle' and 'one of the republicans fired first', has a certain dramatic appeal. Collins would have liked that!

6. *Peace by Ordeal:*   (Frank Pakenham, Lord Longford, 1935).

'Michael Collins walked behind his (i.e. Arthur Griffith's) coffin, revealed to an adoring populace at closer quarters than ever before. A week later he was fighting for his life not many miles from his home at Clonakilty . . . Living, he enriched and exalted Ireland. Dying, he reduced and impoverished mankind' . . . The 'adoring populace' phrase brings an Ark of the Covenant aura to a simple human being who happened to be stronger, brighter, quicker, smarter, blunter and stiffer than most men of his time and all men of his place. By contrast, 'fighting for his life' sounds iconoclastic, as well as being untrue. The antithesis of 'living' and 'dying' touches the heart of the matter with regard to someone who had the doubtful good fortune of being born unique. Rem acu tetigisti, your Lordship!

7. *The Irish Republic:*   (Dorothy Macardle, 1937).

'Ten days later (i.e. from Griffith's death) the whole country was shaken by the news that Michael Collins had been killed in action in County Cork . . . The convoy came along the road. It consisted of a scout on a motor-cycle, a Leyland car in which were five staff officers, all armed, a touring car, a Crossley tender with a Lewis gun, and an armoured car . . . For over half an hour the Volunteers lay firing, under fire themselves from the armoured car. They saw an officer fall, shot through the head. The men with him carried him to a car and the convoy drove off. It was Collins who had been shot and he was dead' . . . The multiple inaccuracy of ambush detail, fifteen years after the event, is a small matter in this authentic, copious but biased history, compared to the startling revelation that the great Michael Collins had been 'killed in action' in a military operation set up by those with whom he had attended Third Brigade Council meetings within three years previously, 'in County Cork'.

8. *The Big Fellow:* (Frank O'Connor, 1937).

'It was evening before they struck the back road from Bandon to Macroom. The ambush party had been waiting there since morning. Now, with the failing light, they scattered to their billets, and as Collins' convoy tore up the narrow road through the glen there were only a handful of men left. They opened fire . . . When they (i.e. Dalton and O'Connell) rushed to where he was lying they found him, his head resting on his arms, a great wound in his skull. . . . Dalton then came and bandaged the wound. He had scarcely completed the task when he saw that Collins was dead. Darkness was coming on' . . . Frank O'Connor, Cork City man of letters, who had fled to Macroom and then to Ballyvourney with the retreating Irregulars, seems assured that Macroom was the objective of Michael Collins. O'Connor's retrospective regard for the 'Big Fellow' is not unusual (His book was 'an act of retribution' — Foreword to 1965 edition), but his 'death in a failing light' notion with 'darkness coming on' has imbued much subsequent writing on the subject with a spirit of Golgotha, while the 'Scotch' mist of an hour's duration only partly and temporarily clouded the remaining hours of daylight. *Note:* Nancy McCarthy (Mrs. Allitt) died on ? October 1988. Who was Nancy McCarthy? 'A gifted Cork lady', said the newspaper. Yes, indeed! Actress, story-teller, wit, business woman, and 'a well-known and highly popular figure in the cultural life of the city'. Friend of famous people, she was in the long ago betrothed to Frank O'Connor. Somehow they both married other people, but she figured largely in his written word. It was she who introduced him to Mrs. Collins-Powell, and accompanied him on visits to the Collins-Powell house while he was working on *The Big Fellow.* To the end she referred to him as 'Mickey Donovan'. Nancy was also sister-in-law to Florrie O'Donoghue, and she told me something rather sensational in the context of Béalnabláth. Florrie had let it be known to the family as a secret not to be revealed — until 1990? — that Collins had arranged to meet him in Macroom on the evening of 22 August 1922. I detect a slight collusion here between Mrs. Nancy McCarthy Allitt and Mr. Michael O'Donovan, alias Frank O'Connor. He was the only writer who could and did state categorically, 'It was evening before they struck the back road from Bandon to Macroom'. Thank you, Nancy! (When Nancy McCarthy died in 1988 her body was cremated and the ashes, on her instructions, were scattered into the Atlantic off the west coast of Kerry).

9. *Guerilla Days in Ireland:*   (Tom Barry, 1949).

'Here I may as well kill the canard that the I.R.A. plotted and planned Collins' death in 1922 and in fact assassinated him . . . The main body of the Column had retired over a mile and the small rearguard over a quarter of a mile from the ambush position when a Free State convoy appeared. The main column was out of sight and range but the small rearguard turned and opened fire from nearly five hundred yards range at the passing convoy which immediately stopped. The Free State party dismounted and lying on the road returned the fire, but the rearguard, after firing less than a dozen rounds, hurried on after the main body. One of these long-range shots killed Michael Collins, the only one of his party to be hit. It was almost five hours later when the I.R.A. Column first heard that Collins had been with the Free State convoy and that he had been killed in the skirmish with the Column's rearguard' . . . How could Barry have got it so wrong! A regular — and almost unlettered — country boy, of little erudition, whose writing skill was to equal his fighting skill, whose book became a world best-seller and a classic for soldier laddies in every clime (though Dan Breen's *My Fight for Irish Freedom* was the one I found being used in Africa); the renowned guerrilla leader of Crossbarry, Kilmichael and points west, who 'walked into West Cork (after escaping from prison in Dublin) and interviewed the men who had fired the shots', and got it all wrong with a deliberation and purpose that has to be seen to be believed, and in the process created a 'canard' far greater than the one he had proposed to kill in the first place! A literary overkill as at Crossbarry!

10. *Michael Collins:* (Rex Taylor, 1958).

'Speeding along they came to the valley of Béal na mBláth, a spot north-west of Bandon, but nearer to Crookstown than to Bandon . . . The gloomy valley seemed a likely place for an ambush. And so it proved. Coming out of a blind corner, and with a straight road in front, they saw an old four-wheel brewer's dray lying lopsided across the road with one front wheel and one rear wheel removed. The dray was loaded with cases and bottles and immediately in front of it the road was strewn with broken bottles. Almost at once machine-gun fire commenced, coming from among the shrubs and alder . . . At the time of the commencement of the ambush the armoured car was almost a half mile behind the rest of the convoy. After a time it arrived on the scene, but its usefulness was short-lived. In answer to shouted instructions, the guns commenced to fire but only two pans of ammunition were fired before the belts fell off . . . Collins stood up, the better to see how things were going. He was in the middle of the road, gazing around and reloading his rifle. There was a single shot and Collins went down. At once several men leaped to his assistance, only to be beaten back by a fierce spell of firing. It was almost ten minutes later when they managed to reach the body. Collins was dead. There was a ghastly wound near the left ear' . . . The books proliferate, errors accumulate and absurdity looms as foreigners begin to appreciate the theme: 'Béal na mBláth', the man said, having been misinformed in the Gaelic syntax: The lovely valley is not at all 'gloomy' — the point has been overworked: 'They', in fact, did not come 'out of a blind corner', nor did they see 'an old four-wheel brewer's dray'. What the motor-cyclist saw, by way of a makeshift barricade, was a two-wheeled horse-cart, or 'common-car', with the off-side wheel removed and set to lean against the near side: There was no machine-gun in action on the republican side, and 'the shrubs and alder' were, according to the text, on the right, or eastern, side of the road where there were no ambushers at that particular time: the armoured car was not 'almost half a mile', but fifty to seventy yards 'behind the rest of the convoy': And I love this one, 'Only two pans of ammunition were fired before the belts fell off'. It reminds me of a disastrous threshing operation of my childhood. 'Pans' were for Lewis light machine-guns, 'belts' were for medium heavy Vickers ditto and they never fell off: 'Retreating in the direction of Cork' — Cork City was east, while the ambushers went westwards towards Kilmurry and Newcestown. 'Almost ten minutes later' — Dalton got to Collins in seconds. And so on. The nature and location of Collins' wound, as well as the controversy surrounding it, still urgently await a resolution.

11. *The Civil War in Ireland.*   (Eoin Neeson, 1966).
'On 22 August 1922, a small mobile column of pro-Treaty soldiers was ambushed between 8.30 p.m. and 9.30 p.m. at a place in West Cork called Béal na mBláth, the Gap of the Blossoms. In that action General Michael Collins, the 32-years old Commander-in-Chief of the pro-Treaty forces was killed. Even to-day, notwithstanding the spate of recent biographical studies in newspaper articles and in book form, the facts relating to the ambush have not yet been fully gathered . . . It was

decided to lay an ambush for the party about 400 yards from the cross
. . . The pro-Treaty machine-guns, that in the armoured car and those
in the tender, immediately opened a tremendous fire on the attackers
. . . The last shots in the action were fired by pro-Treaty forces . . .
The column then moved off eastwards towards Crookstown and
Aherla. The anti-Treatyites did not then know that Collins had been
killed . . . But, about noon, de Valera did pass through the cross going
north — very likely from Ballyvourney — but he had no connection
with the meeting there or with the ambush' . . . Time variations now
enter into the problem of Béalnabláth. 'Ambushed between 8.30 p.m.
and 9.30 p.m.', Neeson says. Is he referring to 'Old Time' or 'New
Time'? Elsewhere in his book he remarks that Summer Time was not in
use in West Cork just then. Daylight-saving Time was discontinued in
England after the Great War but had been resumed there in April of
1922. The new National Army was, to some extent, a British-run outfit. Dalton was C.O. in Cork. Is it possible that the Provisional
Government, and consequently their man in the South, did not work
by British time? Corry, the driver, in his statement, said that they left
Bandon about eight o'clock G.M.T. If that is the case then Dalton,
placing the ambush around 7.30 p.m., was talking in terms of 6.30
p.m., West-Cork time, and Neeson would be placing the start of the af-
fray around 9.30-10.30 p.m., G.M.T.! . . . A small point, perhaps, but
Michael Collins was thirty-one, not thirty-two, at the time of his death
. . . 'It was decided to lay an ambush . . . about 400 yards from the
cross'. Liam Deasy mentions 'about half a mile', which is exactly the
entrance to the vital by-road. Local evidence (cf. 'Five Local People')
places the barricade at the S-bend over 600 yards from the village cross
. . . Dalton does not deny the 'last shot' idea — in his documentary
(1978) he swings around and points to the spot from where it came . . .
Posterity may see these things as important!

12. *Ireland's Civil War:* (Calton Younger, 1968).
'Seán Hales expressed anxiety for Collins' safety. His escort was small
and the country he had to travel through was rife with bands of
Republicans. Hales wanted to escort him by way of Innishannon until
he had seen him safely over a precariously improvised bridge but Collins . . . insisted . . . If *Slievenamon* could have been driven off the
main road and on to the track which led away to the left, curved and
climbed and finally ran level along the ambushers' ridge and parallel to
the main road, the story might have ended differently . . . But the gun

was firing only spasmodic single shots and the armoured car served little purpose other than to ensure the safety of her own crew . . . "The fire was going on for the most part of half an hour", O'Connell relates, "and we could see the road being split up with bullets. In fact, I'm sure if they wanted to, they could have killed us all". Dalton doubts it. There was a lull in the firing and Collins got to his feet and, as O'Connell puts it, "had a gaze around him" . . . "I heard someone say the C.-in-C. was hit", says Dolan. "I didn't know how bad it was until I saw Seán O'Connell whisper an Act of Contrition close to his head". That head, behind the ear, had been slashed open . . . The soldiers removed the last cases and broken bottles which had been spilled from the dray' . . . With the Australian writer open speculation on a vital Irish historical issue begins to draw the case once more towards the realm of the novel. Adroit reconstruction adds verisimilitude . . . 'Men hidden in the hillsides could see the winding road for miles etc.' states an utter impossibility on the ground . . . The idea of an armoured car of massive weight being brought round to Ahalarick bridge, as an obvious military manoeuvre, thereby travelling along a parallel laneway and taking the attackers in the rear, an idea developed more fully and with more conviction by John Feehan, has one outstanding fault — there was NO laneway, just a farm track through a field; unless the ordnance survey maps before and afterwards were in error, the thing was a later construction, the entrance being a ford in a stream. Moreover, the old *Slievenamon* had solid tyres then, not pneumatic as at present, and schoolboys in Gougane Barra — still living — were made to follow the old crate about, even on fine days, brushing off the deep-cut tracks from detection . . . 'Firing from a prone position' — the mud still clinging to the left sleeve of Collins' overcoat, in the National Museum in Dublin, indicates his supporting elbow on the low mud wall. When 'he moved further back' his only prone position was his death-lie . . . 'The ambushers, realising that they had won some kind of advantage, intensified their fire' — arbitrary declarations of this nature are quite mischievous. The 'ambushers' were, in fact, running for their lives over the hills and far away!

13. *Michael Collins: the Lost Leader:*   (Margery Forester, 1971).
'Collins, however, leant forward and commanded him to stop. If only, Joe Dolan was to lament, it had been one of Collins' own drivers, the Hyland brothers, at the wheel! They knew their impetuous Chief and

would almost certainly have obeyed Dalton's order and driven on at full speed for a couple of miles before pausing to enquire of Collins, "What's that you were saying?". But the driver had no such happy disregard for his Commander-in-Chief's wishes and halted at once . . . Michael Collins knew no master, and that quality of leadership which had brought him on this last journey south now made him jump from the car to share in the fight . . . Now the Republicans turned their fire instead on those who had left the touring car. The main body of their force, hearing the shots, had begun to work its way back along the northern hillside. Collins lay on the road between Dalton and O'Connell . . . McPeake had started off with a burst of machine-gun fire, but after a short time the gun no longer opened properly, but fired single shots like a rifle. Only later, when McPeake deserted to the Republicans, taking the *Slievenamon* with him, would this failure take on a sinister significance . . . A mist was rising, and this, with the encroaching darkness, reduced visibility . . . Dolan had the impression that Collins had now knelt upon one knee, and was firing ahead and to the left. The shot that found him was almost certainly a ricochet, possibly off the armoured car. It penetrated the back of his head, above the right ear . . . Firing continued a while, then ceased' . . . Ah, yes, the lady from New Zealand! How did she get involved in Irishmen's killings? How did she develop such an exuberant devotion for a man who died long before she was born, far, far from where she was born? Why this Pygmalion-wise love for a lifeless ivory statue? John Ford, ancient film director, in readjusting Seán O'Casey's *The Plough and the Stars* for his own purposes in the Thirties, added to the script the poignant words: 'For men must fight and women must weep!' Perhaps we shall now weep for 'Michael' and his opponents! 'The long day's clear light was' far from 'fading' at seven o'clock (G.M.T., or even West Cork time) on the twenty-second of August anytime . . . 'Deserted' the road certainly was by any computation . . . 'Ambush position since morning' — it was well into the afternoon, though Neeson says 'ten hours' and Deasy remarks on their being 'uncomfortable' . . . 'The main ambush body . . . set off round the bend' — they were not on the road at all but on the high ground across the stream from the barricade! The 'interrupted Brigade meeting' had not yet begun; in fact it was not a brigade meeting but a general conference of the First Southern Division of which Liam Deasy was O/C and at which most high ranking officers of the Third (West

Cork) Brigade were present as well as the new Fifth (Bantry) and representatives from the First, Second and Fourth Brigades, and men from Limerick, Dublin and other parts of the country, including one Vincent O'Doherty from Derry who had been with Liam Lynch and Deasy at a similar conference in O'Connor's of Glashabee, near Mallow, eight days before (cf. Mrs. Lankford's, *The Hope and the Sadness*) . . . 'The main body ahead' was in no immediate danger and in need of being warned. It was already safely ensconced in its favourite pub of the moment . . . 'Joe Dolan was to lament' — Captain Joseph Dolan's sententiousness, as quoted, sits badly on this hard man of the Dublin Brigade who was eventually to help engineer the dreadful atrocity at Ballyseedy, near Tralee, Co. Kerry . . . 'Michael Collins knew no master' — amply categorical, but doubtful! There was the Provisional Government which, he claimed, was his 'boss' of the moment. There were the British, whose wishes he was obliged to carry out and whose return in force, in the event of his own failure, he certainly feared. Even still perhaps he 'knew no master', but he certainly knew a mistress whose whims were a daily torment . . . 'A mist was rising'? Do I have to say, No! but some light rain was falling!

14. *Brother Against Brother:*   (Liam Deasy, 1975).
'I left Gurranereagh and walked the three miles to Béalnabláth arriving there at about 7 p.m. Jerh Long told me that the Column was in ambush position and I walked down the Bandon road in that direction. There I met Tom Hales who was standing in the middle of the road . . . About twelve men of the Column left in the direction of Newcestown, while others, with Tom Hales and myself, walked back along the road to Béalnabláth Cross . . . We were there in the pub about ten minutes when we heard the sound of machine-gun and rifle fire coming from the direction of the ambush position. We rushed out to a higher road . . . From where we were, some three hundred yards from the actual position, we could see very little — just a lorry and the turret of the armoured car with a few soldiers darting from one position to another. We had fired a few shots when suddenly the whole convoy moved off . . . This meeting began at 9.30 p.m. . . . Seán Galvin, of Crookstown, rushed in and excitedly told us that Michael Collins had been shot dead in the ambush and the convoy had taken his body to Cork via Crookstown, Cloughduv and Killumney' . . . Tom Barry has been rated the best guerrilla fighter of the era, but Liam Deasy was the most important Republican leader in the South, after Liam Lynch: 'I met

Tom Hales who was standing in the middle of the road' — How aptly reminiscent of another tragic civil war — the American, and another gallant soldier of like calibre!: 'And there stood Jackson like a stone wall!' However, the statement that the men were in position 'all day' requires careful analysis. Deasy had the girth and appearance of Collins himself. They might have been identical twins. He had leadership. He surely knew that Collins did not come from Dublin merely to stop in Bandon and turn back! Free State troops were in charge almost everywhere and in need of inspection. Tom Hales was a true Jackson, Deasy's man on the spot. Dev had left at four having agreed in principle to an ambush effort . . . 'He (Hales) also ordered the Battalion Engineer to remove the mine' — I am told that two local men, under John O'Callaghan's direction, both set and removed the barricade mine. Their names are known but not for publication. Jim Kearney's story is that one half of the mine was sitting on the fence. O'Callaghan had just hoisted the other onto his shoulder when the motor-cyclist arrived, and he pitched it inside the fence. On the Free State side John O'Connell said that he and another man examined the site and found only a black oilskin coat and some 'black' powder. Some sections of landmine certainly found their way later to Willie Murray's house on the hill. John Feehan's passing remark that some road workers engaged in repairs, many years later, found and removed the mine is quite puzzling . . . Where were the 'twelve men of the column' who 'left in the direction of Newcestown'? They were walking directly towards the Free State convoy. In the allotted fifteen minutes they would be about where the monument now stands, or between it and Ahalarick bridge. . . 'We rushed out to a higher road' — an impossible feat! The old Bandon road is half a mile away up one of the steepest by-roads in the country. Maggie Long (Mrs. Shorten), Ellen's sister, clearly remembers seeing them 'filtering through the trees at the back of the public house'. Only thus could Deasy be where he claimed to be in fifteen minutes i.e. mid-way between the positions of the now departed Mike Donoghue and Jimmy Ormond. Meda Ryan places Deasy by Coleman's Rock, above Murray's, half a mile from, and out of sight of, the battle scene. The O/C's precaution not to be present when the show started is passing strange!

5. *Ourselves Alone:*   (Robert Kee, 1976).

Ten days later Collins himself was dead . . . They had just given up hope and were dispersing in the fading light when the convoy of a motor-cycle outrider, Collins's open touring Rolls, a Crossley tender and an armoured car drove into the position . . . Note: Forester, *Collins*, pp. 332-9. Many myths and suspicions have accumulated round the manner of Collins's death. This most recent account seems the best summary of all available evidence' . . . Collins's open 'touring Rolls' and the wrong disposition of the vehicles in the convoy apart, it is pleasant to know that this 'most distressful country' has one reputable historian on her side, especially in these times when so many of the breed, who actually live in the glass house, feel it incumbent on them to throw googly cricket-balls just about all of the time.

16. *The Singing Flame:* (Ernie O'Malley, 1978).
'Michael Collins was killed in an ambush in Co. Cork. Those Free State people who had once glorified the ambush now spoke of it as a cowardly form of murder' . . . The die-hard, indestructible and impossible Connaughtman, who died so many times himself for the Republic, and would have died as many more, whom Dan 'Sandow' O'Donovan did not like and would not enlighten despite his many note-taking visits to the Ballybeg office, finally, and posthumously was given his chance to piss on Collins' grave!

17. *Michael Collins:* (Leon Ó Broin, 1980).
'On the reasonable assumption that the blocked roads would force the convoy to return by the same route, it was decided to lay an ambush. A dray was dragged out into the middle of the road at a chosen spot in the valley of Béal na mBláth and its wheels removed, and the ambushing party lay around all day waiting for an eventuality which they almost despaired of when, at about half-past seven, the convoy was seen approaching. What then happened is related by Emmet Dalton, whom we paraphrase' . . . the now familiar 'mixture as before' has become an astute selectivity where brevity is the motivating force. The inherited errors tend to become self-evident and less numerous. The 'reasonable assumption' that Collins was 'forced' to return to Macroom because of 'the blocked roads', true or false, is vital to the issue. That he had a rendezvous with a messenger-boy is, to my mind, far more of a reasonable assumption, to be resolved only with the serious purpose the case deserves. The late Professor Ó Broin's job of work for Gill's *Irish Lives* is decidedly the 'Everyman' reader on the perennial theme of Michael Collins.

18. *The Hope and the Sadness:*   (Siobhán Lankford, 1980).
'Suddenly Con Healy burst into the crowd. "Michael Collins was killed in West Cork", he shouted. There was a stunned silence, which Mr. de Valera broke: "My God, it is too bad; there's no hope for it now", he said . . . The report was confused, but it appeared that only two men took part in the ambush. The remainder of the force of six had gone away . . . They had no idea that Collins was in the vicinity, or in the convoy they fired at' . . . Probably the most delightfully written book on the whole period of 'The Troubles', except possibly Mick O'Sullivan's, *Where Mountainy Men have Sown*, two clearly factual books that read like a good novel, the late Mrs. Siobhán Lankford's effort is helpful on the De Valera Saga and the this-is-how-it-must-have-been approach which is about all one has to work on in 1990 . . . 'There's no hope for it now!', Dev said on hearing of Collins' death. For what? A settlement? An all-Irish republic? A sense of personal loss was not in evidence — but then he was an academic and an idealist. 'The play's the thing!' — personalities were apart. Or were they? About Collins Dev said, 'He must have felt badly, being bottled up in the city (i.e. Dublin) so long. I would say he came to be refreshed in his native county'. Was this a case of the sublime to the ridiculous? Was it 'black' humour at the expense of the Big Fellow? Or naïveté? How about the frogs at Gougane? Perhaps John Devoy was right about him! Dev certainly did cloud the issue, in an extremely sly manner, for his friends in North Cork, with regard to his day's activities on 22nd of August. Was 'the previous day' of Mrs. Lankford part of the subterfuge? Then, perhaps, John Devoy was wrong? . . . Liam Deasy is, therefore, seen to have connived in a necessary cover-up!

19. *The Shooting of Michael Collins:*   (John M. Feehan, 1981. Revised, 1988).
They did, however, leave behind five armed men to clear away an old cart which they had dragged across the road as a block, and to remove a mine. Two of these men came down towards where the cart was and three remained on the high parallel laneway as a look-out and protection . . . At Shanakiel the Matron and Friel washed Collins' face and bandaged his head. They both said there was an entry wound on the hair line and an exit wound at the back of the head. It was Commandant Friel's opinion that a rifle .303 bullet would not have made such a wound. He felt it was more likely that the wound was caused by a Mauser revolver bullet . . . Dalton, it should be remembered, was a

close friend of Collins but not everyone on the Free State side trusted him. There were many who believed that he, like Childers, was a British agent. It is true that this charge, and many other serious ones, were made against him in the public press by an erstwhile colleague. Dalton was aware of these charges but he did not take any action to have them publicly refuted. This fact did not help to allay the suspicions of his critics. Nevertheless it must be pointed out that there is no solid evidence to show that Dalton was a British agent or that any of the other charges are true. I feel it necessary to emphasise this point since it has been said that I pointed the finger of suspicion at him. This is simply not correct' . . . Captain John Feehan got a good deal of attention, some years ago, for trying to pin a murder on Major-General Emmet Dalton. The family would have taken legal proceedings but for the fact that one cannot libel the dead. Mr. O'Shannon, who did the Dalton documentary in 1978, asked me if Feehan were still on that Dalton jag. He appeared to be highly amused. What I personally find far more amusing is the captain's grasp of ballistics, a vital issue in the death of Michael Collins. There never was such a thing as a 'Mauser revolver'. A Mauser automatic pistol, yes (or, more properly, semi-automatic calibre 7.63mm, not 7.45mm as stated), the famous 'Peter the Painter', with hard metal slug which entered and left a man's skull almost without trace, while a 'three-oh-three' could blow the back of his head away (as explained in detail by Dr. Harbison, State Pathologist, in the documentary 'The Shadow of Béalnabláth'). Emmet Dalton carried a British officer's Webley .45 revolver, inaccurate at thirty yeards. He left it on the fence at Béalnabláth where it was retrieved by Tom Foley on the following morning with all six chambers unfired. As Feehan would say, 'Perhaps in the light of all this we might conclude . . .'

20. *Mícheál Ó Coileáin:* (Pádraig Ó Braoin, 1985).

'Nuair a sheol na gluaisteáin isteach sa luíochán, scaoileadh cioth piléar leo ón gcnoc ar an dtaobh chlé den bhóthar . . . Léimeadar anuas agus thosnaigh ag lámhach. Tar éis tamaill bhig, mhaolaigh an ionsaí, d'éirigh Ó Coileáin ina sheasamh agus shiúil taobh thiar den charr armúrtha. Ansan rith sé thar n-ais timpeall le cúig shlat déag de an dtaobh theas den charr armúrtha. Chaith sé é féin ar a bholg a lámhach agus tar éis tamaillín buaileadh go marfach é . . . Bhuail a leor piléar an carr armúrtha agus sciorr timpeall i ngach treo. Ní raibh fhios ag McPeak i dtosach go raibh Ó Coileáin buailte mar bhí a aiste dúnta' . . . Mr. Patrick Breen, ex-teacher, decided it was time that someone wrote about Michael Collins in the native language. And now right he was! This is the studied diction of the new books rather than the traditional language of the old places. Even still, the interpolations in English seem to be directed at a different readership which makes for contradiction. On the language theme it may be remarked that while 'Mícheál Ó Coileáin' means 'Michael Collins', 'Ó Coileáin' does not properly stand for 'Collins' — that would be 'An Coileánach' according to the native frame of mind. Those who are privileged to read and understand this delightful and ancient language will find, in the summary of events, a neat selection and arrangement of items, a shrewd assessment of situations. Otherwise, two items of particular interest might be regarded as naïve and amusing but for the seriousness of the occasion. Of two quoted sources, one gives Collins' death-lie as being behind, the other south of the armoured car. Then there were the two officers — unnamed, though all Free State officers on the ground are well known — who squeezed themselves into the revolving gun-turret (where there was only room for one man crouching and bare clearance to swing the contraption — I keep thinking of the three Marx brothers on a roller-coaster), and how the gun jammed (literally 'went on strike'), and one of the officers tried to refill the empty belt but through inexperience managed to do so only irregularly, so there were irregular shots thereafter. It is hard to resist saying here that a Vickers machine-gun works on a continuous gas feed-back, one shell needing its fellow ('a chéile', as Ó Braoin would say), and can get off eight shots to the second. Margery Forester's 'single shots' is also out of the question, except for the Lewis or Hotchkiss type, and then only in the hands of an expert using the second joint of the middle finger on the trigger. Hopefully we live and learn.

21. *Survivors:* (Uinseann Mac Eoin, 1987).

'Gogarty was the surgeon who performed the autopsy on Collins. Years afterwards in New York he described it (the wound) to me (Connie Neenan). "You see that finger nail; it was about that size. It was a one in a million chance of being fatal". Of course I knew Gogarty intimately. He talked candidly to me. I knew that he had been anti-Republican, that he had been violently opposed to De Valera, but the atmosphere in America was different. People sought me out. They were happy to meet me because I dealt in facts' . . . It is a great pity that Dr. Gogarty, with his acute sense of literary detail, as displayed in his writings, and his acknowledged surgical skill, was not more specific o finger nails which may range from one-quarter to three-quarter-inch i width, and that veteran Connie Neenan did not bother to say which, c that the author did not display a necessary ingenuity. Just the same, th 'one in a million chance of being fatal' is wildly erroneous, like s many of Buck Mulligan's 'obiter dicta'. The smallest calibre bulle ever manufactured (2mm) could be fatal through the eye! (Note: c Chapter Thirteen and a living witness to the 'two-penny' wound).

22. *Green Against Green:* (Michael Hopkinson, 1988).
'Near the end of the shooting Collins was hit by a bullet which left gaping wound in the back of his neck. He died soon afterwards, an was the only fatal casualty on either side. Once the ambush party ha been forced to retreat, the convoy, with Collins's body draped over th armoured car, made an extremely uncomfortable and confuse journey back to Cork city . . . It has been argued that the ambush di not take place, that Collins was killed by a man in his own convoy, o by a British intelligence agent who had infiltrated himself into Collins' entourage and found the ambush a convenient cover. Lately it ha been claimed that one of two Republican soldiers returning home t Kerry from duty in Cork city was unintentionally responsible for th shooting when they came upon the ambush . . . Any implications tha Emmet Dalton was involved in a conspiracy appear patently absurd . . . So the first of the 'Centenary Crop' arrived, and exactly two year beforehand! The 'Collins Problem' has been elevated to the academi Holy of Holies in a standard In-Group Study for advanced universit students by a university professor (Stirling). The diction is clear, readable and matter-of-fact, the expertise extensive, the feeling 'sim- patico', but the title is inept and the cover design (based on a far too familiar picture), showing a Free State soldier back-to-back and left- to-right of himself, is historically misleading and philosophically unac- ceptable. One throws up one's hands at the compounded errors in the mere passing statement of Béalnabláth. It is why the present writer has chosen to give Synoptics and Antithetics so that posterity may be in a position to judge for itself. And one more outsider, kindly as is, has presumed to write about my country's ills. Desist, ye troops of Midian! Leave the problem of Michael Collins to the native-born Republicans and Free Staters who, like the tinkers, are still very much in our midst! The contention is far more at home in Irish pub-land than in foreign Groves of Academe!

3. *The Day Michael Collins was Shot:* (Meda Ryan, 1989).

On Wednesday, 23 August, the day after the Béal na mBláth ambush, Liam Deasy sent a dispatch to Liam Lynch. Lynch stated in his acknowledgement: "Considering the very small number of men engaged this was a most successful operation, and they are to be complimented on the fight made under such heavy fire, and against such odds. Considering you were aware of the fact that the convoy contained an armoured car, it is surprising you had not mines laid to get his" '. . . (Lynch continued) — 'Nothing could bring home more forcibly the awful unfortunate national situation at present than the fact that is has become necessary for Irishmen and former comrades to shoot such men as M. Collins . . .' . . . The few lines from the correspondence of General Liam Lynch, Republican Commander-in-Chief, crystallize in contrasting manner the stark polarization of the leaders' minds: It is a pity that the armoured car was not blown up at Béalnabláth on 22 August 1922; it is a pity that Michael Collins had to be killed anywhere, anytime! . . . By way of observation, Mrs. Ryan's book has promoted a strange phenomenon. Vital recorded interviews with significant people still in their vigour, in the early Seventies, remained silently over many years (running almost to a couple of decades) of acrimonious controversy, then suddenly sprung on the world of history in due time for the centenary celebrations, found firstly a startled public and secondly a new form of contention as errors come to light and, as the terms of reference had been laid away forever in the grave, just a set form of response in a series of repeated categoricals! Seems like the pity of dedicated and persistent labour in vain!

4. *Michael Collins, a Biography:* (T.P. Coogan, 1990).

The Mouth of Flowers' . . . Will we never see the end of that disreputable interpretation! Seán McBride, in a documentary made shortly before his death, remarked that the one thing remaining to be done for Michael Collins was an analysis in depth of the battle scene where he died. Since that time two have come — Meda Ryan's intense effort at reconstruction and Tim Pat's mish-mash of all available material. It is uncertain what purpose either has served. At both ends of the Collins spectrum now stand two literary blockbusters, Béaslaí's and Coogan's. Two diametrically opposed types of publication, they have one thing in common — they both run to two hundred and thirty thousand words. I have heard them described, at fifty years remove, as a fiasco and a farce. Think it over!

APPENDIX B

Cruce to Crauma:
A Chronology

1921

July 11: Announced on July 9, a cessation of hostilities between Ireland and England came into operation whereby both belligerents were to retain the 'status quo' without prejudice. It is known to History as 'The Truce'. The precise time was Monday Noon, July 11, 1921.

July 20: The British Prime Minister, David Lloyd George, proposed terms of a Treaty 'to end the unhappy divisions between Great Britain and Ireland' (as already suggested by King George the Fifth in Belfast). Up till then Ireland was part of what was called 'The British Isles'. The proposed Treaty purported to be an offer of 'Dominion Status', as in Canada.

August 10: Initial terms rejected by the Republican Cabinet in Dublin.

August 23: 'Dáil Éireann' (Parliament) unanimously endorsed the rejection.

August 26: Eamon de Valera was declared 'President of the Irish Republic'. His ministers in Cabinet were Arthur Griffith (Foreign Affairs), Austin Stack (Home Affairs), Cathal Brugha (Defence), Michael Collins (Finance), William Cosgrave (Local Government), and Robert Barton (Economic Affairs).

September 14: The Dáil sanctioned the appointment of the delegates to the projected Imperial Conference in London. They were termed 'Envoys Plenipotentiary'. They were Arthur Griffith, Michael Collins, Robert Barton, Edmund J. Duggan, and George Gavan Duffy.

September 19: President de Valera proposed a 'Treaty of Accommodation and Association' to Prime Minister Lloyd George.

September 23:   Winston Churchill, Secretary of State for the Colonies, and Chairman of the Cabinet Committee on Irish Affairs, repeated his threat of 'real war, not mere bush-ranging' (Australian phrase for guerrilla fighting).

September 28:   Lloyd George sent an invitation to De Valera himself to attend the Conference to be held in London on October 11.

October 7:   The delegates appointed to the Conference were given their credentials. Each carried a copy of 'Draft Treaty A'. De Valera declined to go for tactical reasons. The secretaries were Erskine Childers, Finian Lynch, Diarmuid O'Hegarty and John Chartres. They were also accompanied by an office staff. Childers assumed a consultative role during the Conference.

October 11:   They met across the ancient and historic Cabinet Table at Number Ten, Downing Street, London. Contradictions, at least literary, were already in the making . . . 'Lloyd George greeted the Irish Delegation at the door, shook hands with them warmly and led them to their places along one side of the table' (Frank Pakenham, *Peace by Ordeal*); 'Art O'Brien (President of the Irish Self-Determination League of Great Britain, a sort of legal version of 'Sinn Féin') presented the Irish delegates individually to Lloyd George, who received them cordially but, to their relief, without offering to shake hands' (Dorothy Macardle, *The Irish Republic*).

October 16:   Ulster, in the context of the Conference, was 'a rock of granite', according to Sir James Craig, Premier of the new (1920) Six-County Government. Time proved this insolent assertion all too true!

October 19:   Pope Benedict XV, always concerned for faithful Ireland, sent a telegram of good will to King George V. His reply and that of De Valera, individually designed and interpreted, caused an atmosphere of tension at the Conference table but brought the fundamental issue of Ireland's independence to the fore in the discussions for the first time.

October 24:   The seventh — and last — plenary session of the Conference. 'External Association' was proposed. Its definition was the issue. It was set out in a Memorandum to the British Delegation before the meeting and embodied the Irish offer approved by the home Cabinet, but tactfully avoided the rather crucial issue of Unionist Ulster.

October 27: A corresponding Memorandum was sent across by the British. It declared, 'A man must be either a subject of the King (of England), or an alien'. It ignored the Irish offer of 'External Association'. The Conference was now reduced to committee stage with occasional meetings in private between chosen members of the delegations

October 29: The Irish reply to the British Memorandum — they might consider the 'Crown' as a symbol if otherwise allowed to go free

November 8: A 'Boundary Commission' was proposed by the British. It would, they said, delimit the Six-Counties (which the Northern Unionist interest called 'Ulster') in keeping with the concentration of Catholic and Protestant inhabitants, if Craig refused to come under an All-Ireland parliament in Dublin. Craig and his cabinet refused.

November 17: A crucial Unionist Conference was held in Liverpool P.M. Lloyd George was ready to withstand them on a verbal promise of co-operation from Arthur Griffith. (He held Griffith to this 'gentleman's agreement' right to the end). Consequently, a Unionist motion to halt the London Conference was defeated. Negotiations would, therefore, continue.

November 18: Arthur Griffith wrote to De Valera stating his verdict on the situation: 'The crucial question, "Crown and Empire", must be next week!'

November 22: A new Irish Memorandum was sent to the British. It was an amendment of the unacceptable 'Draft Treaty A', and allowed for a certain consultative relation with the British Commonwealth on matters of peace and war, while retaining the Republic and essential unity. It 'filled Lloyd George with despair', according to a confidant

November 25: Cabinet meeting in Dublin with Griffith and Collins present. The 'Crown Symbol' was agreed to. Continuing outbreaks of Protestant violence in the North, and the murder of Catholics in Belfast. Martyrdom for the Faith had become commonplace — but canonization was remote!

November 28: MONDAY. Another Memorandum sent to the British. It was returned with a request to adapt it somehow to the terms of a Treaty already being drawn up. Canada appeared to be the model as a Dominion (but this was never made quite clear). Childers alone while having no executive authority, feared for the future of the

Republic. At home in Ireland, Tyrone County Council pledged itself and included Fermanagh) to Dáil Éireann, and the country prepared or war.

December 1: THURSDAY. A document entitled 'Proposed Articles of Agreement' was delivered to the Irish delegation. Dominion Status, and the title of 'Irish Free State', was the final offer.

December 3: SATURDAY. The Cabinet met in Dublin. They were divided on the issue of 'Dominion Status', but most were against an Oath of Allegiance to the King of England. The problem of signing or not signing a Treaty started here.

December 5: MONDAY. To Griffith and Collins (the appointed leaders of the Irish Delegation) Lloyd George gave his ultimatum — this was Peace or War! Of two prepared letters on the table — 'Which letter am I to send?', he asked (i.e. to Sir James Craig in Belfast). 'Both saw the shadow of doom . . .' (Lloyd George in *Is it Peace?*').

December 6: TUESDAY. 2.15 a.m. The signing of the Anglo-Irish Treaty.

December 8: The sad Cabinet meeting in Dublin. The vote was four to three in favour of the Treaty. The reasons why had a sevenfold diversity. Nonetheless, the three dissenters, while diverse in character, had one common trait — they were not personal friends of Michael Collins.

December 9: Lloyd George explained the proposed 'Boundary Commission' (Article Twelve) to Craig, but the Northern Prime Minister was dissatisfied.

December 14: The Treaty Debates began in Dublin and London. Lloyd George emerged as a restless and energetic referee in a four-sided game, and a broad and reasonable political mind would have given him the greatest sympathy, as he himself, in fact, gave to Collins and Griffith. Fair Jews!, as an Irishman would say. And Winston, now responsible for the Colonies, admitted that the reconquest of Ireland would have been, at best, a mere Pyrrhic victory.

December 16: London approved the Treaty.

December 22: Dublin disagreed over it, and adjourned to January 3.

1922

January 3: The 'Second Dáil' assembled in the Convocation Hall o
the National University of Dublin. It had been three eventful year
since the First, the 'Rebel' Dáil. Now the divided mind, the notoriou
'Split' over the Treaty, became evident throughout the whole spectrun
of Sinn Féin, the Dáil, the Cabinet, the Army, the Volunteers in
general, and the I.R.B. And a 'We, the People' motif was pathetically
interposed, from time to time, by both sides in the acrimonious
debates.

January 4: President de Valera was forced to withdraw his 'Document No. 2', an amendment to the 'External Association' document
(i.e. 'Draft Treaty A'), which he put forward as an alternative to the
already signed Treaty.

January 7: The 'Treaty Motion' was carried in the Dáil by a small
majority of seven deputies (64 to 57).

January 9: Eamon de Valera resigned as President and Arthur Griffith was elected in his place, albeit reluctantly. Michael Collins became
Minister for Finance and Richard Mulcahy, for Defence, gave an
assurance of 'status quo' for the Republican Army.

January 11: A proposal for an Army Convention was refused by the
Minister for Defence.

January 14: The Dáil reassembled at the request of Arthur Griffith.
Only pro-Treaty (a new and soon to be familiar term) members attended. A 'Provisional Government' was formed with Michael Collins
as Chairman.

January 16: Dublin Castle, the centre of British Administration in
Ireland for centuries, was formally 'surrendered' to Collins who made
a wry and rather bitter comment on the occasion. Henceforth,
Winston Churchill began the evacuation of British troops, and the new
Government set up the Civic Guards (now known as the 'Garda
Síochána', the 'guardians of the peace'), and the C.I.D. (the 'Criminal
Investigation Department'). The new authorities also began reorganiz-
ing the Army (hitherto seen merely as 'Volunteers') on a professional
basis.

January 21: An amended 'Boundary Commission' was agreed upon
between Craig and Collins, to be followed shortly by disagreement.

January 31:   The new National Army took over Beggar's Bush Barracks, in Dublin, as its headquarters, and its troops became identified accordingly.

February 5:   'Cumann na mBan' (militant 'Society of the Women') held their Convention in Dublin. Countess Markievicz (Constance Gore-Booth), veteran of the Rebellion of 1916, was elected President. There was an almost unanimous rejection of the Treaty.

February 13:   The evacuation of British troops was halted because of an escalation of trouble at the Northern border.

February 22:   'Sinn Féin', the over-riding national movement, North and South, held its 'Ard-Fheis' (Convention) in Dublin. De Valera and Griffith agreed to an election in three months, with a provisional Constitution to be put before the people.

February 28:   Winston Churchill promised the Provisional Government an unlimited supply of weapons and other war materials as, and when, required.

March 2:   The Dáil ratified the Sinn Féin Ard-Fheis agreement, and ajourned to April 25. A cargo of German arms for the I.R.A. was landed at Helvic Head, Co. Waterford.

March 3:   Limerick City was occupied by sections of the two now clearly opposed factions of the Army, creating an explosive situation.

March 10:   Liam Lynch, Commandant of the First Southern Division, and Oscar Traynor, Commandant of the anti-Treaty Dublin Brigade, went down to Limerick in an effort to defuse the situation.

March 23:   The deferred Army Convention was summoned against the wishes of Griffith and the orders of Mulcahy.

March 26:   The Army Convention met in the Mansion House, Dublin, and declared allegiance to the Irish Republic, towards which they had already sworn an oath . . . 'In the fall of the year (1919) Richard Mulcahy, Chief of Staff, Irish Republican Army, came to Ballyvourney accompanied by Florrie O'Donoghue, Brigade Adjutant, to administer the Republican Oath, which they duly proceeded to do in the salubrious atmosphere of Jim Connie Paddy Lehane's cowshed. So Ballyvourney swore its allegiance to Dáil Éireann and to the Irish Republic amid real democratic surroundings, and Jerh O'Riordan of "The Rookery", as orderly for the night, had a lively time trying to keep the hens, roosting on rafters and couplings, from flying at the candle and throwing a deep gloom over the whole proceedings'. (From *Green Tears for Hecuba*).

March 29:   'Volunteers of the First Southern Division carried out a daring capture of arms and ammunition from a British Admiralty vessel at Cobh (still known as Queenstown); a great quantity of explosives and machine-guns (equipment of evacuated barracks, which was being removed to England) was seized' (Dorothy Macardle, *The Irish Republic*). Politicians and writers have invariably tended to maximize the extent of the cache of arms removed from the *Upnor* at Ballycotton. Even Churchill spoke on the matter in the House of Commons. (Still, a first hand witness of my acquaintance minimizes the incident to the extent of a joke. Neilus Sheehan of Ballyvourney, still going strong at ninety-one, was one of the men who took the arms. This is his story. The *Upnor*, he said, was moored at Passage West — where Emmet Dalton was to land a few months later — with only the slipway between it and the quay. Two men from Cork City were already in the hold. They were Jim Counihan and Dan 'Sandow' O'Donovan. The operation was, he says, 'the quickest thing ever!' The crew took no notice, even helped to some extent. They talked of nothing but 'Peace — Peace — Peace', and all were anxious to get away, but knew the action was still a violation of the Truce. The men had a truck. While Neilus and Mickey O'Leary from Cork City remained in the truck the two brothers, Jim and Miah Grey, with Denis O'Leary, all from Cork City, went on board the ship to find the ammunition boxes already lying on the deck. There were two large cases of .303 rifle ammunition and four other small boxes, two each of hand-guns and ammunition for same, including surprisingly a 'Peter the Painter' which Neilus himself held on to for the remainder of the trouble. At Penrose Quay the 'stuff' was transferred to the red Buick motor-car, quite a famous vehicle in Ballyvourney during the Black-and-Tan times, and was thus transported to the cottage home of Bob Hallissey, at Shanacloon, Ballyvourney — or so the man said. The evidence, however, is for the regulation 'Upnor Scoop' as reported, though with varying details and even dates. Sorry, Neilus! It had to be another boat, another time!).

March 31:   Royal assent was given to the Irish Free State (Agreement) Bill which had been debated in Parliament throughout the month of March; and so the 'Treaty' became Law, at least as far as England was concerned.

April 8: 'It is possible that things (in Ireland) will get worse before they get better' (Winston Churchill).

April 9: An Army Convention was held, once again, regardless of the Provisional Government's embargo. A 'Constitution' was drawn up for the 'Irish Republican Army', and an 'Executive' was formed with Liam Lynch as Chief-of-Staff and Florence O'Donoghue as Adjutant-General. Two other Cork men, Brigadier Seán O'Hegarty and Commandant Tom Hales, were made members of the Executive. Later on the three (i.e. apart from Lynch) resigned, and O'Hegarty and O'Donoghue took a neutral (rather than aloof) stance for the future.

April 13: The Republican Army Council ordered the Dublin Brigade to occupy the 'Four Courts', beside the Liffey, and set up a Military H.Q. of their own.

April 26: A peace conference was called by the Archbishop of Dublin, with the Lord Mayor. It began in the Mansion House in Dawson Street (the official residence of the Lord Mayor since 1715, where the First Dáil met in January, 1919, and the Truce with Britain was signed in July, 1921), with proposals and counter-proposals leading to failure; and one quaint note, to wit, the suggestion from Michael Collins for 'a chapel gates on Sunday' plebiscite to determine the mind of the people of Ireland on current affairs.

May 2: A number of peace proposals, from officers on both sides of the Army divide, were presented to Dáil Éireann by Brigadier Seán O'Hegarty.

May 4: An Army truce was declared, followed by a series of conferences.

May 10: The Army failed to agree among themselves and the appointed committee reported to the Dáil with regard to this failure.

May 16: Separate reports were presented by the Army to Dáil Éireann on the progress and outcome of the conferences. They differed in essentials.

May 17: A debate was held on the issue in the Dáil. Cathal Brugha proposed a united front to protect Catholics in the North. Collins proposed a Party Coalition, which was well received by De Valera, and showed a certain softening of attitude in the Big Fellow — which raises the interesting, but now merely hypothetical, question: Was Ireland's successful War of Independence with its dire consequences, designed solely by that unique and powerful mind?

May 20:   De Valera and Collins signed a 'Pact' agreeing to a National Coalition Government, with an election in June.

May 23:   The Sinn Féin Ard-Fheis ratified the Pact, as did Michael Collins and the National Army Executive.

May 27:   The 'Parliament of Southern Ireland' (in the words of Lord Fitzalan, the *Catholic Viceroy*) was dissolved, and an election set for June.

May 29:   Field-Marshal Sir Henry Wilson, Chief of the Imperial General Staff, denounced the Pact, and Churchill sent reinforcements to the North. In Dublin General Sir Nevil Macready, G.O.C., reluctantly prepared to shell the city from his headquarters in the Phoenix Park.

May 31:   The House of Commons denounced the Pact . . . 'The resources of our (British) civilization' would be thrown into 'the inevitable bloody struggle' (Lord Birkenhead). One wonders what happened to 'the freedom of small nations', the stated crusade of the Great War!

June 6:   Arthur Griffith took a draft Constitution with him to London, but Michael Collins stayed at home. The draft was badly received.

June 8:   The 'Second Dáil' formally adjourned. The 'Third Dáil' was decreed to meet on July 1. (This curious enumeration still obtains).

June 9:   The election campaign opened in the Mansion House, Dublin, where Collins and De Valera both spoke.

June 12:   Collins was called to London to meet Churchill.

June 14:   Collins was back in Cork and effectively repudiated the Pact, before the electorate, at a monster meeting at which some Republicans fired pistol shots in the air (there is a picture). In Dublin, in an effort to unite the Army, some officers from the Four Courts and Beggar's Bush met in conference. The crux was the posts of Minister of Defence and Chief of Staff. Florrie O'Donoghue, still an anti-Treaty officer, was to be Director of Intelligence. This effort also failed.

June 16:   FRIDAY.   Polling Day. The draft Constitution, amended in London, was published in the national newspapers only that morning, giving most of the electorate no opportunity of studying it before going to the polls.

June 18: At a Republican Army convention, in the Mansion House, Dublin, Tom Barry proposed an immediate attack on the British Army H.Q. in the Phoenix Park. Shades of Kilmichael and Crossbarry! The motion was defeated and split the Four Courts Executive itself.

June 22: Sir Henry Wilson was shot dead in London by two Irish ex-British soldiers 'justified by the verdict of our own consciences'. Wilson was also an Irishman, from Edgeworthstown, Co. Longford, and, like the Duke of Wellington (who said — 'If a man is born in a stable, do you call him a horse?'), disdainfully repudiated his Irish origins.

June 23: Prime Minister David Lloyd George, in a fever of uncertainty, sent an ultimatum to Michael Collins on the Four Courts situation.

June 24: Election results. The situation was left more confused and self-contradictory than ever, with the proposed Constitution seen to be almost totally, or at least gravely, at variance with national aspirations.

June 25: The Four Courts garrison decided to attack the North of Ireland in an effort to relieve the persecuted Catholics there.

June 26: Churchill again threatened war in the House of Commons, but his 'sham Augustan prose' (Evelyn Waugh) sounded futile and frustrated. At the same time the Four Courts garrison seized motor cars, newly imported from Belfast, for transport to the North. In the process an anti-Treaty officer was arrested and in response the Four Courts men arrested American-born pro-Treaty Lieutenant-General J.J. ('Ginger') O'Connell.

June 27: At the Four Courts the garrison, with Cumann na mBan, prepared to go North but, unknown to them, the Provisional Government, with the distrait connivance of Michael Collins, had made a decision to attack the building.

June 28: WEDNESDAY. Early in the morning a message was sent to the Four Courts garrison calling on them to surrender by 4 a.m. They made no reply. At 4.07 a.m. some field guns, borrowed temporarily from the Phoenix Park, opened up on the building. The CIVIL WAR had started. (Even then the situation had its comic moments. While Collins 'tore his hair' in despair, Macready thought the attack was on his own H.Q. The shooting was so bad that the shells were falling all about him. Dalton, in charge of the operation, amusedly tells of a Clare man, ex-British Army, who came along offering to help, claiming to know something about cannon, and started a personal duel with a rifleman high up in a window of the dome. He was Andy O'Neill — sometimes confused with Sonny O'Neill — who incredibly still lives down on the Shannon, near Cahircon in Co. Clare). From the Clarence Hotel (Wellington Quay) Liam Lynch, as Chief of Staff, made a proclamation to the country on behalf of the Irish Republican Army. At this stage the River Liffey approximately divided the opposing forces. One side or other might be the eventual winners. (In fact all became the losers — all are still politically and emotionally at a loss). In the South of Ireland a state of war was declared, and never retracted but for a cease-fire order in April of 1923.

June 30: Oscar Traynor (O/C anti-Treaty Dublin Brigade and Member of the I.R.A. Executive) by messenger ordered the Four Courts garrison to surrender (by reason of his authority over them). They did so. Ernie O'Malley escaped while on the way to imprisonment. The fight continued from a number of hotels and other buildings in O'Connell Street and adjacent Abbey Street.

July 1: Liam Lynch, having escaped to the country, occupied part of Limerick City. He and pro-Treaty Commandant Michael Brennan signed a provisional Treaty. It was repudiated by the Government, and the fighting spread.

July 3: De Valera and Traynor escaped from the Hamman Hotel. Cathal Brugha stayed on to keep his rendezvous with destiny.

July 5: Cathal Brugha fell fighting in a back lane at the rear of the hotel and died two days later. (The tough, dour little ex-Minister for Defence had been severely wounded and lamed for life in 1916. Director of a Church Supplies firm, his English extraction and name — Charles William St. John Burgess — have been frequently pointed to, with scant logic, by his detractors).

July 6: There were indications of rejoicing in London. Churchill exulted that the new Irish Government had destroyed their own property n 'that great historic street in the historic capital of Ireland'. A 'Call to Arms' was issued by the Provisional Government for men to join the new Army, or, as they still persisted in putting it, 'The Irish Volunteers'.

July 8: Frank Aiken, Commandant of the Fourth Northern Division, Dundalk, went to Limerick to remonstrate with Lynch but in vain. The die was cast.

July 11: Lynch moved his H.Q. Staff to Clonmel where he was joined by Seán Moylan, Director of Operations, and De Valera, as Moylan's adjutant. The terms 'National Army' and 'Irregulars' came into vogue officially, for the opposing sides, but unofficially they were known as the 'Free State Army' and the 'I.R.A.' respectively — otherwise 'Staters' and 'Rebels'.

July 13: The overdue Parliament was prorogued for the second time. The first time was June 30, the day the Four Courts surrendered). A War Council was formed, an *ad hoc* arrangement with Richard Mulcahy as Chief-of-Staff and Michael Collins as Commander-in-Chief of the Army. ('After all, he reflected, his whole uniform was a disguise, his whole new calling a masquerade'! Guy Crouchback in Waugh's *Men at Arms*).

July 15: Liam Lynch moved his G.H.Q. to Fermoy Military Barracks.

July 20: Frank Aiken, now in prison, made a written appeal to Richard Mulcahy stating that no Irishman (Aiken was a Northern Protestant) should be required to take an Oath of Allegiance to the King of England.

July 25: Parliament was postponed once again.

July 31: The final suppression of all Republican Courts, originally set up by a decree of the Dáil, came as a shock to friend and foe alike.

August 4: Dáil Éireann, even in its subservient role, was once again prorogued and set to meet on Saturday, August 26.

August 8: Major-General Emmet Dalton sailed with an expeditionary force into Cork Harbour, landed at Passage West, and in two days of hard fighting worked his way into Cork City.

August 11: Liam Lynch and Eamon de Valera left Fermoy having arranged for the burning down of the great British military barracks which had been the mainstay of the town for generations.

August 12:   Arthur Griffith died suddenly in Dublin.

August 21:   The Provisional Government published a refutation o‹ George Gavan Duffy's statement of their motive for suppressing th‹ Republican courts. He was not only the recently resigned Minister fo‹ Foreign Affairs but a signatory of the Treaty. Robert Barton, cousi‹ of Erskine Childers and another of the six original signatories, ha‹ already reneged on grounds of principle.

August 22:   General Michael Collins was shot dead in a mistaken am‹ bus situation at Béalnabláth (prn. 'Bale-nu-Blaw'), at the entrance t‹ a valley near the village of Crookstown, while on a military inspectio‹ of County Cork.

*   *   *

CODA: The man who first twisted the Lion's Tail was gone! A ma‹ of wild dreams, could he have imagined, in his wildest, that the ver‹ next generation of English men and women would be singing:

> 'Who do you think you are kidding, Mr. Hitler,
> If you think old England's done!'